新时代商务英语专业系列教材
New Era Business English Series

总主编 / 翁凤翔　郭桂杭

A Listening Course in Business English

国际贸易法

主　编 / 陈建平

内 容 提 要

教材共16个单元,重点介绍两大法律体系、联合国国际货物销售合同公约、国际贸易术语解释通则、国际海上货物运输法、国际货物运输保险法、国际结算法、反倾销法、合同法、代理法、产品责任法、世界贸易组织、国际货币基金组织、世界银行、知识产权法、国际商事仲裁等内容,旨在使读者在英语语境中较为系统地学习国际贸易法律知识,熟悉和掌握英文国际贸易法律术语、基本概念及基础理论知识,进而提高专业英语技能。

图书在版编目(CIP)数据

国际贸易法:英文/陈建平主编.—重庆:重庆大学出版社,2017.1

商务英语专业系列教材

ISBN 978-7-5689-0382-0

Ⅰ.①国… Ⅱ.①陈… Ⅲ.①贸易法—高等学校—教材—英文 Ⅳ.①D996.1

中国版本图书馆CIP数据核字(2017)第006855号

国际贸易法

GUOJI MAOYIFA

主 编 陈建平

责任编辑:陈 亮 版式设计:高小平

责任校对:关德强 责任印制:张 策

*

重庆大学出版社出版发行

出版人:易树平

社址:重庆市沙坪坝区大学城西路21号

邮编:401331

电话:(023) 88617190 88617185(中小学)

传真:(023) 88617186 88617166

网址:http://www.cqup.com.cn

邮箱:fxk@cqup.com.cn(营销中心)

全国新华书店经销

重庆市正前方彩色印刷有限公司印刷

*

开本:787mm×1092mm 1/16 印张:11.25 字数:277千

2017年2月第1版 2017年2月第1次印刷

ISBN 978-7-5689-0382-0 定价:35.00元

总　序

商务英语作为本科专业获得教育部批准进入我国大学本科教育基本目录已经好些年了。商务英语本科专业的身份与地位获得了我国官方和外语界的认可。迄今为止，据不完全统计，有300所左右的大学开设了商务英语本科专业。各种商务英语学术活动也开始活跃。商务英语专业与英语语言文学专业、翻译专业成为我国英语教学的"三驾马车"。商务英语教学在全国已经形成较大规模，正呈良性发展态势，越来越多的大学正在积极准备申报商务英语本科专业。可以预计，将来在我国，除了研究性大学外的大部分普通本科院校的外语学院都可能开设商务英语本科专业。这是大势所趋，因为随着我国改革开放和经济全球化、世界经济一体化进程的加快，各个融入经济一体化的国家和地区急需有扎实英语功底的，熟悉国际商务基本知识的，具备国际商务领域操作技能的跨文化商务交际复合型、应用型商务英语人才。

高校商务英语专业教育首先必须有充足的合格师资；其次，需要有合适的教材。目前，虽然市面上有很多商务英语教材，但是，完整的四年商务英语本科专业教材并不多。重庆大学出版社出版的商务英语本科专业系列教材一定程度上能满足当前商务英语本科专业的教学需要。

本套系列教材能基本满足商务英语本科专业1—4年级通常开设课程的需要。商务英语专业不是商务专业而是语言专业。所以，基础年级的教材仍然是英语语言学习教材。但是，与传统的英语语言文学专业教材不同的是：商务英语专业学生所学习的英语具有显著的国际商务特色。所以，本套教材特别注重商务英语本科专业教育的特点，在基础阶段的英语技能教材中融入了商务英语元素，让学生在学习普通英语的同时，接触一些基础的商务英语语汇，通过听、说、读、写、译等技能训练，熟悉掌握商务英语专业四级和八级考试词汇，熟悉基础的商务英语篇章，了解国际商务常识。

根据我国《高等学校商务英语本科专业教学质量国家标准》（以下简称《标准》），本套教材不仅包含一、二年级的基础教材，还包含高年级的继续夯实商务英语语言知识的教材，如《高级商务英语教程》1—3册等。此外，还包括英语语言文学专业学生所没有的突出商务英语本科专业特色的国际商务知识类教材，如《国际商务概论》《国际贸易实务》《国际贸易法》《市场营销》等。本套教材的总主编都是教育部商务英语专业教学协作组成员，参与了该《标准》的起草与制定，熟悉《标准》的要求，这为本套教材的质量提供了基本保障。此外，参与编写本套教材的主编及编者都是多年从事商务英语教学与研究的有经验的教师，因而，在教材的内容、体例、知识、练习以及辅助教材等方面，都充分考虑到了教材使用者的需求。教材的编写宗旨是：力求传授实用的商务英语知识和国际商务有关领域的知识，提高学生的商务英语综合素质和跨文化商务交际能力以及思辨创新能力。

教材编写考虑到了以后推出的全国商务英语本科专业四级和专业八级的考试要求。在教材的选材、练习、词汇等方面都尽可能与商务英语本科专业四级、八级考试对接。

本套教材特别适合培养复合型、应用型的商务英语人才的商务英语本科专业的学生使用，也可作为商务英语爱好者学习商务英语的教材。教材中若存在不当和疏漏之处，敬请专家、学者及教材使用者批评指正，以便我们不断修订完善。

翁凤翔

2016 年 3 月

前　言

《国际贸易法》教材旨在使读者在英语语境中较为系统地学习国际贸易法律知识，熟悉和掌握英文国际贸易法律术语、基本概念及基础理论知识，从而提高专业英语技能。本书共16个单元，重点介绍两大法律体系、联合国国际货物销售合同公约、国际贸易术语解释通则、国际海上货物运输法、国际货物运输保险法、国际结算法、反倾销法、合同法、代理法、产品责任法、世界贸易组织、国际货币基金组织、世界银行、知识产权法、国际商事仲裁等内容。

本书在编写上具有以下特点：

1. 在编排结构上，呈现立体式趋势。各个单元首先明确了重要概念和学习目标，课后配有参考文献、阅读书目、课文注释、问题讨论、案例分析等栏目，便于教师有效地组织课堂教学及学生自主学习。

2. 在内容体系上，注重国际商务法律知识与专业英语知识的有机统一，使学生能在专业英语语境中较为系统地学习国际商务法律知识，强化专业英语技能。

3. 课文注释注重背景知识和专业词语介绍。对专有名称、专业词汇、难词及难点进行中文翻译和解释，以帮助学生更好地理解课文内容，拓展知识面。

本书主要用作高等院校商务英语本科专业国际商务法律教材，也可作为其他英语专业、法律专业及经济、管理类专业的国际贸易法双语教材、法律英语教材或教学参考用书，此外，还可作涉外经济部门的法律英语和国际商法的培训教材或自学参考书。

本书的多数章节已在本校学生中使用多年，效果较好。本书配有教学课件，如有需要请与我们联系(chenjianping@nbu.edu.cn)。

在本书的编写、出版过程中，翁凤翔教授给予悉心指导和关心，在此谨表衷心的谢意。也感谢重庆大学出版社高小平先生以及作者单位宁波大学国际交流学院同事的支持和帮助。

由于编者水平有限，书中错误或不当之处在所难免，敬请学界同仁及读者批评指正。

编　者

2016年8月

Contents

Unit 1 Introduction to Two Major Legal Systems 1

Unit 2 Introduction to United Nations Convention on Contracts for the International Sale of Goods 8

Unit 3 Incoterms 19

Unit 4 The Law of International Marine Cargo Transport 26

Unit 5 The Law of Insurance in International Cargo Transport 35

Unit 6 The Law of International Settlement of Payment 43

Unit 7 Anti-dumping Law 59

Unit 8 Contract Law 70

Unit 9 The Law of Agency 88

Unit 10 Product Liability Law 103

Unit 11 World Trade Organization 117

Unit 12 International Monetary Fund and the World Bank 132

Unit 13 TRIMs Agreement 139

Unit 14 Introduction to Intellectual Property 145

Unit 15 Introduction to Paris Convention for the Protection of Industrial Property 152

Unit 16 Disputes Settlement in International Trade 158

References 169

UNIT 1 Introduction to Two Major Legal Systems

Key Concepts

common law	civil law	adversarial procedure	inquisitorial procedure
natural law	cross-examinations		

Learning Objectives

1. Understand the concepts of civil law system and common law system.
2. Understand the differences between adversarial procedure and inquisitorial procedure.
3. Be familiar with the differences between civil law system and common law system.

Civil Law System[1]

The Civil Law System is the oldest and most influential of the legal families. It is derived from Roman and Germanic practice. As distinguished from public law, the body of the law deals with rights of private citizens. It is also called Romano-Germanic Family or Continental System. The French Civil Code of 1804 and the German Civil Code of 1896 are now regarded as the very basis of the modern civil law.

Civil law is a legal system inspired by Roman law[2], the primary feature of which is that laws are written into a collection, codified, and not (as in common law) interpreted by judges.

Conceptually, it is the group of legal ideas and systems ultimately derived from the Code of Justinian[3], but heavily overlaid by Germanic, ecclesiastical, feudal, and local practices, as well as doctrinal strains such as natural law[4], codification, and legislative positivism.

Materially, civil law proceeds from abstractions, formulates general principles, and distinguishes substantive rules from procedural rules. It holds legislation as the primary source of law, and the court system is usually inquisitorial, unbound by precedent, and composed of specially trained judicial officers with a limited authority to interpret law. Juries separate from the judges are not used, although in some cases, volunteer lay judges participate along with legally trained career judges.

The principle of civil law is to provide all citizens with an accessible and written collection of the laws which apply to them and which judges must follow. It is the most widespread type of legal system in the world, applied in various forms in approximately 150 countries and oldest surviving legal system in the world. Colonial expansion spread the civil law system and European civil law has been adopted in much of Latin America as well as in parts of Asia and Africa.

The civil law system takes as its major inspiration Roman law, and in particular the Corpus Juris Civilis of Emperor Justinian, and subsequent expounding and developments in Medieval Roman Law. Roman law was received differently in different countries. In some it went into force wholesale by legislative act, i.e., it became positive law, whereas in others it was diffused into society by increasingly influential legal experts and scholars.

Roman law was in place in the Byzantine Empire until its final fall in the 15th century. However, subject as it was to multiple incursions and occupations in the latter Middle Ages, its laws became widely available in Western Europe. It was first received into the Holy Roman Empire partly because it was considered imperial law, and it spread in Europe mainly because its students were the only trained lawyers. It became the basis of Scots law, though partly rivaled by feudal Common law. In England, it was taught academically at Oxford and Cambridge, but underlay only probate and matrimonial law, inherited by canon law when secularized, and maritime law, adapted from the law merchant through the Bordeaux trade.

Consequently, neither of the two waves of Romanism completely dominated in Europe. Roman law was a secondary source that was applied only when local customs and laws were found lacking on a certain subject. However, after a time, even local law came to be interpreted and evaluated primarily on the basis of Roman law (it being a common European legal tradition of sorts), thereby in turn influencing the main source of law. Eventually, the works of Civilian glossators and commentators led to the development of a common body of law and writing about law, a common legal language, and a common method of teaching and scholarship, all termed the *jus commune*, or law common to Europe, which consolidated canon law and Roman law, and to some extent, feudal law.

An important characteristic, beyond Roman law foundations, is the extended codification of the adopted Roman law, i.e. its inclusion into civil codes. The system of codification has its origins in the Code of Hammurabi, written in ancient Babylon during the 18th century BC.

The concept of codification was further developed during the 17th and 18th centuries AD, as an expression of both Natural Law and the ideas of the Enlightenment. The political ideal of that era was expressed by the concepts of democracy, protection of property and the rule of law. That ideal required the creation of certainty of law, through the recording of law and through its uniformity. So, the aforementioned mix of Roman law and customary and local law ceased to exist, and the road opened for law codification, which could contribute to the aims of the above mentioned political ideal.

Another reason that contributed to codification was that the notion of the nation state required the recording of the law that would be applicable to that state.

Certainly, there was also reaction to the aim of law codification. The proponents of codification regarded it as conducive to certainty, unity and systematic recording of the law; whereas its opponents claimed that codification would result in the ossification of the law.

In the end, despite whatever resistance to codification, the codification of European private laws moved forward. Codifications were completed by Denmark (1687), Sweden (1734), Prussia (1794), France (1804), and Austria (1811). The French codes were imported into areas conquered by Emperor Napoleon and later adopted with modifications in the Netherlands (1838), Italy and Romania (1865), Portugal (1867), Spain (1888), Germany (1900), and Switzerland (1912). These codifications were in turn imported into colonies at one time or another by most of these countries. The Swiss version was adopted in Brazil (1916) and Turkey (1926).

Because Germany was a rising power in the late 19th century and its legal system was well organized, when many Asian nations were developing, the German Civil Code became the basis for the legal systems of Japan and South Korea. In China, the German Civil Code was introduced in the later years of the Qing Dynasty and formed the basis of the law of the Republic of China, which remains in force in Taiwan.

Some authors consider civil law to have served as the foundation for socialist law used in Communist countries, which in this view would basically be civil law with the addition of Marxist-Leninist ideas. Even if this is so, civil law was generally the legal system in place before the rise of socialist law, and some Eastern European countries reverted back to the pre-Socialist civil law following the fall of socialism, while others continued using their Socialist legal systems.

Several legal institutions in civil law are similar to institutions in Islamic law and jurisprudence during the Middle Ages, and some have suggested a borrowing. For example, the Islamic *Hawala* institution is the basis of the *Avallo* in Italian civil law and the *Aval* in French civil law.

Common Law System[5]

Common Law System is also called Anglo-American Law System (British-American Law System). It is the legal system of England and countries that were once English colonies. It is based on court-made rules and precedents. An import aspect of the common law is its basis in the customary practice of the courts, and the term itself is often used to describe that part of English law that is not based on statutory law or legislation.

Common law (also known as case law or precedent) is law developed by judges through decisions of courts and similar tribunals rather than through legislative statutes or executive branch action. A "common law system" is a legal system that gives great precedential weight to common law, on the principle that it is unfair to treat similar facts differently on different occasions. The body of precedent is called "common law" and it binds future decisions. In cases where the parties disagree on what the law is, an idealized common law court looks to past precedential decisions of relevant courts. If a similar dispute has been resolved in the past, the court is bound to follow the reasoning used in the prior decision (this principle is known as *stare decisis*). If, however, the court finds that the current dispute is fundamentally distinct from all previous cases (called a "matter of first impression"), judges have the authority and duty to make law by creating precedent. Thereafter, the new decision becomes precedent, and will bind future courts.

In practice, common law systems are considerably more complicated than the idealized system described above. The decisions of a court are binding only in a particular jurisdiction, and even within a given jurisdiction, some courts have more power than others. For example, in most jurisdictions, decisions by appellate courts are binding on lower courts in the same jurisdiction and on future decisions of the same appellate court, but decisions of lower courts are only non-binding persuasive authority. Interactions between common law, constitutional law, statutory law and regulatory law also give rise to considerable complexity. However *stare decisis*, the principle that similar cases should be decided according to consistent principled rules so that they will reach similar results, lies at the heart of all common law systems.

Common law legal systems are in widespread use, particularly in England where it originated in the Middle Ages, and in nations or regions that trace their legal heritage to England as former colonies of the British Empire, including the United States, Malaysia, Singapore, Bangladesh, Pakistan, Sri Lanka, India, Ghana, Cameroon, Canada, Ireland, New Zealand, South Africa, Zimbabwe, Hong Kong, and Australia.

Main Differences Between the Two Legal Systems

The common law is based on court decision or precedents whereas the civil law's grounds for deciding cases are found in codes, statues, and prescribed texts. The way in which the common law spread around the world is different from how the civil law was distributed. Those nation in which the common law developed are Australia, Canada, India, Ireland, New Zealand, and the United States. Most European continental nations and Latin American nations are civil law nations.

Common law is a matrix of case law and statutes; it uses the jury system and the doctrine of supremacy to limit the actions of the government. The common law adopts adversarial procedure[6] while the civil law uses inquisitorial procedure[7]. The adversarial system (or adversary system) of law is the system of law that relies on the contest between each advocate representing his or her party's positions and involves an impartial person or group of people, usually a jury or judge, trying to determine the truth of the case. As opposed to that, the inquisitorial system has a judge (or a group of judges who work together) whose task is to investigate the case. The adversary procedure requires the opposing sides to bring out pertinent information and to present and cross-examine witnesses. This procedure is observed primarily in countries in which the Anglo-American legal system of common law predominates.

Under the adversary system, each side is responsible for conducting its own investigation. In criminal proceedings, the prosecution represents the people at large and has at its disposal the police department with its investigators and laboratories, while the defense must find its own investigative resources and finances. Both sides may command the attendance of witnesses by subpoena. If the defendant is indigent, his attorney's opportunities for a broader investigation are limited by the provisions of the jurisdiction in which the trial is conducted. In criminal law under the adversary system, the accused need not be present in grand jury indictment proceedings (no longer conducted in Great Britain and recommended by some authorities for eventual abolition in the United States). If an indictment is handed down by the grand jury, its proceedings are available to the defendant. Under civil law the adversary system works similarly, except that both plaintiff and respondent must prepare their own cases, usually through privately engaged attorneys.

In any adversary trial, the opposing sides present evidence, examine witnesses, and conduct cross-examinations[8], each in an effort to produce information beneficial to its side of the case. Skillful questioning can often produce testimony that can be made to take on various meanings. What seemed absolute in direct testimony can raise doubts under cross-examination. The skills of the attorneys are also displayed at the time of summation, especially in a jury trial, when their versions of what the jury has heard may persuade the jury to interpret the facts to the benefit of the side that is most persuasive.

In adversary proceedings before juries the judge functions as moderator and referee on points of law, rarely taking part in the questioning unless he or she feels that important points of law or fact must be made clearer. In a bench trial (without a jury) the judge makes findings of fact as well as of law. Since a witness called by the opposing party is presumed to be hostile, cross-examination does permit leading questions. A witness called by the direct examiner, on the other hand, may only be treated as hostile by that examiner after being permitted to do so by the judge, at the request of that examiner and as a result of the witness being openly antagonistic and/or prejudiced against the opposing party.

The main purposes of cross-examination are to elicit favorable facts from the witness, or to impeach the credibility of the testifying witness to lessen the weight of unfavourable testimony. Cross-examination frequently produces critical evidence in trials, especially if a witness contradicts previous testimony. The advocate Edward Marshall-Hall built his career on cross-examination which often involved histrionic outbursts designed to sway jurors. Most experienced and skilled cross-examiners, however, refrain from caustic or abrasive cross-examination so as to avoid alienating jurors.

Cross-examination is, arguably, the main purpose of a trial. Though the closing argument is often considered the deciding moment of a trial, effective cross-examination wins trials.

An inquisitorial system is a legal system where the court or a part of the court is actively involved in investigating the facts of the case, as opposed to an adversarial system where the role of the court is primarily that of an impartial referee between the prosecution and the defense. Inquisitorial systems are used in some countries with civil legal systems as opposed to case law systems. Also countries using case law, including the United States, may use an inquisitorial system for summary hearings in the case of misdemeanors such as minor traffic violations. In fact, the distinction between an adversarial and inquisitorial system is theoretically unrelated to the distinction between a civil legal and case law system. Some legal scholars consider "inquisitorial" misleading, and prefer the word "nonadversarial".

The inquisitorial system applies to questions of criminal procedure as opposed to questions of substantive law; that is, it determines how criminal enquiries and trials are conducted, not the kind of crimes for which one can be prosecuted, nor the sentences that they carry. It is most readily used in some civil legal systems. However, some jurists do not recognize this dichotomy and see procedure and substantive legal relationships as being interconnected and part of a theory of justice as applied differently in various legal cultures.

In some jurisdictions, the trial judge may participate in the fact-finding inquiry by questioning witnesses even in adversarial proceedings. The rules of admissibility of evidence may also allow the judge to act more like an inquisitor than an arbiter of justice.

Although international tribunals intended to try crimes against humanity, such as the Nuremberg Trials and the International Criminal Court, have generally used a version of the adversarial system, they have also incorporated some key features of the inquisitorial system, such as the use of professional career judges, and in the case of the International Criminal Court, the use of a pre-trial examining or investigative division.

Notes

1. Civil Law System　民法法系

   民法法系又称罗马法系、法典法系、大陆法系、罗马日尔曼法系，是与英美普通法系并列的当今世界两大重要法系之一，覆盖了当今世界的广大区域，德国、法国、中国、日本等均为大陆民法系地区。民法法系是指以古罗马，特别是以19世纪初《法国民法典》和《德国民法典》为传统产生和发展起来的法律的总称。以古罗马法为发端，并以罗马法在中世纪意大利的复兴和神圣罗马帝国中的继受为源流，在近代法国民法和德国民法的基础之上发展形成。始终与罗马法有密切关系，以法典为主要渊源。由于该法系的影响范围主要是在欧洲大陆国家，特别是法国和德国，且主要法律的表现形式均为法典，所以又称为大陆法系、罗马-德意志法系、法典法系。属于这一法系的除了欧洲大陆国家外，还有曾是法国、德国、葡萄牙、荷兰等国殖民地的国家及因其他原因受其影响的国家。

2. Roman law　罗马法

   罗马法一般泛指罗马奴隶制国家法律的总称，存在于罗马奴隶制国家的整个历史时期。它既包括从罗马国家产生至西罗马帝国灭亡时期的法律，以及皇帝的命令、元老院的告示、成文法和一些习惯法在内，也包括公元7世纪中叶以前东罗马帝国的法律。

3. the Code of Justinian 《查士丁尼法典》

东罗马帝国皇帝查士丁尼一世下令编纂的一部汇编式法典,是罗马法的集大成者。法典内容为东罗马帝国时期的皇帝敕令,以及权威的法学家对于法律的解释。《查士丁尼法典》颁布后,又陆续颁布了《查士丁尼法学总论》《查士丁尼学说汇编》和《查士丁尼新律》3 部分,作为《查士丁尼法典》的续编,最后完成于公元 530 年左右。

4. natural law 自然法

在法学中,自然法的学说指在自然状态中固有的正义法则,以及(或者)在解决冲突的自然过程中显现的规律(具体化为习惯法)。

5. Common Law System 普通法系

又称英美法系。是指以英国普通法为基础发展起来的法律的总称。它首先产生于英国,之后扩大到曾经是英国殖民地、附属国的许多国家和地区,包括美国、加拿大、印度、巴基斯坦、孟加拉、马来西亚、新加坡以及非洲的个别国家和地区。到 18 世纪至 19 世纪时,随着英国殖民地的扩张,英国法被传入这些国家和地区,英美法系终于发展成为世界主要法系之一。英美法系的主要特点是以判例法为主要形式。

6. adversarial procedure 抗辩程序

英美法系的诉讼程序以原告、被告及其辩护人和代理人为重心,法官只是双方争论的"仲裁人"而不能参与争论,与这种抗辩式程序同时存在的是陪审团制度,陪审团主要负责作出事实上的结论和法律上的基本结论(如有罪或无罪),法官负责作出法律上的具体结论,即判决。

7. inquisitorial procedure 讯问程序

大陆法系的诉讼程序以法官为重心,突出法官职能,具有讯问程序的特点,而且,多由法官和陪审员共同组成法庭来审判案件。

8. cross-examinations 交叉询问

由一方当事人向另一方当事人所提供的证人提出的诘问,一般是在提供证人的一方首先向自己的证人提问后进行的,交叉询问是意图使证人改变、限定、修正或撤回提出的证据。在交叉询问中允许进行诱导性提问,询问证人的当事人通常比对方当事人有更大的自由。在任何情节上不对证人进行询问,一般就暗示接受证人对该情节的举证。一项证据已经或将要被给予的效力不同于证人所陈述的效力,那么在交叉询问中必须就此证据的效力同证人见面,以使他能够作出承认、否认或解释。英美法系关于证人质证几乎就是交叉询问的同义词。大部分证据包括证人证言、被害人陈述、被告人供述、当事人陈述以及书证、物证均可以交叉询问来进行质证。交叉询问被一些英美法学者视为专业性很强的法庭技术。要求律师有高明的技巧和丰富的经验。

Study Questions

1. Try to define Roman law and natural law.
2. Briefly describe the main features of civil law system and common law system.
3. What are the main differences between two legal systems?
4. What are the main differences between adversarial procedure and inquisitorial procedure?

UNIT 2 Introduction to United Nations Convention on Contracts for the International Sale of Goods[1]

Key Concepts

offer	invitation for offer	acceptance	anticipatory of the contract
fundamental breach of the contract		preservation of the goods	

Learning Objectives

1. Understand the concept of offer and acceptance.
2. Understand the differences between withdrawal of an offer and revocation of an offer.
3. Understand the obligations of the seller and the buyer.
4. Understand remedies of the breach of the contract by the seller and the buyer respectively.

Offer[2]

An offer means a proposal for concluding a contract addressed to one or more specific persons. The offer shall be sufficiently definite and indicates the intention of the offeror to be bound in case of acceptance. A proposal is sufficiently definite if it indicates the goods and expressly or implicitly[3] fixes or makes provisions for determining the quantity and the price. So an effective offer shall be in line with the minimum requirements of this convention. An offer becomes effective when it reaches the offeree.

Invitation for Offer[4]

A proposal other than one addressed to one or more specific persons is to be considered merely as an invitation to make offers, unless the contrary is clearly indicated by the person making the proposal. In practice, catalogues of the goods, price list, public announcement of auction or tender, prospectus[5], commercial advertisements, etc, are usually taken as invitation for offer. In some countries, if the contents of the commercial advertisement are sufficiently definite, and it is made to the public as an offer, it shall constitute an offer. For instance, the commercial advertisement states that it constitutes an offer, or the goods under this advertisement will be sold to those who are the first to pay cash, or open L/C.

Withdrawal and Revocation of an Offer[6]

Withdrawal means that the offeror takes the offer back, making it void, before it reaches the offeree and becomes effective. While revocation means that the offeror revokes it so as to make it void after the offer reaches the offeree, and becomes effective. Withdrawal or revocation has great significance in international trade. The offeror may withdraw or revoke the offer if he makes a mistake in the offer, or due to the fluctuation of the market price. An offer may be revoked if the revocation reaches the offeree before he has dispatched an acceptance. An offer can not be revoked if it states a fixed time for acceptance or otherwise, that it is irrevocable, or if it was reasonable for the offeree to rely on the offer as being irrevocable and the offeree has acted in reliance on the offer. An offer, even if it is irrevocable, may be withdrawn if the withdrawal reaches the offeree before or at the same time as the offer.

Acceptance[7]

An acceptance means a statement made by or other conduct of the offeree indicating assent to an offer. Silence or inactivity does not amount to acceptance. An acceptance of an offer becomes effective at the moment the indication of assent reaches the offeror. An acceptance is not effective if the indication of assent does not reach the offeror within the time he has fixed or, if no time is fixed, within a reasonable time. An oral offer must be accepted immediately unless the circumstances indicate otherwise. The offeree may indicate assent by performing an act, such as one relating to the dispatch of the goods or payment of the price, without notice to the offeror, the acceptance is effective at the moment the act is performed, provided that the act is performed within the period of time.

A reply to an offer which purports to be an acceptance but contains additions, limitations or other modifications is a rejection of the offer and constitute a counteroffer[8]. Nevertheless, if certain additional or different terms in a reply to an offer do not materially alter[9] the terms of the offer, the reply shall constitute an acceptance, unless the offeror, without undue delay, objects orally to the discrepancy or dispatches a notice to that effect. Additional or different terms relating to the price, payment, quality and quantity of the goods, place and time of delivery, extent of one party's liability to the other or the settlement of disputes are considered to alter the terms of the offer materially.

If a notice of acceptance can not be delivered at the address of the offeror on the last day of the period because that day falls on an official holiday or a non-business day at the place of the offeror, the period is extended until the first business day which follows. If its transmission had been normal it would have reached the offeror in due time, the late acceptance is effective as an acceptance unless, without delay, the offeror informs the offeree that he considers his offer as having lapsed. An acceptance may be withdrawn if the withdrawal reaches the offeror before or at the same time as the acceptance would have become effective.

A contract is concluded at the moment when an acceptance of an offer becomes effective in accordance with the provisions of this convention. [10]

Obligations of the Seller

Delivery of the Goods and Handing over of Documents

The seller must deliver the goods, hand over any documents relating to them and transfer the property in the goods as required by the contract. The seller must deliver the goods at the time required by the contract, or in any other case, within a reasonable time after the conclusion of the contract. If the seller is not bound to deliver the goods at any other particular place, he shall hand the goods over to the first carrier for transmission to the buyer, provided that the contract involves carriage of the goods. If the seller is not bound to effect insurance in respect of the carriage of the goods, he must, at the buyer's request, provide him with all available information necessary to enable him to effect such insurance. If the seller is bound to hand over documents relating to the goods, he must hand them over at the time and place and in the form required by the contract.

Conformity of the Goods and Third Party Claims

The quantity, quality and descriptions of the goods delivered by the seller shall be in conformity with those required by the contract. The goods are contained or packaged in the manner required by the contract. The seller is liable in accordance with the contract for any lack of conformity which exists at the time when the risk passes to the buyer, even though the lack of conformity becomes apparent only after that time. The seller is also liable for any lack of conformity which is due to a breach of his obligations, including a breach of any guarantee that for a period of time the goods will remain fit for their ordinary purpose or for some particular purpose or will retain specified qualities or characteristics.

In any event, the buyer loses the right to rely on a lack of conformity of the goods if he does not give the seller notice thereof at the latest within a period of two years from the date on which the goods were actually handed over to the buyer, unless this time limit is inconsistent with a contractual period of guarantee.

The seller must deliver goods which are free from any right or claim of a third party [11], unless the buyer agreed to take the goods subject to that right or claim. The seller must deliver the goods which are free from any right or claim of a third party based on industrial property or other intellectual property, of which at the time of the conclusion of the contract the seller knew or could not have been unaware, provided that the right or claim is based on industrial property or other industrial property, (a) under the law of the State where the goods will be resold or otherwise used, if it was contemplated by the parties at the time of the conclusion of the contract that the goods would be resold or otherwise used in that State; (b) in any other case, under the law of the State where the buyer has his place of business. Nevertheless, the seller's obligation is not governed if, at the time of the conclusion of the contract the buyer knew or could not have been unaware of the right or claim; or the right or claim results from the seller's compliance with technical drawings, designs, formulae or other such specifications furnished by the buyer.

Remedies for Breach of the Contract by the Seller[12]

If the seller fails to perform any of his obligations under the contract, the buyer may act as follows:

(1) The buyer may require performance by the seller of his obligations;

(2) If the goods do not conform with the contract, the buyer may require delivery of substitute goods only if the lack of conformity constitute a fundamental breach of the contract[13];

(3) If the goods do not conform with the contract, the buyer may require the seller to remedy the lack of conformity by repair;

(4) The buyer may declare the contract avoided if the seller's failure to perform any of his obligations under the contract amounts to a fundamental breach of the contract, or in case of non-delivery, if the seller does not deliver the goods within the additional period of time fixed by the buyer;

(5) If the goods do not conform with the contract and whether or not the price has already been paid, the buyer may reduce the price in the same proportion as the value that the goods actually delivered had at the time of the delivery bears to the value that conforming goods would have had at that time[14];

(6) If the seller delivers the goods before the date fixed, the buyer may take delivery or refuse to take delivery;

(7) If the seller delivers a quantity of the goods greater than that provided for in the contract, the buyer may take delivery or refuse to take delivery of the excess quantity. If the buyer takes delivery of all or part of the excess quantity, he must pay for it at the contract rate;

(8) The buyer is not deprived of any right he may have to claim damages by exercising his right to other remedies.

Obligations of the Buyer

The buyer must pay the price of the goods and take delivery of them as required by the contract. If the price is fixed according to the weight of the goods, in case of doubt it is to be determined by the net weight. The buyer must pay the price on the date fixed by or determinable from the contract without the need for any request or compliance with any formality on the part of the seller. The buyer's obligation to take delivery consists in doing all the acts which could reasonably be expected of him in order to enable the seller to make delivery, and taking over the goods.

Remedies for Breach of the Contract by the Buyer

If the buyer fails to perform any of his obligations under the contract,

(1) the seller may require the buyer to pay the price, take delivery or perform his other obligations, unless the seller has resorted to a remedy which is inconsistent with this requirement;

(2) the seller may fix an additional period of time of reasonable length for performance by the buyer of his obligations;

(3) the seller may declare the contract avoided if the failure by the buyer to perform any of his obligations under the contract amounts to a fundamental breach of contract; or if the buyer does not perform his obligations within the additional period of time fixed by the seller, or if he declares that he will not do so within the period so fixed;

(4) the seller is not deprived of any right he may have to claim damages by exercising his right to other remedies;

(5) no period of grace may be granted to the buyer by a court or arbitral tribunal[15] when the seller resorts to a remedy for breach of contract.

Passing of Risks

Loss of or damages to the goods after the risk has passed to the buyer does not discharge him from his obligation to pay the price, unless the loss or damage is due to an act or omission of the seller.

If the contract of sale involves carriage of the goods and the seller is not bound to hand them over at a particular place, the risk passes to the buyer when the goods are handed over to the first carrier for transmission to the buyer in accordance with the contract. If the seller is bound to hand the goods over to a carrier at a particular place, the risk does not pass to the buyer until the goods are handed over to the carrier at that place. The fact that the seller is authorized to retain documents controlling the disposition of the goods does not affect the passage of the risk. The risk in respect of goods sold in transit passes to the buyer from the time of the conclusion of the contract. Nevertheless, if at the time of the conclusion of the contract the seller knew or ought to have known that the goods had been lost or damaged and did not disclose this to the buyer, the loss or damage is at the risk of the seller. In other cases, the risk passes to the buyer when he takes over the goods or, if he does not do so in due time, from the time when the goods are placed at his disposal and he commits a breach of the contract by failing to take delivery.

Anticipatory Breach[16]

A party may suspend the performance of his obligations if, after the conclusion of the contract, it becomes apparent that the other party will not perform a substantial part of his obligations as a result of a serious deficiency in his ability of performance or in his creditworthiness, or his conduct in preparing to perform or in performing the contract. A party suspending performance, whether before or after dispatch of the goods, must immediately give notice of suspension to the other party and must continue with performance if the other party provides adequate assurance of his performance.

Installment Contract[17]

In the case of the contract for delivery of goods by installments, if the failure of one party to perform any of his obligations in respect of any installment constitutes a fundamental breach of the contract with respect to that installment, the other party may declare the contract avoided with respect to that installment. If one party's failure to perform any of his obligations gives the other party good grounds to conclude that a fundamental breach of contract will occur with respect to future installments, he may declare the contract avoided for the future, provided that he does so within a reasonable time. The buyer who declares the contract avoided in respect of any delivery may, at the same time, declare it avoided in respect of deliveries already made or of future deliveries if, by reason of their interdependence, those deliveries could not be used for the purpose contemplated by the parties at the time of the conclusion of the contract.

Damages

Damages for breach of contract by one party consist of a sum equal to the loss, including loss of profit, suffered by the other party as a consequence of the breach. The party claiming damages may recover the difference between the contract price and the price in the substitute transaction as well as any further damages, such as the loss of profit, or the difference between the price fixed by the contract and the current price at the time of avoidance of the contract under differently circumstances.

The party who relies on a breach a contract must take reasonable measures to mitigate the loss, including the loss of profit, resulting from the breach. If he fails to take such measures, the party in breach may claim a reduction in the damages in the amount by which the loss should have been mitigated.

Furthermore, if a party fails to pay the price or any other sum that is in arrears, the other party is entitled to interest on it, without prejudice to any claim for other damages[18].

Exemption

A party who is not liable for any failure to perform any of his obligations if he proves that the failure was due to an impediment beyond his control[19] and he could not reasonably be expected to have taken the impediment into account at the time of the conclusion of the contract or to have avoided or overcome it or its consequences. The exemption has effect for the period which the impediment exists.

A party may not rely on a failure of the other party to perform to the extent that such failure was caused by the first party's act or omission.

Effects of Avoidance

Avoidance of the contract releases both parties from their obligations under it, subject to any damages which may be due. A voidance does not affect any provisions of the contract for the settlement of disputes or any other provisions of the contract governing the rights and obligations of the parties consequent upon the avoidance of the contract.

A party who has performed the contract either wholly or in part may claim restitution from the other party of whatever the first party has supplied or paid under the contract. If both parties are bound to make restitution, they must do so concurrently.

If the seller is bound to refund the price, he must also pay interest on it, from the date on which the price was paid.

The buyer must account to the seller for all benefits which he has derived from the goods or part of them if he must make restitution of the goods or part of them.

Preservation of the Goods[20]

If the buyer is in delay in taking delivery of the goods or, where payment of the price and delivery of the goods to be made concurrently, if he fails to pay the price, and the seller is either in possession of the goods or otherwise able to control their disposition, the seller must take steps as are reasonable in the circumstances to preserve the goods. He is entitled to retain them until he has been reimbursed for his reasonable expenses by the buyer.

If the buyer has received the goods and intends to exercise the right under the contract or this convention to reject them, he must take such steps to preserve them, and is entitled to retain them until he has been reimbursed his reasonable expenses by the seller.

If the goods dispatched to the buyer have been placed at his disposal at their destination and he exercises the right to reject them, he must take possession of them on behalf of the seller, provided that this can be done without payment of the price and without unreasonable inconvenience or unreasonable expenses. This provision does not apply if the seller or a person authorized to take charge of the goods.

A party who is bound to preserve the goods may deposit them in a warehouse of a third person at the expense of the other party provided that the expense incurred is not unreasonable.

A party who is bound to preserve the goods may sell them by any appropriate means if there has been an unreasonable delay by the other party in taking possession of the goods or in taking them back or in paying the price or the cost of preservation, provided that reasonable notice of the intention to sell has been given to the other party. If the goods are subject to deterioration or their preservation would involve unreasonable expense, a party who is bound to preserve the goods must take reasonable measures to sell them. To the extent possible he must give notice to the other party of his intention to sell.

A party selling the goods has right to retain out of the proceeds of sale an amount equal to the reasonable expenses of preserving the goods and of selling them. He must account to the other party for the balance.

Notes

1. *United Nations Convention on Contracts for the International Sale of Goods* 《联合国国际货物销售合同公约》
   该公约于 1980 年通过,并已于 1988 年 1 月 1 日起正式生效。该公约既考虑到大陆法系国家的合同法,亦考虑到英美法系国家的相关法律,是迄今为止关于国际货物买卖的一个最重要的国际公约。至 1998 年 5 月 31 日,已有 51 个国家加入该公约。我国于 1986 年加入该公约,但在加入时就合同形式(form of the contract)及适用范围(sphere of its application)作出了保留,即要求合同采用书面形式,公约的适用范围限于双方的营业地处于不同缔约国的当事人之间所订立的货物买卖合同。
2. offer 要约
   是指希望和他人订立合同的意思表示。要约符合条件:向一个或一个以上的特定的人提出,内容明确,发要约人应明确一旦对方接受,即具有拘束力的意思表示。国际贸易实务中的实盘(firm offer)为要约,虚盘(non-firm offer)为要约邀请。
3. expressly or implicitly 明示或默示
4. invitation for offer 要约邀请
   是指当事人向他人作出的希望对方向自己发出要约的意思表示。
5. public announcement of auction or tender, prospectus 拍卖公告、招标公告、招股说明书。
6. withdrawal and revocation of an offer 要约撤回和撤销
   撤回是指要约在生效前收回,而撤销则指的是要约生效后的收回。
7. acceptance 承诺
   是指受要约人对要约表示无条件接受的意思表示。
8. counteroffer 反要约
   在外贸实务中又称“还盘”,反要约应视为一项新要约。
9. materially alter 实质性变更
   是指对要约中的价格、货物质量、数量、付款、交货时间或地点、赔偿责任、争议解决中的任何一项作出添加或变更。若受要约人对要约作了实质性的变更,那就不能视为对要约的承诺,而是一项反要约。
10. A contract is concluded at the moment… of this convention.
    依照本公约规定,合同于对要约承诺生效时订立。
11. The seller must deliver goods which are free from any right or claim of a third party.
    卖方所交付的货物,应为第三人不得提出任何权利或要求的货物。

值得注意的是,这里的"权利"或"要求"尤其涉及知识产权方面的主张。

12. Remedies for Breach of the Contract by the Seller　对卖方违约的补救方法
比如,要求卖方实际履行、减少价款、宣告合同无效、损害赔偿。应注意的是,买方享有要求损害赔偿的权利,不因其行使其他救济办法的权利而丧失。
13. a fundamental breach of the contract　根本违约
是指一方违反合同,致使另一方根据合同有权期待得到的东西落空。是否构成根本违约,对当事人采取何种救济措施有直接的关系。如果已构成根本违约,受害方有权宣告撤销合同,反之则不能。
14. the buyer may reduce the price in the same proportion... at that time
买方可按货物交付时的实际价值与符合合同要求的货物在当时所应具有的价值之间的比例计算。
15. arbitral tribunal　仲裁庭
16. anticipatory breach　预期违约
是指履约期限到来之前,一方无正当理由而明确表示将不履行合同(明示毁约),或者其行为表明将不可能履约(默示毁约)。
17. installment contract　分批交货合同
18. Furthermore, if a party fails to... without prejudice to any claim for other damages.
此外,如果一方当事人没有支付价款或拖欠其他款项,另一方当事人有权对这些款额收取利息,而且亦不影响其对其他损失的赔偿要求。
此处的 in arrears 及 without prejudice to 可分别理解为"拖欠"和"不影响(不妨碍)"。
19. an impediment beyond his control　非他所能控制的障碍
此处实际上指的是"不可抗力"(force majeure),即一方所难以预见、难以避免、难以克服的客观情况。
20. preservation of the goods　货物保全
通常在买方迟延收取货物、迟延支付价款时,如货物仍在卖方的掌控中,卖方应采取合理措施以保全货物。如果货物已到达目的地或买方在收到货物后打算退货,买方亦应采取保全措施,例如,将货物存放在第三方的仓库,而货物保全的合理费用则由另一方承担。

Study Questions

1. What is offer?
2. What is acceptance of an offer?
3. Briefly explain the seller's obligation.
4. How do you think of the transfer of risks to the goods?
5. Are there any stipulations as regard the transfer of ownership in the convention? Why?

Case Study

Carlill v Carbolic Smoke Ball Company

Facts

The Carbolic Smoke Ball Company made a product called the "smoke ball". It claimed to be a cure for influenza and a number of other diseases, in the context of the 1889-1890 flu pandemic which is estimated to have killed 1 million people. The smoke ball was a rubber ball with a tube attached. It was filled with carbolic acid (phenol). The tube was then inserted into the user's nose. It was squeezed at the bottom to release the vapours into the nose of the user. This would cause the nose to run, and hopefully flush out the viral infection.

The Company published advertisements in the *Pall Mall Gazette* and other newspapers on November 13, 1891, claiming that it would pay £100 to anyone who got sick with influenza after using its product according to the instructions set out in the advertisement.

"£100 reward will be paid by the Carbolic Smoke Ball Company to any person who contracts the increasing epidemic influenza colds, or any disease caused by taking cold, after having used the ball three times daily for two weeks, according to the printed directions supplied with each ball.

£1000 is deposited with the Alliance Bank, Regent Street, showing our sincerity in the matter.

During the last epidemic of influenza many thousand carbolic smoke balls were sold as preventives against this disease, and in no ascertained case was the disease contracted by those using the carbolic smoke ball.

One carbolic smoke ball will last a family several months, making it the cheapest remedy in the world at the price, 10s. post free. The ball can be refilled at a cost of 5s. Address: Carbolic Smoke Ball Company, 27, Princes Street, Hanover Square, London."

Mrs Louisa Elizabeth Carlill saw the advertisement, bought one of the balls and used three times daily for nearly two months until she contracted the flu on January 17, 1892. She claimed £100 from the Carbolic Smoke Ball Company. They ignored two letters from her husband, who had trained as a solicitor. On a third request for her reward, they replied with an anonymous letter that if it is used properly the company had complete confidence in the smoke ball's efficacy, but "to protect themselves against all fraudulent claims" they would need her to come to their office to use the ball each day and be checked by the secretary. Mrs Carlill brought a claim to court. The barristers representing her argued that the advertisement and her reliance on it was a contract between her and the company, and so they ought to pay. The company argued it was not a serious contract.

Judgment

The Carbolic Smoke Ball Company, despite being represented by HH Asquith, lost its argument at the Queen's Bench. It appealed straight away. The Court of Appeal unanimously rejected the company's arguments and held that there was a fully binding contract for £100 with Mrs Carlill. Among the reasons given by the three judges were: (1) that the advert was a unilateral offer to all the world; (2) that satisfying conditions for using the smoke ball constituted acceptance of the offer; (3) that purchasing or merely using the smoke ball constituted good consideration, because it was a distinct detriment incurred at the behest of the company and, furthermore, more people buying smoke balls by relying on the advert was a clear benefit to Carbolic; (4) that the company's claim that £1000 was deposited at the Alliance Bank showed the serious intention to be legally bound.

UNIT 3 Incoterms[1]

Key Concepts

FOB CFR CIF INCOTERMS symbolic delivery of the goods
physical delivery of the goods the charter party

Learning Objectives

1. Understand the essentials of 13 trade terms in *Incoterms* 2000.
2. Understand the differences between symbolic delivery of the goods and physical delivery of the goods.
3. Understand the differences between *Incoterms* 2000 and *Incoterms* 2010.
4. Be familiar with ICC.

Incoterms or International Commercial terms are a series of pre-defined commercial terms published by the International Chamber of Commerce (ICC) widely used in international commercial transactions. A series of three-letter trade terms related to common sales practices, Incoterms are intended primarily to clearly communicate the tasks, costs and risks associated with the transportation and delivery of goods. Incoterms are accepted by governments, legal authorities and practitioners worldwide for the interpretation of most commonly used terms in international trade. They are intended to reduce or remove altogether uncertainties arising from different interpretation of such terms in different countries. In 1936, the first set of Incoterms was published. The first set remained in use for almost 20 years before the second publication in 1953, additional amendments and expansions followed in 1967, 1976, 1980, 1990 and 2000. The eighth and current version of Incoterms—Incoterms 2010—was published on January 1, 2011.

Incoterms 2000

E Term

E Term has only one term—EXW. EX works means that the seller fulfills his obligations to deliver when he has made the goods available at his premises (i. e. works, factory, warehouse, etc) to the buyer. Under this term, unless the contract stipulates otherwise, the seller is not bound to[2] load the goods on board the vehicle provided by the buyer, or to clear the goods for export[3]. The buyer bears all costs and risks involved in taking the goods from the seller's premises to the desired destination. Hence, this term represents the minimum obligation for the seller.

F Terms

F Terms involves three terms—FAS, FOB and FCA.

FAS (Free Alongside Ship) means that the seller fulfills his obligation to deliver when the goods have been placed alongside the vessel on the quay or in the lighters[4] at the named port of shipment. From that moment the buyer has to bear all costs and risks of the loss or damage to the goods. Under this term, the seller is bound to clear the goods for export.

FOB (Free on Board) means that the seller fulfills his obligations to deliver when the goods, cleared for export, have passed over the rail of the vessel at the named port of shipment. This means that the buyer shall, from that point, be responsible for all costs and risks of the loss or damage to the goods. Under this term, it is the buyer who arranges the ship for the shipment of the goods. So, the parties must try to ensure that the goods and the ship arrive at the same loading port concurrently. The loss caused by the untimely arrival or delay of the ship shall be compensated by the buyer while the loss arising from the untimely arrival or delay of the goods will be covered by the seller. At the request of the buyer, the seller may make the charter party[5] or book shipping space on behalf of the buyer, but the cost as well as the risk shall be covered by the buyer.

FCA (Free Carrier) means that the seller fulfills his obligations to deliver when he has handed over the goods, cleared for export, into the charge of the carrier named by the buyer at the appointed place or point. If the seller hands over the goods to the carrier at his own premises, the seller is bound to load the goods on board the vehicle, while the seller is not bound to unload the goods from the vehicle if the goods are handed over to the carrier at the place appointed by the buyer. This term may be used for any mode of transport, including the carriages by air, road, rail, sea, inland waterway, or by a combination of such modes.

C Terms

C Terms includes CFR, CIF, CPT, CIP.

CFR (Cost and Freight) means that the seller covers the cost of carriage but does not bear the risk arising from the carriage of the goods. That is to say, the seller must pay the cost and freight necessary to bring the goods to the named port of destination but the risk of the loss or damage to the goods, as well as any additional cost due to the events occurring after the goods have been delivered on board the vessel, is transferred from the seller to the buyer when the goods pass over the rail of the vessel in the port of shipment. This term is only used for sea and inland waterway transport. Under this term, the buyer shall effect the insurance.

CIF (Cost, Insurance and Freight) means that the seller shall not only have the same obligations as under CFR, but also procure marine insurance against the buyer's risk of loss of or damage to the goods during the carriage.

CPT (Carriage Paid To) means that the seller pays the freight for the carriage of the goods to the named destination. The risk of the loss of or damage to the goods, as well as any additional costs due to the event occurring after the time the goods have been delivered to the carrier, shall be transferred from the seller to the buyer when the goods have been handed over into the custody of the carrier. This term may be used for any mode of transport.

CIP (Carriage Insurance Paid To) means that the seller shall have the same obligations as under CPT; in addition, the seller shall procure the insurance against the buyer's risk of loss of or damages to the goods during the carriage.

Under C and F terms, the symbolic delivery of the goods[6] is applied, that is, once the seller has delivered the goods and acquired the necessary documents; he is entitled to the payments of the goods even if the carriages are lost during the transit. If the goods are lost during the transit, the buyer, instead of the seller, is to ask the insurance company to cover the losses. So such delivery also means to transfer the necessary documents at the stipulated time.

D Terms

This group contains five terms: DAF, DES, DEQ, DDU and DDP.

DAF (Delivered at Frontier) means that the seller fulfills his obligation to deliver when the goods have been made available, cleared for export, at the named point or place at the frontier, but before the customs border of the adjoining country. This term is primarily intended to be used when the goods are to be carried by rail or road, but it may also be used for any other mode of transport.

DES (Delivered Ex Ship) means that the seller fulfills his obligation to deliver when the goods have been made available to the buyer on board the ship at the named port of destination. The seller has to bear all costs and risks involved in bring the goods to the named port of destination. The buyer shall clear the goods for import. This term can only be used for sea or inland waterway transport.

DEQ (Delivered Ex Quay) means that the seller fulfills his obligation to deliver when the goods have been made available to the buyer on the quay at the named port of destination. The seller shall bear all risks and costs of delivering the goods thereto. But the buyer shall clear the goods for import.

DDU (Delivered Duty Unpaid) means that the seller fulfills his obligation to deliver when the goods have been made available to the buyer at the named place in the country of importation. The seller shall bear the risks and costs involved in bring the goods thereto. The buyer shall clear the goods for import and pay customs duties[7].

DDP (Delivered Duty Paid) means that the seller fulfills his obligation to deliver when the goods have been made available at the named place in the country of importation. Under this term, the seller shall not only bear costs and risks involved in bringing the goods thereto, but also clear the goods for import and pay customs duties. This term represents maximum obligations for the seller.

E Term and D terms may be called physical delivery of the good[8], that is, the seller shall deliver the contracted goods at agreed time, place and in the agreed manners to the buyer. Before the goods have been made available for the buyer's disposal, the seller shall be responsible for all costs and risks.

Incoterms 2010[9]

The eighth published set of pre-defined terms, *Incoterms* 2010 defines 11 rules, reducing the 13 used in *Incoterms* 2000 by introducing two new rules ("Delivered at Terminal", DAT; "Delivered at Place", DAP) that replace four rules of the prior version ("Delivered at Frontier", DAF; "Delivered Ex Ship", DES; "Delivered Ex Quay", DEQ; "Delivered Duty Unpaid", DDU). In the prior version, the rules were divided into four categories, but the 11 pre-defined terms of *Incoterms* 2010 are subdivided into two categories based only on method of delivery. The larger group of seven rules applies regardless of the method of transport, with the smaller group of four being applicable only to sales that solely involve transportation over water.

General Mode of Transportation

The seven rules defined by *Incoterms* 2010 for general modes of transportation are:

EXW—Ex Works (named place)

The seller makes the goods available at his premises. The buyer is responsible for all charges. This trade term places the greatest responsibility on the buyer and minimum obligations on the seller. The Ex Works term is often used when making an initial quotation for the sale of goods without any costs included. EXW means that the seller has the goods ready for collection at his premises (works, factory, warehouse, plant) on the date agreed upon. The buyer pays all transportation costs and also bears the risks for bringing the goods to their final destination. The seller delivers the goods at seller's premises or named place (works, factory and warehouse, etc), but not loaded on collecting vehicles and not cleared for export. The seller has no obligation to load the goods, even though in practice he may be in a better position to do so. If the seller does load the good, he does so at buyer's risk and cost. If parties wish seller to be responsible for the loading of the goods on departure and to bear the risk and all costs of such loading, this must be made clear by adding explicit wording to this effect in the Contract of sale.

FCA—Free Carrier (named places)

The seller hands over the goods, cleared for export, into the custody of the first carrier (named by the buyer) at the named place. This term is suitable for all modes of transport, including carriage by air, rail, road, and containerized / multimodal sea transport. This is the correct "freight collect" term to use for sea shipments in containers, whether LCL (less than container load) or FCL (full container load).

CPT—Carriage Paid To (named place of destination)

The general/containerized/multimodal equivalent of CFR. The seller pays for carriage to the named point of destination, but risk passes when the goods are handed over to the first carrier.

CIP—Carriage and Insurance Paid (To) (named place of destination)

The containerized transport/multimodal equivalent of CIF. Seller pays for carriage and insurance to the named destination point, but risk passes when the goods are handed over to the first carrier.

DAT—Delivered at Terminal

The seller pays for carriage to the terminal, except for costs related to import clearance, and assumes all risks up to the point that the goods are unloaded at the terminal.

DAP—Delivered at Place (named place of destination)

The seller pays for carriage to the named place, except for costs related to import clearance, and assumes all risks prior to the point that the goods are ready for unloading by the buyer.

DDP—Delivered Duty Paid (destination place).

Water Transportation

The four rules defined by *Incoterms* 2010 for sales where transportation is entirely conducted by water are:

FAS—Free Alongside Ship (named loading port)

The seller must place the goods alongside the ship at the named port. The seller must clear the goods for export. Suitable only for maritime transport but NOT for multimodal sea transport in containers (see *Incoterms* 2010, ICC publication 715). This term is typically used for heavy-lift or bulk cargo.

FOB—Free on Board (named loading port)

The seller must load the goods on board the ship nominated by the buyer, cost and risk being divided at ship's rail. The seller must clear the goods for export. Maritime transport only but NOT for multimodal sea transport in containers (see *Incoterms* 2010, ICC publication 715). The buyer must instruct the seller the details of the vessel and port where the goods are to be loaded, and there is no reference to, or provision for, the use of a carrier or forwarder. It does not include Air transport. This term has been greatly misused over the last three decades ever since *Incoterms* 1980 explained that FCA should be used for container shipments.

CFR—Cost and Freight (named destination port)

The seller must pay the costs and freight to bring the goods to the port of destination.

However, risk is transferred to the buyer once the goods are loaded on the ship. Maritime transport only and Insurance for the goods is NOT included. Insurance is at the Cost of the Buyer.

CIF—Cost, Insurance and Freight (named destination port)

Exactly the same as CFR except that the seller must in addition procure and pay for insurance for the buyer. Maritime transport only.

Notes

1. Incoterms 《国际贸易术语解释通则》

   Incoterms 的副标题为 *International Rules for the Interpretation of Trade Terms*,故译为"国际贸易术语解释通则"。Incoterms 这一缩略词则源于 International Commercial Terms 三词。该套术语由国际商会 ICC(International Chamber of Commerce)于 1936 年制订。为了适应国际贸易的不断发展,国际商会于 1953 年、1967 年、1976 年、1980 年、1990 年、2000 年、2010 年先后对 Incoterms 作了修订和补充。该套贸易术语在国际上得到广泛的承认和采用,为国际货物买卖最为重要的贸易惯例。此外,有关贸易术语的国际贸易惯例还有《1932 年华沙—牛津规则》(*Warsaw-Oxford Rules* 1932)及《1941 年美国对外贸易定义修订本》(*Revised American Foreign Trade Definitions* 1941)。
2. is not bound to 没有义务
3. to clear the goods for export 办理货物出口清关手续

   此处主要是指买方应办理货物出口所需的一切海关手续,包括交纳关税及其他相关费用
4. lighters 驳船

   驳船通常在货轮不能靠港时使用,由其将货物从码头运至停于港外的货轮,再将货物从驳船装上货轮。
5. the charter party 租船合同

   在 FOB 合同中,应有买方负责安排运输,办理租船或订舱手续,并支付运费。在实务中,对于大宗货物,包括散装货,需作整船装运时,买方通常自行租船,而货物只需部分舱位时,则常委托卖方向班轮公司订舱,而相关费用及风险则由买方承担。
6. symbolic delivery of the goods 象征性交货

   2000 年版《国际贸易术语解释通则》的 F 组、C 组项下,卖方是通过向买方提交货运单据(主要有提单、商业发票、装箱单、保险单等)来完成其交货义务的。卖方所提交的单据等同于交付货物。由于这两组术语下都具有在装运港(装运地)交货的性质,因此其性质属于装运合同。
7. customs duties 关税
8. physical delivery of the good 实际交货

   依照 2000 年版《国际贸易术语解释通则》,D 组术语成交时,卖方应承担货物运至目的地的所有费用及风险,即在目的地履行其交货义务,因此,其性质上属于到达合同。
9. Incoterms 2010 《2010 年国际贸易术语解释通则》

   《2010 年国际贸易术语解释通则》(*International Rules for the Interpretation of Trade Terms*

2010，缩写 Incoterms® 2010）是国际商会根据国际货物贸易的发展，对《2000 年国际贸易术语解释通则》的修订，2010 年 9 月 27 日公布，于 2011 年 1 月 1 日实施。《2010 年国际贸易术语解释通则》删去了《2000 年国际贸易术语解释通则》4 个术语：DAF（Delivered at Frontier）边境交货、DES（Delivered Ex Ship）目的港船上交货、DEQ（Delivered Ex Quay）目的港码头交货、DDU（Delivered Duty Unpaid）未完税交货，新增了 2 个术语：DAT（Delivered at Terminal）在指定目的地或目的港的集散站交货、DAP（Delivered at Place）在指定目的地交货。即用 DAP 取代了 DAF、DES 和 DDU 三个术语，DAT 取代了 DEQ，且扩展至适用于一切运输方式。

DAP（Delivered at Place）目的地交货，类似于取代了的 DAF、DES 和 DDU 三个术语，指卖方在指定的目的地交货，只需做好卸货准备无需卸货即完成交货。术语所指的到达车辆包括船舶，目的地包括港口。卖方应承担将货物运至指定的目的地的一切风险和费用（除进口费用外）。如卖方欲在目的地指定地点交货，且愿意承担货物运送到该地点的费用（卸货费除外）和风险时，可考虑选择 DAP。本术语适用于任何运输方式、多式联运方式及海运。

DAT（Delivered at Terminal）目的地或目的港的集散站交货，类似于取代了的 DEQ 术语，指卖方在指定的目的地或目的港的集散站卸货后将货物交给买方处置即完成交货，术语所指目的地包括港口。卖方应承担将货物运至指定的目的地或目的港的集散站的一切风险和费用（除进口费用外）。如卖方除承担 DAP 所必须履行的义务外，还愿意承担货物运送到该地点时从运输工具上卸货产生的费用，可考虑选择 DAT。本术语适用于任何运输方式或多式联运。

修订后的《2010 年国际贸易术语解释通则》取消了“船舷”的概念，卖方承担货物装上船为止的一切风险，买方承担货物自装运港装上船后的一切风险。在 FAS、FOB、CFR 和 CIF 等术语中加入了货物在运输期间被多次买卖（连环贸易）的责任义务的划分，考虑到对于一些大的区域贸易集团内部贸易的特点，*Incoterms*® 2010 不仅适用于国际销售合同，也适用于国内销售合同。

尽管 *Incoterms* 2010 于 2011 年 1 月 1 日正式生效，但并非 *Incoterms* 2000 就自动作废。国际贸易惯例本身不是法律，对国际贸易当事人不产生必然的强制性约束力。国际贸易惯例在适用的时间效力上并不存在“新法取代旧法”的说法，即 *Incoterms* 2010 实施之后并非 *Incoterms* 2000 就自动废止，当事人在订立贸易合同时仍然可以选择适用 *Incoterms* 2000 甚至 *Incoterms* 1990。

Study Questions

1. Briefly describe the essentials of 13 trade terms in *Incoterms* 2000.
2. What are the differences between symbolic delivery of the goods and physical delivery of the goods?
3. What are the differences between *Incoterms* 1990 and *Incoterms* 2000?
4. What are the differences between *Incoterms* 2000 and *Incoterms* 2010?
5. What do you think of *Incoterms* 2010?

UNIT 4 The Law of International Marine Cargo Transport[1]

Key Concepts

liner transport	charter transport	B/L	order B/L
Hague Rules	*Hamburg Rules*		

Learning Objectives

1. Understand the differences between liner transport and charter transport.
2. Understand the varieties of Bill of Lading.
3. Understand the carrier's responsibilities in marine transport.
4. Understand the differences between *Hague-Visby Rules* and *Hamburg Rules*.

There are different ways to carry the goods to their destination, such as marine transport, land transport, air transport and multimode transport, etc. In choosing one mode of transport, one shall consider such elements as the availability of the transport vehicles, the time of transport, the quantity of the goods and the safety of the goods, etc.

Modes of Marine Transport

Marine transport falls into two groups: liner transport and charter transport[2]. Liners operate on a scheduled service between a group of ports. Liners sail on the scheduled dates and times irrespective of whether the ships are full or not. The respective obligations and liabilities of the consignors and the carriers are listed in the bill of lading issued by the liner companies.

The freight of liners comprises basic charges and additional charges. There are several ways to be used to calculate the basic charges. The cargoes are usually charged by W/T, M/T, A/V[3], the numbers of the goods, or as arranged by the consignor and carrier. The additional charges may contain long length surcharge, over weight surcharge, currency adjustment factor, optional charge, port congestion surcharge, transshipment surcharge, bunker adjustment factor, alternation surcharge, and port surcharge[4], etc.

The goods are usually classified into 20 grades which are listed in the liner's freight tariff[5]. The basic freight rates are charged according to their respective grades. One may acquire such information in the liner's freight tariff of the shipping company.

Charter transport, also called tramp transport, unlike the liner transport, does not operate on a fixed route and a fixed schedule. The tramps go all over the world in search of the goods, primarily bulk shipments, like coal, grain, timber, mineral ores, fertilizers, etc. They are usually carried in complete shiploads. Tramp vessels are engaged under charter on a time, voyage or demise basis[6]. Voyage charter might be determined by one single or consecutive single voyages or one return or consecutive return voyages, while time charter is on time basis. It might be several months, a year, or even many years. Under demise, or bareboat charter, the charterer has to supply by himself the crew, and the vessel is completely under his control.

Marine Transport Bill of Lading

Marine Transport Bill of Lading, shortened as B/L, is issued by the captain or the shipping company or its agent. It is a document to testify that the goods have been received or shipped on board, and will be delivered to a certain place of destination by the carrier. In legal sense, it is a receipt issued by the carrier to have received the goods. It is also a document of title, with which the seller may come to the bank for negotiation of payment, and the bearer can get the goods at the port of destination from the carrier. Furthermore, B/L is the evidence of the carriage contract between the consignor and the carrier.

In general, B/L may contain the following information:

(1) Carrier;

(2) Shipper;

(3) Consignee[7] (This column shall be filled in with great care, if L/C is involved, with instructions of L/C);

(4) Notified party;

(5) B/L No.;

(6) Name of vessel and V/N;

(7) Port of discharge;

(8) Port of delivery;

(9) Shipping marks;

(10) Description of the goods;

(11) G/W, N/W, Measurement;

(12) Freight prepaid or to collect[8];

(13) Signature of the master or his agent and the date.

While an air way bill (AWB) must have the name and address of the consignee, a B/L may be consigned to the order of the shipper. Where the word order appears in the consignee box, the shipper may endorse it in blank or to a named transferee. A B/L endorsed in blank is transferable by delivery. Once the goods arrive at the destination they will be released to the bearer or the endorsee of the original bill of lading. The carrier's duty is to deliver goods to the first person who presents any one of the original B/L. The carrier need not require all originals to be submitted before delivery. It is therefore essential that the exporter retains control over the full set of the originals until payment is effected or a bill of exchange is accepted or some other assurance for payment has been made to him. In general, the importer's name is not shown as consignee. The bill of lading has also provision for incorporating notify party. This is the person whom the shipping company will notify on arrival of the goods at destination. The B/L also contains other details such as the name of the carrying vessel and its flag of nationality, the marks and numbers on the packages in which the goods are packed, a brief description of the goods, the number of packages, their weight and measurement, whether freight costs have been paid or whether payment of freight is due on arrival at the destination. The particulars of the container in which goods are stuffed are also mentioned in case of containerized cargo. The document is dated and signed by the carrier or its agent. The date of the B/L is deemed to be the date of shipment. If the date on which the goods are loaded on board is different from the date of the bill of lading then the actual date of loading on board will be evidenced by a notation on the B/L. In certain cases a carrier may issue a separate on board certificate to the shipper.

B/L may fall into the following varieties:

(1) On board B/L and Received for shipment B/L[9];

(2) Straight B/L, Order B/L and Open B/L[10];

(3) Clean B/L and Unclean B/L[11];

(4) Direct B/L, Transshipment B/L and Through B/L.

Straight Bill of Lading

In this importer/consignee/agent is named in the bill of lading, it is called straight bill of lading. It is a document, in which a seller agrees to use a certain transportation to ship a good to a certain location, where the bill assigned to a certain party. It details to the quality and quantity of goods.

Order Bill of Lading

This bill uses express words to make the bill negotiable, e. g. it states that delivery is to be made to the further order of the consignee using words such as "delivery to A Ltd. or to order or assigns". Consequently, it can be indorsed (legal spelling of endorse), maintained in all statute, including *Bills of Exchange Act* 1909 (CTH)) by A Ltd. or the right to take delivery can be transferred by physical delivery of the bill accompanied by adequate evidence of A Ltd.'s intention to transfer.

Clean Bill of Lading

A clean bill of lading states that the cargo has been loaded on board the ship in apparent good order and condition. Such a B/L will not bear a clause or notation which expressively declares a defective condition of goods and/or the packaging. Thus, a B/L that reflects the fact that the carrier received the goods in good condition. The opposite term is a soiled bill of lading, which reflects that the goods are received by the carrier in anything but good condition.

A straight bill of lading by land or sea, or sea/air way bill are not documents that can convey title to the goods they represent. They do no more than require delivery of the goods to the named consignee and (subject to the shipper's ability to redirect the goods) to no other. This differs from an "order" bill of lading which are possessory title documents and negotiable, i. e. they can be endorsed and so transfer the right to take delivery to the last endorsee. Nevertheless, bills of lading are "documents of title", whether negotiable or not, under the terms of the *Uniform Commercial Code*.

Multimodal Transport Documents

The advent of unitization in air and sea transportation brought about many innovations in international transportation of goods. Multimodal or combined transport is one such innovation. Cargo today can be moved from an inland freight station in the exporting country to an inland destination in the importing country. Goods may be picked up and transported using different modes of transport. E. g. a consignment of garments may be containerized at a factory in Mysore, customs cleared at ICD Bangalore, moved by rail to Cochin, by sea to Dubai, by air to Frankfurt and road to Düsseldorf, all under a single transport document. In such an operation, involving one or more land legs and/or air or sea legs, one carrier makes itself responsible for the entire transport operation. The contracting carrier is referred to as a multimodal or a combined transport operator (MTO). He is liable in contract to the shipper if the goods are damaged at any stage of the carriage. The multimodal transportation document may be issued either in non-negotiable or negotiable form. The multimodal transportation document (MTD), whether negotiable or non-negotiable, is prima facie evidence of the MTO taking charge of the goods for transportation. MTDs are of two types, the COMBIDOC evolved by the Baltic International Maritime Council (BIMCO) and FBL or FIATA MT Bill of Lading evolved by the International Federation of Freight Forwarders' Associations (FIATA). This document (FBL) has been approved by the International Chamber of Commerce (ICC) for the purpose of documentary credit. FIATA has evolved specific norms for the use of FBLs. Having seen what is covered by sea, air and multimodal transport, let us look at other modes, including courier and charter movements. The ICC has a publication called the *Uniform Customs and Practices*, *UCP* 600 (*UCP* 500 and *UCP* 400 were the earlier editions) which among other things deals with various transport documents, including those we have already looked at. Articles 20 to 24 of the *UCP* 600 deal with these documents.

Carrier's Responsibilities[12]

According to the maritime law of China, the responsibilities of the carrier with regard to the goods carried in containers cover the entire period during which the carrier is in charge of the goods, starting from the time the carrier has taken over the goods at the port of loading, until the goods have been delivered at the port of discharge. The responsibilities of the carrier with respect to non-containerized goods cover the period during which the carrier is in charge of the goods, starting from the time of loading of the goods onto the ship until the time the goods are discharged therefrom. During the period the carrier is in charge of the goods, the carrier shall be liable for the loss of or damage to the goods, except as otherwise provided for in the law. The carrier may enter into any agreement concerning carrier's responsibilities with regard to non-containerized goods prior to loading onto and after discharging from the ship.

The carrier shall, before and at the beginning of the voyage, exercise due diligence to make the ship seaworthy, properly man, equip and supply the ship and to make the holds, refrigerating and cool chambers and all other parts of the ship in which goods are carried, fit and safe for their reception, carriage and preservation[13].

The carrier shall properly and carefully load, handle, stow, carry, keep, care for and discharge the goods carried. The carrier shall carry the goods to the port of discharge on the agreed or customary or geographically direct route.

The carrier shall be liable for the loss of or damage to the goods caused by delay in delivery due to the fault of the carrier, except those arising or resulting from causes for which the carrier is not liable.

The carrier shall be liable for the economic losses caused by delay in delivery of the goods due to the fault of the carrier, even if no loss of or damage to the goods had actually occurred, unless such economic losses had occurred from causes for which the carrier is not liable.

The carrier shall not be liable for the loss of or damage to the goods occurred during the period of carrier's responsibility arising or resulting from any of the following causes:

(1) Fault of the Master, crew, pilot or servant of the carrier in the navigation or management of the ship;

(2) Fire, unless caused by the actual fault of the carrier;

(3) Force majeure[14] and perils, dangers and accidents of the sea or other navigable waters;

(4) War or armed conflict;

(5) Act of the government or competent authorities, quarantine restrictions or seizure under legal process;

(6) Strikes, stoppages or restraint of labor;

(7) Saving or attempting to save life or property at sea;

(8) Act of the shipper, owner of the goods or their agents;

(9) Nature or inherent vice of the goods;

(10) Inadequacy of packing or insufficiency of illegibility of marks;

(11) Latent defect of the ship not discoverable by due diligence;

(12) Any other causes arising without the fault of the carrier or his servant or agent.

The carrier who is entitled to exonerate from the liability[15] for compensation under the above-mentioned causes, shall, with the exception of the fir cause, bear the burden of proof[16].

The carrier shall not be liable for the loss of or damage to the live animals arising or resulting from the special risks inherent in the carriage thereof. However, the carrier shall be bound to prove that he has fulfilled the special requirements of the shipper with regard to the carriage of the live animals and that under the circumstances of the sea carriage, the loss or damage has occurred due to the special risks inherent therein.

The amount of indemnity for the loss of the goods shall be calculated on the basis of the actual value of the goods so lost, while that for the damage to the goods shall be calculated on the basis of the difference between the values of the goods before and after the damage, or on the basis of the expenses for the repair. The actual value shall be the value of the goods at the time of shipment plus insurance and freight.

Where the performance of the carriage or part of the carriage thereof has been entrusted to an actual carrier, the carrier shall nevertheless remain responsible for the entire carriage. The carrier shall be responsible, in relation to the carriage performed by the actual carrier, for the act or omission of the actual carrier and of his servant or agent acting within the scope of his employment or agency. Where a contract of carriage by sea provides explicitly that a specified part of the carriage covered by the said contract is to be performed by a named actual carrier other than the carrier, the contract may nevertheless provide that the carrier shall not be liable for the loss, damage or delay in delivery arising from an occurrence which takes place while the goods are in the charge of the actual carrier during such part of the carriage.

Where both the carrier and the actual carrier are liable for compensation, they shall be jointly liable[17] within the scope of such liability.

International Conventions on Marine Transport[18]

Hague-Visby Rules

The *Hague-Visby Rules* are a set of international rules for the international carriage of goods by sea. The official title is "International Convention for the Unification of Certain Rules of Law Relating to Bills of Lading" and was drafted in Brussels in 1924. After being amended by the Brussels Amendments (officially the "Protocol to Amend the International Convention for the Unification of Certain Rules of Law Relating to Bills of Lading") in 1968, the Rules became known as the *Hague-Visby Rules*. The premise of the *Hague-Visby Rules* (and of the earlier English Common Law) is that a carrier has far greater bargaining power than the shipper; and that to protect the interests of the shipper/cargo-owner, the law should impose minimum obligations upon the carrier. Key provisions are as follows:

(1) Basis of liability: imperfect liability with fault[19];

(2) Period of responsibility: tackle to tackle;

(3) Amount of limitation of liability: 100 pounds/unit;

(4) Limitation of actions: 1 year.

Hamburg Rules

The *Hamburg Rules* are a set of rules governing the international shipment of goods, resulting from the United Nations International Convention on the Carriage of Goods by Sea adopted in Hamburg on 31 March, 1978. The Convention was an attempt to form a uniform legal base for the transportation of goods on oceangoing ships. A driving force behind the convention was the attempt of developing countries' to level the playing field. It came into force on 1 November, 1992. As of May 2011, the convention had been ratified by 34 countries. Key provisions are as follows:

(1) Basis of liability: presumed liability with fault[20];

(2) Period of responsibility: reception to delivery;

(3) Amount of limitation of liability: 835 SDR/unit;

(4) Limitation of actions: 2 years.

Rotterdam Rules

The "*Rotterdam Rules*", formally the United Nations Convention on Contracts for the International Carriage of Goods Wholly or Partly by Sea is a treaty comprising international rules that revises the legal and political framework for maritime carriage of goods. The convention establishes a more modern, uniform legal regime governing the rights and obligations of shippers, carriers and consignees under a contract for door-to-door shipments that involve international sea transport. The aim of the convention is to extend and modernize international rules already in existence and achieve uniformity of admiralty law in the field of maritime carriage, updating and/or replacing many provisions in the *Hague Rules*, *Hague-Visby Rules* and *Hamburg Rules*.

The final draft of the *Rotterdam Rules*, which was assembled by the United Nations Commission on International Trade Law, was adopted by the United Nations on December 11, 2008 and a signing ceremony commenced in Rotterdam, Netherlands (the convention's informal namesake) on September 23, 2009. Signers included United States, France, Greece, Denmark, Switzerland and the Netherlands; in all, signatures were obtained from countries which are said to make up 25 percent of world trade by volume. The World Shipping Council is a prominent supporter of the *Rotterdam Rules*.

The following are critical provisions and law changes found in the *Rotterdam Rules*.

(1) It extends the period of time that carriers are responsible for goods to cover the time between the point where the goods are received to the point where the goods are delivered. (Note: This applies only if there is a sea leg involved in the transport. Thus, the *Rotterdam Rules* are not completely multimodal since all multimodal carriage excluding a sea leg is outside of the scope of application.)

(2) It allows for more e-commerce and approves more forms of electronic documentation.

(3) It obligates carriers to have ships that are seaworthy and properly crewed throughout the voyage. The level of care is set to due diligence, which is the same as in the *Hague Rules*.

(4) It increases the limit liability of carriers to 875 units of account per shipping unit or three units of account per kilogram of gross weight.

(5) It eliminates the "nautical fault defence" which had prevented carriers and crewmen from being held liable for negligent ship management and navigation.

(6) It extends the time that legal claims can be filed to two years following the day the goods were delivered or should have been delivered.

(7) It allows parties to certain "volume" contracts to opt—out of some liability rules set in the convention.

Notes

1. International Marine Cargo Transport 国际海上货物运输
   国际货物运输是指采用一种或多种运输方式将货物从一国或地区运至另一国或地区的某一地点。国际货物运输涉及多种运输方式,包括海运(marine transport)、空运(air transport)、铁路运输(rail transport)、公路运输(road transport)、邮政运输(parcel post transport)、内陆水道运输(如江河运输、湖泊运输)(inland waterway transport)、管道运输(pipe transport)、国际多式联运(international multimodal transport)等。其中,海上运输为最重要的运输方式,它具有货运量大、成本低等优点,国际贸易业务中约有三分之二的货物采用海运。此外,现在的运输规则也大都是从海运发展起来的。因此,本单元重点讨论国际海运方面的实务和法律知识。
2. liner transport and charter transport 班轮运输和租船运输
   班轮运输是指货轮按固定的航线、固定的停靠港口、固定的航运时间表及相对固定的费率进行航行。租船运输又称不定期船(tramp)运输,它没有班轮运输中的"四个固定",而需经过租船人(charterer)与船东(ship owner)在租船契约(charter party)中进行约定。租船运输主要有定程租船、定期租船、光船租船三种形式。
3. W/T, M/T, A/V "重量吨""尺码吨""从价"
   分别为 weight ton, measurement ton, Ad Valorem 的缩略词,可理解为:货物的运费按货物毛重、货物体积、货物价值计收。
4. long length surcharge, over weight surcharge, currency adjustment factor, optional charge, port congestion surcharge, transshipment surcharge, bunker adjustment factor, alternation surcharge, and port surcharge 超长附加费、超重附加费、货币贬值附加费、选择港附加费、港口拥挤费、转船附加费、燃油附加费、变更卸货港附加费及港口附加费
5. liner's freight tariff 班轮运价表
6. Tramp vessels are engaged under charter on a time, voyage or demise basis 租船运输采用定期租船、定程租船或光船租船的方式

7. consignee 收货人
8. freight prepaid or to collect 运费付讫、运费到付
9. On board B/L and Received for shipment B/L 已装船提单和备运提单
10. Straight B/L, Order B/L and Open B/L 记名提单、指示提单、不记名提单
11. Clean B/L and Unclean B/L 清洁提单和不洁提单
12. carrier's responsibilities 承运人责任
13. The carrier shall, before and at the beginning of the voyage, exercise due diligence to make the ship seaworthy, properly man, equip and supply the ship and to make the holds, refrigerating and cool chambers and all other parts of the ship in which goods are carried, fit and safe for their reception, carriage and preservation. 承运人在开航前和开航时,应当谨慎处理,使船舶处于适航状态,妥善配备船员、装备船舶和配备供应品,并使货舱、冷藏舱、冷气舱和其他载货处所适于并能安全收受、载运和保管货物。
14. force majeure 不可抗力
15. exonerate from the liability 免除责任
16. bear the burden of proof 承担举证责任
17. be jointly liable 连带责任
18. International Conventions on Marine Transport 国际海运公约
    国际货物海上运输规则主要包括1924年的《海牙规则》(*Hague Rules*),1968年的《维斯比规则》(*Visby Rules*)及1978年的《汉堡规则》(*Hamburg Rules*)。我国未参加上述三个公约,但我国的海商法在有关班轮运输方面的法律规定,借鉴了这三个规则的相关内容。
19. imperfect liability with fault 不完全过错责任
20. presumed liability with fault 推定过错责任

Study Questions

1. Which methods are often used in calculation of the basic freight charges in liner transport?
2. Can a straight B/L be negotiable? Why?
3. What are the differences between clean B/L and unclean B/L?
4. What are the legal functions of B/L?
5. What are the differences between imperfect liability with fault and presumed liability with fault?

UNIT 5 The Law of Insurance in International Cargo Transport[1]

Key Concepts

insurance policy	right of subrogation	general average	franchise	abandonment
F. P. A.	W. A.	all risks		

Learning Objectives

1. Understand the basic principles of insurance.
2. Be familiar with right of subrogation.
3. Appreciate the differences between insurance policy and insurance certificate.
4. Be familiar with F. P.A. , W. A. , and all risks.

Insurance is a form of risk management in which the insured transfers the cost of potential loss to another entity in exchange for monetary compensation known as the premium. Insurance allows individuals, businesses and other entities to protect themselves against significant potential losses and financial hardship at a reasonably affordable rate. Insurance works by pooling risk. What does this mean? It simply means that a large group of people who want to insure against a particular loss pay their premiums into what we will call the insurance bucket, or pool. Because the number of insured individuals is so large, insurance companies can use statistical analysis to project what their actual losses will be within the given class. They know that not all insured individuals will suffer losses at the same time or at all. This allows the insurance companies to operate profitably and at the same time pay for claims that may arise. For instance, most people have auto insurance but only a few actually get into an accident. You pay for the probability of the loss and for the protection that you will be paid for losses in the event they occur.

Insurance against perils is an important aspect of international commercial transactions. In the event of loss or damage to cargo due to hazards during voyage, an insured party will be able to recover losses from the insurer. The type of insurance required depends on the mode of transport agreed between parties to transport the cargo. Such insurance forms include marine, aviation and land.

The type of insurance contract depends on the *Incoterms* adopted by the parties in a sale contract. A CIF sale contract requires the seller to obtain insurance cover for the voyage. An FOB contract however places no obligation on the buyer or seller to obtain insurance, although it is prudent for the buyer to protect against potential losses. It is not uncommon for the buyer in an FOB contract to request the seller to arrange insurance on an understanding that they will reimburse the insurancfe costs incurred.

General Principles of Insurance

(1) Indemnity—The insurance company indemnifies, or compensates, the insured in the case of certain losses only up to the insured's interest.

(2) Insurable interest—The insured typically must directly suffer from the loss. Insurable interest must exist whether property insurance or insurance on a person is involved. The concept requires that the insured have a "stake" in the loss or damage to the life or property insured. What that "stake" is will be determined by the kind of insurance involved and the nature of the property ownership or relationship between the persons.

(3) Utmost good faith—The insured and the insurer are bound by a good faith bond of honesty and fairness. Material facts must be disclosed.

(4) Subrogation—The insurance company acquires legal rights to pursue recoveries on behalf of the insured; for example, the insurer may sue those liable for insured's loss.

(5) Proximate cause—The cause of loss (the peril) must be covered under the insuring agreement of the policy, and the dominant cause must not be excluded.

(6) Principle of loss minimization—In case of any loss or casualty, the asset owner must attempt to keep the loss to a minimum, as if the asset was not insured.

Insurance Policy[2]

A contract of marine insurance is a contract whereby the insurer undertakes, as agreed, to indemnify the loss to the subject matter insured[3] and the liability of the insured caused by perils covered by the insurance against the payment of an insurance premium by the insured[4]. A contract of marine insurance comes into being after the insured puts forth a proposal for insurance and the insurer agrees to accept the proposal and the insurer and the insured agree on the terms and conditions of the insurance. The insurer shall issue to the insured an insurance policy or other certificate of insurance in time, and the contents of the contract shall be contained therein. Insurance policy is an evidence for conclusion of the insurance contract. It is issued by the insurer and has legal effect and shall be binding upon the insurer and the insured. The insurance policy may involve the following contents on its front page:

(1) the insurer and the insured

(2) invoice No. and insurance policy No.

(3) description of the goods and packing , quantity and marks

(4) the insured amount and the currency

(5) premium[5]

(6) date and place of shipment and place of destination

(7) risks to be covered

(8) inspection agent and place where claim may be made

(9) date of issuance

(10) signature and seal by the insurer

In addition, on the back of the insurance policy, standard clauses[6] have been made, which may involve the obligations and rights between the insurer and the insured. But in respect to the insurance certificate[7], it is just the simplified insurance policy, and has no such clauses on its back.

Upon failure of the insured to truthfully inform the insurer of the material circumstances[8] due to his intentional act, the insurer has the right to terminate the contract without refunding the premium. The insurer shall not be liable for any loss arising from the peril insured against before the contract is terminated.

Unless otherwise agreed in the contract, neither the insurer nor the insured may terminate the contract after the commencement of the insurance liability.

Right of Subrogation[9]

To prevent the insured from recovering twice from the same loss, the insurer is entitled to be subrogated to all the rights and claims the insured has against the third party which has caused the damages of the goods provided he has duly indemnified the insured. This is called the right of subrogation. In practice, the insured usually will sign a letter of subrogation for the insurer after he has received the indemnity. Then the insurer, with the right of subrogation and the required documents, such as the bill of lading, will claim against the third party.

Franchise[10]

For the goods which are easy to be breakable and lose weight, franchise is usually claimed by the insurer. Franchise falls into nondeductible franchise and deductible franchise[11]. If the loss does not exceed the franchise, the insurer does not cover the loss. If the loss has exceeded the franchise, the insurer who claims nondeductible franchise will cover the losses including that with the franchise while the insurer who claims deductible franchise will only cover the losses in excess of the franchise.

Actual Total Loss and Constructive Total Loss[12]

It means the whole lot of the consignment has been lost or damaged or found valueless upon the arrival at the port of destination.

Constructive total loss takes place in case the actual loss of the insured goods is unavoidable, or the ship or the consignment has to be abandoned because the cost of the salvage or recovery[13] would exceed the value the ship and the consignment in sound condition upon the arrival at the port of destination.

Abandonment[14]

In case of occurrence of constructive total loss, the insured may ask the insurer to cover the actual loss or total loss of the insured goods. Under the latter case, the insured must present to the insurer a notice of abandonment by which he means to transfer all his interest and obligations to the insurer so that he might cover his total loss. The abandonment is effective only after it is accepted by the insurer.

General Average[15]

Partial loss means the loss of or damage to the goods is only partial. Partial loss can either be general average or particular average[16]. Particular average means a particular consignment is only partially damaged.

When both the ship and the consignments on board are endangered and the captain, for the safety of the ship and the consignments on board, intentionally and reasonably does some sacrifices or makes some expenses. The losses or expenses arising to that effect, shall be borne by both the carrier and consignors in proportion to the value of their interest thus saved. It is called general average contribution[17]. In practice, the typical example is when the ship goes aground and both the ship and consignments on board are in peril, the captain, after all his efforts to refloat the ship have failed, may decide to jettison part of consignments on board to lighten the ship. Thus the losses shall be borne by both the carrier and the consignors.

Perils of the Sea

A. Natural Calamity

Natural calamity refers to the perils under force majeure such as vile weather, thunder storm and lightning, tsunami[18], earthquake, flood, etc. The ordinary action of the winds and waves is not taken as natural calamities.

B. Fortuitous Accidents

Fortuitous accidents are such risks as ship stranding, ship collision, ship sinking, ship missing, striking upon the rocks, colliding with icebergs or other objects, fire and explosion and the like.

C. Extraneous Risks[19]

Extraneous risks can further be general extraneous risks and special extraneous risks. Risks caused by theft, rain and fresh water, leakage, shortage, breakage, dampness, mildewing, heating, taint of odor, hooking and rusting are called general extraneous risks. Risks caused by on deck, war, strikes, failure of delivery and rejection, etc. are called special extraneous risks.

Ocean Marine Insurance Under China Insurance Clause

A. F. P. A. (Free from Particular Average)[20]

It covers the following losses:

(1) Actual total loss or constructive total loss of the consignment caused by natural calamities.

(2) Total loss or partial loss caused by fortuitous accidents.

(3) Partial loss of the insured goods attributable to vile weather, where the ship has been in peril of fortuitous accidents, irrespective of whether the event took after or before such accidents.

(4) Partial or total loss consequent on falling of an entire package or packages into the sea during loading, unloading and transshipment.

(5) Reasonable expenses the insured makes for salvages of the goods insured, and for averting or minimizing the losses, provided the expenses do not exceed the insured amount.

(6) Expenses incurred by discharge of the insured cargo at the port of distress following a sea peril as well as special charges arising from loading, warehousing and forwarding of the goods at an intermediate port of call or refuge.

(7) Sacrifice in and contribution to general average and salvage charges.

(8) Such proportion of losses sustained by the ship owners as is to be reimbursed by the insured under the contract of carriage "both to blame collision"[21].

B. W. A. (With Average)[22]

Aside from the risks covered under F. P. A., W. A. also covers partial losses of the insured goods caused by natural calamities.

C. All Risks[23]

Aside from the risks under F. P. A. and W. A., all risks also cover partial or total loss of the insured goods arising from general extraneous risks during transit.

Institute Cargo Clauses (ICC)

Institute Cargo Clauses are made out by the Institute of London Underwriters. This set of clauses has played a vital role in the development of international insurance. Most countries in the world have referred more or less in making their own insurance clauses. The ocean marine cargo clauses of the People's Insurance Company of China are basically the same as the old clauses of ICC. ICC has undergone revisions for many times. The latest revision came into effect on January 1, 1982.

Clause A

Clause A does cover all risks except for the exclusions under its coverage. Its exclusions fall into five groups:

(1) General exclusions—The insurer does not cover the losses or expenses caused by deliberate or illegal activities of the insured, the loss or expenses caused by natural leakage, ordinary wear or tear, or inappropriate or insufficient packing, or by the innate defects of the goods, or by delay, or by bankruptcy of the owner or manager or the ship charterer, or by atomic or nuclear bombs.

(2) Exclusions of unseaworthiness or uncargoworthiness[24].

(3) Exclusion of war (antagonistic activities, capture, detention, underwater mines or torpedoes, except those by pirates).

(4) Exclusion of strikes.

(5) Exclusion of malicious damages (caused by terrorists or people with outer political motives).

Clause B

Clause B covers all of the risks listed under its coverage.

(1) Fire, explosion.

(2) Striking upon rocks, sinking or capsizing of the cargo-carrying ship or barge.

(3) Overturn or derail of the overland transport vehicles.

(4) Striking of the carrying ship, barge, or transportation vehicle upon other objects.

(5) Unloading of the goods at the port of distress.

(6) Earthquake, eruption of volcano, lightning.

(7) General average contribution.

(8) Jettison either because of general average or some other reasons.

(9) Loss overboard.

(10) Entering of sea water, lake water, river water into the cargo carrying ship, barge, vehicle, container, or storehouse.

(11) The total loss caused by cargo dropping into sea or on the ground while loading or unloading.

(12) Such proportion of losses sustained by the ship owners as is to be reimbursed by the consignors under "both to blame collision" clause.

Clause C

Clause C covers the losses due to the perils listed under Clauses B except for (6), (9), (10) and (11) as shown above.

Notes

1. Insurance in International Cargo Transport 国际货物运输保险

国际货物运输保险是国际货物贸易的重要组成部分,而保险人和被保险人在保险活动中应遵循保险利益原则(the principle of insurable interest)、最大诚信原则(the principle of utmost good faith)、损失补偿原则(the principle of indemnity)及近因原则(the principle of proximate cause)。由中国人民保险公司制定的《中国保险条款》(*China Insurance Clause*)(包括海洋、陆地、航空和邮政运输保险条款)在我国对外贸易中被广泛采用。此外,伦敦保险业协会所制定的《协会货物条款》(*Institute Cargo Clauses*)对国际货物运输保险的影响也很大,实际上,我国的保险条款制定就是以此为基础的。

2. insurance policy　保险单
3. the subject matter insured　保险标的
4. the insured　投保人
5. premium　保险费
6. standard clauses　格式条款
7. insurance certificate　保险凭证

   实务中又称"小保单"。
8. the material circumstances　重要情况

   在订立保险合同前,被保险人应将其知道的或应知道的有关影响保险人据以确定保险费率或确定是否承保的"重要情况"如实告知保险人,这也是最大诚信原则的体现。
9. right of subrogation　代位权

   代位权或代位求偿权也是保险业务中的一个重要概念,它体现了保险补偿性原则。
10. franchise　免赔率

    免赔率通常为那些易碎和易短量的货物而设定的。
11. nondeductible franchise and deductible franchise　相对免赔率和绝对免赔率

    两者区别在于,如果损失数额超过免赔率,前者不扣除免赔率,予以全部赔偿,而后者则要扣除免赔率,只赔超过部分。
12. actual total loss and constructive total loss　实际全损和推定全损
13. the salvage or recovery　救助或修复
14. abandonment　委付

    委付仅适用于推定全损的场合,被保险人将保险标的转让给保险人,而向保险人请求赔付全部保险金额。这种转让保险标的的权利称之为"委付"。而对于保险人而言,可以接受委付,也可拒绝之。
15. general average　共同海损

    其构成要件:危险必须是确实存在或难以避免的,所采取的措施是有意识且合理的,作出的牺牲和支出的费用最终是有效的(即避免了危险)。
16. particular average　单独海损
17. general average contribution　共同海损分摊
18. tsunami　海啸
19. extraneous risks　外来风险
20. free from particular average　平安险
21. both to blame collision　船舶互撞责任

22. With Average　水渍险
23. All Risks　一切险
24. unseaworthiness or uncargoworthiness　不适航或不宜载货
即船舶不能经受航程中的一般风险，或者船舶不适宜接收、保管和运输货物。

Study Questions

1. What are the principles of insurance?
2. What is an insurance policy?
3. What are the differences between insurance policy and insurance contract?
4. Briefly explain the marine perils.
5. What are the basic risks for ocean transportation to be covered under CIC?

UNIT 6 The Law of International Settlement of Payment[1]

Key Concepts

draft	check	promissory note	D/A	D/P
endorsement	L/C	acceptance	right of recourse	

Learning Objectives

1. Understand negotiable instruments, remittance and collection.
2. Understand the differences between D/A and D/P.
3. Be familiar with the procedures of the L/C.
4. Understand the changes of UCP 600.

Draft

A draft or a bill of exchange is an instrument signed by the issuer, authorizing the payer to pay unconditionally a certain sum of money to the payee or the bearer when the bill is presented at a specified time. A draft shall specify the following information: the word of "draft", authorization of unconditional payment, a fixed sum, the name of the payer, the payee, the issuing date, signature of the drawer. A draft may become null and void if any of the above-mentioned items is not specified therein.

Types of Draft

Banker's Draft and Commercial Draft

Banker's draft or bill is drawn by the bank, which is chiefly used in remittance, while commercial draft or bill is issued by a commercial firm.

Sight Draft and Usance Draft[2]

Under a sight draft, the draft is payable on demand or at sight, that is, the drawee is required to pay immediately when the draft is presented to him. In case of the usance or time draft, the draft will be payable within a fixed period after the date of the draft, e. g. "pay three months after date…". A draft may be expressed as being payable within a fixed period after sight; here sight means the presentation of the draft to the drawee for acceptance.

Clean Draft and Documentary Draft[3]

In the transfer of the draft, if the draft is accompanied by the shipping documents it is a documentary draft; if not, it is a clean bill. In international trade, the documentary draft is frequently employed for the settlement of payment, while the clean draft is occasionally used to collect the small amount of payment or sundry charges.

Endorsement[4]

Endorsement refers to the act of putting relevant items in writing and making signature or seal on the back of the bill or on an allonge[5]. The bearer must endorse the draft where he intends to transfer his rights to the draft to other persons. When the issuer writes the term "non-transferable" on the draft, then it cannot be transferred. If the draft is transferred by means of endorsement, there shall be an uninterrupted series of endorsement in a draft. Here "an uninterrupted series of endorsement"[6] denotes that, in the course of transfer of an instrument, the endorsement of the person endorsing the transfer of the draft shall be made by immediate prior endorsee to acquire the draft. A person to whom a draft is transferred by means other than endorsement or who acquires a draft by other legitimate means shall provide evidence in accordance with the law showing his rights to it.

No conditions can be attached to the endorsement, any conditions attached to endorsements shall have no effect on the bill. After the draft has been endorsed and transferred, the endorser shall be liable for guaranteeing the acceptance and payment of the draft held by the subsequent party[7]. In cases of non-acceptance or non-payment of the draft, the endorser shall compensate the bearer with the sum of the unpaid draft, interest and other relevant expenses. When the endorser writes the term "non-transferable" on the draft and his subsequent party reendorses and transfers it, the original endorser shall not bear any responsibility for any guarantees made to the subsequent party's endorsee.

Acceptance[8]

Acceptance denotes the act whereby the payer of the draft promises to pay the sum of the money in the draft at its maturity. Where a draft is payable on a fixed date or within a fixed period after the date of issue, the bearer shall present the draft to the payer for acceptance before the date of maturity. When accepting a bill, the payer shall write the word "accepted" and the date of acceptance on the draft and sign it. In addition, the payer shall accept it unconditionally; if conditions have been added, this is deemed to be a refusal. When the payer has accepted the draft, he shall bear the liability of paying it at maturity.

Guaranty

The responsibility of guaranteeing the payment of the draft shall be borne by the guarantor. The guarantor shall be someone other than the debtor of the draft. Where the draft is guaranteed, the guarantor and the person to whom the guaranty is given shall undertake joint liability to the bearer. In case the guaranteed draft has not been paid at its maturity, the bearer is entitled to demand payment from the guarantor who shall pay the draft in full. If there two or more guarantors, they shall undertake joint liability. After the guarantor has paid the debt in the draft, the guarantor may exercise his right of recourse[9] against the person to whom the guaranty is given and his prior parties.

Payment

The bearer shall present the draft for payment or acceptance within the prescribed period as stipulated in the relevant laws and regulations. According to the negotiable instruments law[10] of PRC, a draft payable on sight should be presented to the payer within one month of the date of issue; while a draft payable on a fixed date, within a fixed period after the date of issue or within a fixed period after sight shall be presented for acceptance within 10 days of the date of maturity. Presentation for payment made to the payer by an authorized bank or by means of exchanging system for the instruments shall be deemed as that by the bearer. When paying a draft, the payer or his agent shall check the continuity of the series of endorsement, as well as the legitimacy of the identification of the person presenting the draft and other valid certificates. In case the payer or his agent makes payment out of malice or with gross negligence[11], they shall bear liability accordingly. Once the draft has been paid in full, all debtors shall be discharged from liability.

Right of Recourse

When the payer dishonors the draft or refuses to accept it, the bearer may exercise the right of recourse against the endorsers, the issuer and other debtors of the draft. If the acceptor dies or flees, or has been declared bankrupt according to the law or has been ordered to cease business activities due to the violations of the law, the bearer may also exercise the right of recourse. In exercising the right of recourse, the bearer shall provide sufficient evidences such as the protest[12] or a statement noting reasons for non-acceptance, or relevant judicial documents, etc.

The issuer, endorser, acceptor and guarantor of the draft are jointly liable to the bearer. The bearer may exercise the right of recourse against any one or all of the persons hereto without being required to observe the order in which the debtors have become bound.

Promissory Note[13]

A promissory note is an instrument issued and signed by the issuer promising to pay unconditionally the payee or bearer a certain sum of money when the note is presented or at a specified time. Under a promissory note, there are only two parties concerned, that is, the issuer and the payee. A promissory note can be sight promissory note or time promissory note. As a promissory note is a promise by the issuer to pay to the payee, it is not necessary for the bearer to present a time note for acceptance by the payer. A promissory note can also be made by a commercial firm or a banker. If it is issued by the banker, it is also called cashier's check or cashier's order, and shall be a sight one.

According to the negotiable instruments law of PRC, a promissory note denotes a banker's promissory note.

Check

A check is an instrument issued and signed by the issuer authorizing any bank or any other financial institution handling business of depositing checks to unconditionally pay a certain sum of money to the payee or to the bearer at sight. Checks may be payable in cash or payable into an account. If a check is payable only into an account, this shall be specified on the face of the check. A cash check can only be used for payment in cash, while a crossed check[14] can not be used for payment in cash but only for settlement into an account. A check shall specify the following information such as the word of "check", authorization of unconditional payment, a certain sum, the name of the payer, the date of issue and the signature of the issuer. The sum specified on a check by the issuer shall not exceed the issuer's balance in the bank paying it, otherwise the check is a rubber one, and it will be dishonored by the paying bank. The issuer is prohibited to issue a rubber check[15]. If the paying bank marked "certified" with signature on the check, then it is a certified check[16] which will not be dishonored.

Remittance[17]

Remittance means the remitter remits a certain sum of money to the beneficiary by the bank transfer. It is also called favorable exchange[18]. In remittance, there are four parties involved: the remitter, the beneficiary, the remitting bank, and the receiving bank. In international trade, remittance is chiefly used in those sales under the terms of payment in advance, cash on delivery or open account[19].

Remittance falls into Mail Transfer (M/T), Telegraphic Transfer (T/T), Demand Draft (D/D).

Mail Transfer

By mail transfer, on receipt of the customer's instruction, the remitting bank will advise the overseas bank which is usually its branch or correspondent bank in the beneficiary's country to pay a specific amount to the beneficiary. The payment instruction is made by ordinary or airmail, and must be signed by the authorized signatories.

Telegraphic Transfer

If T/T is used, the same procedure as for mail transfer is adopted. However, the payment instruction to the overseas bank is sent by telegraphic means, such as cable, telex or SWIFT. In case of telex, the overseas bank will require a special authenticating code word, which is called "test key", before it will act.

Demand Draft

D/D is in effect a bill of exchange drawn by one bank on another payable on demand. The customer will forward the draft to the beneficiary who will obtain the money from the paying bank on presenting it.

Collection[20]

Collection is also called adverse exchange, under it, the exporter takes initiative to collect the payment from the importer. The exporter draws a bill of exchange on the importer for the sum due, with or without relevant shipping documents attached, and authorizes his bank to effect the collection of the payment through its branch or correspondent bank in the importer's country. Collection falls into clean collection and documentary collection. In case of collection on clean draft, only a draft is needed, no shipping documents are attached to it. This type of collection is occasionally used in the payment of the balance, sundry charges, and the like. Documentary collection is frequently used in international settlement. The operation of documentary credit is as follows:

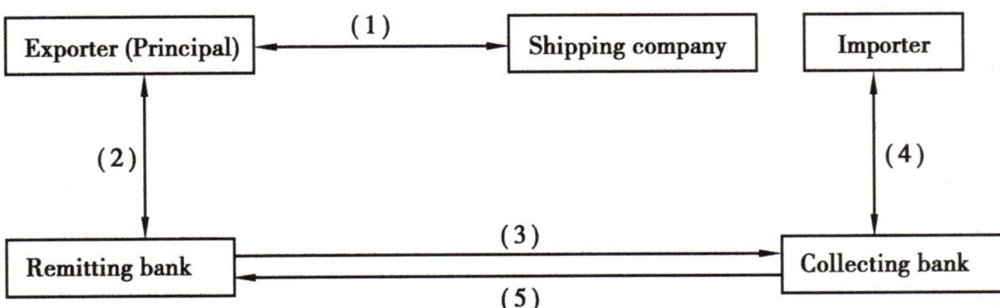

(1) The exporter ships the goods and obtains documents of title from the shipping company.

(2) The exporter who is known as the principal, hands over the shipping documents and the draft to his bank (the remitting bank) for collection.

(3) The remitting bank sends collection instruction and documents to the importer's bank (the collecting bank).

(4) The collecting bank will release the documents to the importer against payment under D/P, or against acceptance under D/A.

(5) If and when the draft is paid, the collecting bank sends funds to the remitting bank for credit to the principal's account.

Documentary collection falls into D/P (Documents Against Payment) and D/A (Documents Against Acceptance). Under D/P, the shipping documents will be released to the importer only when he effects the full payment of the goods. In case of D/A, the shipping documents will be released to the buyer when he duly accepts the draft.

Documentary Credit[21]

Definition

According to UCP 500, a documentary credit is an arrangement, however named or described, whereby a bank (the issuing bank) acting at the request and on the instructions of a customer (the applicant) or on his behalf

(1) is to make a payment to or to the order of a third party (the beneficiary), or is to accept and pay draft drawn by the beneficiary, or

(2) authorizes another bank to effect such payment, or to accept and pay such draft, or

(3) authorizes another bank to negotiate, against stipulated documents, provided that the terms and conditions of the credit are complied with.

Parties to a Documentary Credit

(1) Applicant, this is the party at whose request or for whose account a letter of credit is issued.

(2) Beneficiary, this is the party who under the terms of L/C is entitled to have its complying presentation honored.

(3) Issuing bank, this is the bank that issues L/C in favor of beneficiary.

(4) Advising bank, this is the bank which, at the request of an issuing bank, a confirming bank, or another advising bank, notifies the beneficiary that L/C has been issued, confirmed, or amended.

(5) Confirming bank, this is a nominated bank which undertakes, at the request or with the consent of the issuing bank, to honor a presentation directly under L/C issued by another.

(6) Nominated bank, this is a bank which the issuing bank designates or authorizes to pay, accept, negotiate, or otherwise give value under L/C or undertakes by agreement or custom and practice to reimburse.

How a Documentary Credit Operates

Assume that an importer and exporter have agreed that the payment terms will be by way of an irrevocable, confirmed documentary credit. The procedures are as follows:

(1) The importer asks his bank (issuing bank) to issue an irrevocable credit and to request confirmation by another bank (confirming bank).

(2) The issuing bank requests a bank (advising bank) to advising the beneficiary (the exporter) of the details.

(3) After consignment, the beneficiary obtains the shipping documents and presents the documents to the confirming bank. The confirming bank pays the beneficiary provided that the documents are in full compliance with the terms and conditions of the credit.

(4) The confirming bank sends the documents to the issuing bank and gets reimbursement from it.

(5) The issuing bank settles the payment with the importer, and then the importer is given the documents for delivery of the goods.

Types of Documentary Credit

Payment Credit

The meaning of the term "payment" is self-evident. The nominated bank will pay the beneficiary on receipt of the specified documents and on fulfillment of all terms of the credit.

Sometimes the issuing bank nominates itself as paying bank, in which case payment will be made on receipt of the correct documents at their counters abroad. On other occasions, usually with confirmed credits, the issuing bank will nominate the advising to pay. The term "payment" only applies to the sight drafts, and sometimes, deferred payment.

Negotiation Credit

Sometimes the issuing bank will nominate the advising bank to negotiate a credit, or it may even make the credit freely negotiable, in which case any bank is a nominated bank. If a bank negotiates a credit, it will advance the money to the beneficiary on presentation of the required documents and will charge interest on the advance from the date of the advance until such time as it receives reimbursement from the issuing bank. Under such negotiation, the negotiating bank enjoys the right of recourse. If payment is not ultimately forthcoming from the issuing bank, the negotiating bank will be able to claim repayment from the beneficiary of the advance, plus interest.

Acceptance Credit

The acceptance credit is also referred to as usance credit, which means that the seller draws a draft on the nominated bank, and demand payment at some determinable future date, e. g. at 60 days' sight instead of at sight.

The term "acceptance" can only apply when the credit calls for usance bills, i. e. bills of exchange payable at a specified time after acceptance by the drawee. And bills should be drawn on a bank.

In practice, this means that instead of receiving immediate payment on presentation of the documents, the seller's draft is returned to him accepted on face by the nominated bank.

Deterred Payment Credit

In deferred payment credits, there is no need for the exporter to draw a draft. The issuing bank simply promises that the payment will be made on a fixed or determinable future time date, provided that the other conditions have been fulfilled.

One benefit of deferred credits is that they avoid the need for payment of stamp duty on drafts.

Transferable Credit

A transferable credit is defined in Article 48 of UCP 500. Under UCP, a credit is only transferable if it is expressly indicated as being transferable by the issuing bank. The transferable credit may be used when the supplier of the goods sells them through a middleman and does deal with the ultimate buyer. In such case, the supplier is in effect the second beneficiary while the middleman is the first beneficiary.

A transferable credit can be transferred only once. Under it, L/C can be transferred to several suppliers at the same time, provided that the total amount transferred does not exceed that of the original L/C.

Back-to-Back Credit

Back to back consists of two entirely separately documentary credits, but one credit may act as security for the other. They apply in transactions when original suppliers and ultimate buyers deal through a middleman. Under such case, the middleman will first receive a L/C from the buyer, then on hypothecation of the original credit (master or prime credit), he will ask his bank to open another credit in favor of the supplier. In fact, back to back credit are used in the same situations as transferable credits, but the rights and obligations of the parties differ between the two types of credit. In addition, under transferable credits, the ultimate buyer is aware that he is dealing with a middleman while under back to back credits, he is not.

Revocable Credit and Irrevocable Credit

A revocable credit involves risks to the beneficiary, since it can be amended, revoked or cancelled without the beneficiary's consent and even without prior notice to the beneficiary. The revocable credit is normally accepted as usage between affiliated parties or subsidiary companies, or as a substitute for a promise to pay.

An irrevocable credit gives the beneficiary greater assurance of payment. It can not be cancelled or modified without the express consent of the issuing bank, the confirming bank (if any) and the beneficiary. It constitutes a definite undertaking of the issuing bank, provided that the stipulated documents are presented to the nominated bank or to the issuing bank and that the terms and conditions of the credit are complied with, to pay, accept the draft and or documents presented under the documentary credit.

Confirmed Credit

A confirmation of an irrevocable documentary credit by a bank (the confirming bank) upon the authorization or request of the issuing bank constitutes a definite undertaking of payment by the confirming bank, in addition to that of the issuing bank, provided that the stipulated documents are presented to the confirming bank or to any other nominated bank on or before the expiry date and the terms and conditions of the documentary credit are complied with.

Revolving Credit

A revolving credit is one by which, under the terms and conditions thereof, the amounts is renewed or reinstated without specific amendments to the documentary credit being required. A documentary credit in this nature can be cumulative or non-cumulative. If it is stated to be "cumulative", any sum not utilized during the first period carries over and may be utilized during the subsequent period. If it is "non-cumulative", any sum not utilized in a period ceases to be available, i. e. it is not carried over to a subsequent period.

Anticipatory Credit

Under anticipatory credit or prepaid credit, the issuing bank authorizes the paying bank to effect the payment in advance to the exporter. The payment can be made in full or partial amount. In such case, the beneficiary is usually required to draw a draft upon the paying bank, and present a statement declaring the required documents will be produced in due time.

Reciprocal Credit

Under reciprocal credits, the beneficiary of the first credit is the applicant of the second credit. The credits can take effect either simultaneously or at different times. Under the former case, the first credit does not take effect upon its arrival until the advising bank has received the notice that the returned credit has been received. Under the latter case, the credit takes effect when it reaches the beneficiary.

Stand-by Credit

Like a commercial credit, stand-by credit is a promise by the issuer to honor the beneficiary's presentation of the document(s) specified in the credit. In a stand-by credit, the parties do not normally expect that the presentation of documents will occur. The issuer is merely "stand-by", just in case the obligation in the underlying transaction is not performed by the obligor. A stand-by credit anticipates the possibility that something will go wrong or a negative event will occur while a commercial credit, by contrast, is a method of payment that anticipates a positive event, the consummation of the underlying transaction.

UCP 500[22]

The Uniform Customs and Practice for Documentary Credits is a set of internationally accepted rules and definitions which involve the liabilities and obligations of all parties to documentary credits. All bank authorities and advices of documentary credits shall state the credit is subject to UCP 500. UCP was first published by ICC in 1933. Revised versions were issued in 1951, 1962, 1974 and 1983. UCP 500 was adopted by the ICC Executive Board in April 1993, and first published as ICC Publication No. 500 in May 1993.

Some Main Provisions of UCP 500

Article 3:

Banks are concerned only with the documents presented under the credit. Even when the underlying sales contract is mentioned in the credit, the bank's decision to pay depends solely on whether the documents presented conform to the credit.

Article 4:

Banks are only concerned with documents, not goods nor the performance of the underlying contract.

Article 6:

Credits should clearly indicate whether they are revocable or irrevocable. In the absence of any such indication, the credits are deemed irrevocable.

Article 7:

The advising bank must take reasonable care to check that the credit is genuine, if it elects to advise the credit. If the advising bank cannot establish authenticity, it must inform the bank from which the instructions appear to have been received without delay. The advising bank may advise an unauthenticated credit but if it does so it must inform the beneficiary that authenticity has not been established. In all cases, there is no obligation on the part of the advising bank to advise a credit, but if it elects not to do so, it must inform the issuing bank without delay.

Article 13:

Banks must examine all documents with reasonable care to ensure that on the face of it they appear to be in order. Documents with on the face of it appears to be inconsistent with one another will be considered as not appearing to comply with credit terms. Any documents which are not called for by the credit will not be examined by the banks.

Article 15:

Banks shall have a reasonable time, not to exceed seven banking days following the day of receipt of documents, to examine the documents and determine whether to take up or refuse the documents and to inform the party from which the documents were received of the decision.

If the credit contains terms and conditions without stating the document(s) to be presented in compliance with such conditions, then banks will disregard the conditions.

Banks assume no liability for the genuineness of documents.

Article 17:

Banks assume no liability or liability or responsibility for the consequences arising out of the interruption of their business by Acts of God, riots, civil commotions, insurrections, wars or any other causes beyond their control, or by any strikes or lockouts. Unless specifically authorized, banks will not, upon resumption of their business, pay, incur a deferred payment undertaking, accept draft(s) or negotiate under credits which expired during such interruption of their business.

Article 32:

A clean transport document is one which bears no clause or other indication which declares that the goods or the packing are defective. Where such clauses exist, banks must reject the documents, unless the credit specifically authorizes such clauses or notations.

Article 39:

The word "circa" or "about" or "approximately" indicate that a difference of 10% either way can be allowed. Where the goods are described by volume or weight, a 5% tolerance in the amounts actually shipped is allowed, provided the monetary amount claimed is adjusted accordingly.

Article 40:

Partial shipments are allowed, unless the credit states otherwise.

Articles 44:

When the expiry date of a credit falls on a non-business day, banks will accept presentation on the following business day.

UCP 600[23]

The latest revision of UCP is the sixth revision of the rules which was made in July 2007. It is the fruit of more than three years of work by the ICC's Commission on Banking Technique and Practice.

Main Changes of UCP 600

A major theme in the revision was to ensure clarity and consistency in approach. This was achieved by means of changes to the overall structure of the rules and more fundamental changes in content of certain key rules. UCP 600 both clarifies how certain pre-existing rules should be interpreted and also adds new conditions and parameters for documentary credit practice. ICC Position Papers and a number of the ICC Banking Decisions will no longer be used to interpret the rules. The restructuring condenses the provisions from 49 to 39 articles and streamlines the procedure and should, in theory at least, leave less room for inconsistent application. It is clear that the rules have been carefully considered both individually and as a whole. There are a number of provisions or amendments to provisions which should aid clear interpretation and consistent application:

Fuller definitions are provided, including full definitions of "advising" and "confirming" banks, "issuing bank" and also the concept of "honour" (i.e. "honour" means to pay immediately or, alternatively, to pay at maturity having either incurred a deferred payment undertaking or accepted a "draft"/bill of exchange).

The term "negotiation", which was previously unclear, has now been defined properly. It means the purchase of drafts or documents under a complying presentation by advancing or agreeing to advance funds to the beneficiary on or before the banking day on which reimbursement is due to the nominated bank. This appears to apply to silent confirmations as well.

Defining "honour" and "negotiation" should create an improvement in practice since these terms have been the subject of disputes in the past.

A "banking day" is defined and can be distinguished from a business day since the drafters wanted to exclude days on which a bank would be open for business but not for checking documents presented under credits. Unfortunately, the wording arguably does not achieve this aim since it provides that a "banking day means a day on which a bank is regularly open at the place at which an act subject to these rules is to be performed".

An entirely new section containing interpretations aims to ensure clarity and consistency in application of the rules.

Some of the interpretations are not new. For instance, the requirement to disregard terms such as "prompt", "immediately" and "as soon as possible" appear under UCP 500 but only towards the end of the rules, like an afterthought. The new interpretations section in UCP 600 is given prominence as the third article under the rules. Here a note of caution is given in relation to calculating time in the context of a shipment period. In particular, the new rules provide that calculation of the number of days "from" a certain date in the context of a shipment period must include the date mentioned. This is not the way most people would approach such a calculation.

Further quite simple changes provide clarity and remove previous problem areas. For instance, the phrases "without delay" and "reasonable time...which must not exceed seven banking days", being the period in which banks previous had to accept or reject documents under UCP 500, have now been replaced with a defined period of five days without any qualification.

Similarly, banks cannot now impose a time limit for rejection of amendments to the credit. This effectively puts a halt on some banks' previous practice under the UCP 500 of setting down a time limit within which an amendment had to be accepted or rejected and, if the deadline was not complied with by the due date, the amendment would, somewhat unfairly, be deemed accepted.

Standard for Examination of Documents

The conflict between the doctrine of strict compliance in documentary credit practice and the need to ensure commercial workability was raised in the introduction to this article. One of factors driving the need for revision of the UCP was the high level of rejections of documents on first presentation. Indeed, the introduction to UCP 600 specifically refers to concerns that documentary credits will be undermined as international payment mechanisms if certain issues are left unaddressed. A major concern was banks being able to continue rejecting documents on purely technical grounds when, in fact, there is no real or actual discrepancy.

One key change under UCP 600 which goes to the root of the problem is the fact that documents presented under a credit are now not required to be an exact replica or mirror image of each other. Rather, the data in documents must not be inconsistent or, as set out in Article 14, must "not conflict" with other data. This alters the previous requirement under the UCP 500 that such data had to be consistent. This is sensible in that data in two documents which is not "consistent" might at the same time not actually conflict. It is a matter of degree, and by changing the requirement to a lack of conflict, the drafters have lowered the threshold slightly.

Typographical errors have in the past been a sticky area when it comes to technical as opposed to real discrepancies. There are numerous examples of typographical errors in documents causing problems and particularly common are typing errors in addresses. In this situation, the document checker might not be aware whether he is considering two entirely different addresses or whether the discrepancy is merely a typographical error. Under UCP 600, with the exception of addresses in transport documents, the addresses of the beneficiary and the applicant need not be identical provided that they are in the same country as the addresses provided in the credit. Moreover, contact details such as telex, telephone, fax and the like will be disregarded. This change will go some way towards ensuring that documents presented under a credit cannot be rejected on purely technical grounds.

In the same vein, Article 14 requires that non-documentary conditions are disregarded. A non-documentary condition would be a condition in the credit which does not stipulate a corresponding document to indicate compliance with the condition. For instance, a credit may specify that goods are carried on a first class vessel but not require a class certificate to be tendered establishing the vessel's classification. Similarly, the credit may state that the goods be of a certain origin but not call for presentation of a certificate of origin for those goods.

The aim of these changes is to reduce the number of rejections of documents tendered under documentary credits. It is still early days but the outlook is favorable in that it is easier for a document to be compliant under UCP 600 and there is less room for rejecting documents presented under a credit on purely technical grounds. If this is wrong and the figure of 70% of documents rejected on first presentation is not reduced, there are likely to be further changes by the ICC.

URC 522[24]

For many years, this practical set of rules help banks, buyers and sellers in the collections process. The first revision was issued in 1971 and the latest revision became effective as of January 1st, 1996. It describes the rules governing collections, including those for the presentation, payment and acceptance terms. The articles also specify the responsibilities of the banks and the principals.

Some Main Provisions

Article 4:

The principal should insert the complete address of the drawee in the collection order. If the complete address is not shown, the collecting bank may try and ascertain the information, but it is under no obligation to do so. Any loss or delay caused by an incomplete drawee's address will rest with the principal. In practice the remitting bank should check that the full address appears on the collection order.

Article 7:

The collection order should indicate D/A or D/P. In the absence of such a statement, documents can only be released on payment.

Articles 9 and 10:

These two articles state that bank will act in good faith and exercise reasonable care. Banks must check that they appear to have received the documents which are specified in the collection order, but they have no obligation to examine the documents any further.

Articles 11:

Where the principal specifies a collecting bank, the remitting bank will use that bank. Where no collecting bank is specified, the remitting bank will choose a collecting bank. In practice, it is better for the choice to be left to the remitting bank. Not all overseas banks can be relied upon, and it is much safer for the remitting bank to select one of the collecting overseas banks, which it knows will carry out instructions properly.

Articles 12 and 14:

Banks have no liability for any delay or loss caused by postal or telecommunication failure.

Article 21:

A collection order must state whether charges and interest can be waived if refused.

Article 24:

The collection order should give specific instructions about whether or not to protest in the event of non-payment or non-acceptance. In the absence of such instructions no protest need be made. Any legal fees incurred by the presenting bank in a protest will be charged to the remitting bank who will debit the principal's account.

Article 25:

Where the collection order indicates a case of need, an agent of the exporter who is resident in the importer's country, his powers must be clearly stated. In the absence of such indication banks will not accept any instruction from the case of need.

Notes

1. The Law of International Settlement of Payment 《国际结算法》
   与国内货款结算相比,国际货款结算要复杂得多,它不仅涉及不同的货币和结算工具,而且还涉及不同国家的法律和国际惯例。票据(negotiable instruments)是国际结算的重要支付工具,票据包括汇票、本票和支票三种,而流通性、无因性、文义性和要式性为票据的四个特性。国际贸易中的常见支付方式主要有三种,即汇付、托收和信用证。本单元重点介绍有关国际结算中的支付工具及支付方式的实务及相关法律知识。
2. usance draft 远期汇票
   又称 time draft。
3. clean draft and documentary draft 光票和跟单汇票
4. endorsement 背书
   背书是一种以转让票据权利为目的的票据行为。票据的流通就是通过票据转让来实现的,例如,持票人转让汇票应当背书并交付汇票。背书可分为记名背书(special endorsement)和空白背书(blank endorsement)。
5. allonge 粘单
   票据凭证如果不能满足背书人记载事项的需要,可以加附粘单,粘附于票据凭证上。
6. an uninterrupted series of endorsement 背书的连续性
7. the subsequent party 后手
   “前手”为 prior party。
8. acceptance 承兑
   是指汇票付款人承诺在汇票到期日支付汇票金额的票据行为。

9. right of recourse 追索权
10. the negotiable instruments law 票据法
11. out of malice or with gross negligence 处于恶意或重大疏忽
12. the protest 拒绝证明
 又称 certificate of dishonor。
13. promissory note 本票
14. crossed check 划线支票
15. rubber check 空头支票
16. certified check 保付支票
17. remittance 汇付
18. favorable exchange 顺汇
19. payment in advance, cash on delivery or open account 预付款、货到付款或赊购
20. collection 托收
 与汇付不同,托收是由出口商委托银行向进口商收款的一种方式,因此,又称之“逆汇”(adverse exchange)。
21. documentary credit 跟单信用证
 目前,信用证已成为国际贸易中使用最广、最为重要的一种结算方式。信用证是指银行按进口商的请求,向出口商开具的,凭符合规定的单据进行付款的一项书面保证。信用证项下,银行负首要付款责任(primary liability for payment),信用证是一项自足文件(独立于买卖合同以外的约定)(self-sufficient instrument),信用证是纯单据业务(pure documentary transaction)。值得注意的是,通过SWIFT 网络开立的信用证,即 SWIFT 信用证,又称“环银电协信用证”,因其安全、高效率、低成本等优点,使其在银行间也广泛使用。
22. UCP 500 《跟单信用证统一惯例国际商会第 500 号出版物》
23. UCP 600 《跟单信用证统一惯例国际商会第 600 号出版物》
 UCP 600(《跟单信用证统一惯例——2007 年修订本,国际商会第 600 号出版物》)共有 39 个条款、比 UCP 500 减少了 10 条,但却比 500 更准确、清晰,更易读、易掌握、易操作。它将一个环节涉及的问题归集在一个条款中,将 L/C 业务涉及的关系方及其重要行为进行了定义,如第二条的 14 个定义和第 3 条对具体行为的解释。
 UCP 600 纠正了 UCP 500 造成的许多误解:第一,把 UCP 500 难懂的词语改变为简洁明了的语言,取消了易造成误解的条款,如“合理关注”“合理时间”及“在其表面”等短语。第二,UCP 600 取消了无实际意义的许多条款。如“可撤销信用证”“货运代理提单”及 UCP 500 第 5 条“信用证完整明确要求”及第 12 条有关“不完整不清楚指示”的内容也从 UCP 600 中消失。第三,UCP 600 的新概念描述清楚准确。如兑付(Honor)定义了开证行、保兑行、指定行在信用证项下,除议付以外的一切与支付相关的行为;议付(Negotiation),强调是对单据(汇票)的买入行为,明确可以垫付或同意垫付给受益人,按照这个定义,远期议付信用证就是合理的。另外还有“相符交单”“申请人”“银行日”等。第四,更换了一些定义。如对审单作出单证是否相符决定的天数,由“合理时间”变为“最多为收单翌日起第 5 个工作日”。又如,“信用证”UCP 600 仅强调其本质是“开证行一项不可撤销的明确承诺,

即兑付相符的交单”。再如开证行和保兑行对于指定行的偿付责任,强调是独立于其对受益人的承诺的。第五,方便贸易和操作。UCP 600 有些特别重要的改动,如拒付后的单据处理,增加了“拒付后,如果开证行收到申请人放弃不符点的通知,则可以释放单据”;增加了拒付后单据处理的选择项,包括持单候示、已退单、按预先指示行事。这样便利了受益人和申请人及相关银行操作。又如,转让信用证方面,UCP 600 强调第二受益人的交单必须经转让行。但当第二受益人提交的单据与转让后的信用证一致,而第一受益人换单导致单据与原证出现不符时,又在第一次要求时不能做出修改的,转让行有权直接将第二受益人提交的单据寄开证行。这项规定保护了正当发货制单的第二受益人的利益。再如单据在途中遗失,UCP 600 强调只要单证相符,即只要指定行确定单证相符,并已向开证行或保兑行寄单,不管指定行是兑付还是议付,开证行及保兑行均对丢失的单据负责。这些条款的规定,都促进了国际贸易及结算的顺利运行。

24. URC 522 《托收统一规则国际商会第 522 号出版物》

Study Questions

1. What are the legal features of negotiable instruments?
2. What are the differences between UCP 500 and UCP 600?
3. Briefly describe the procedures of D/A and D/P.
4. Briefly describe the procedures of the establishment and negotiation of L/C.

UNIT 7 Anti-dumping Law[1]

Key Concepts

dumping	normal value	anti-dumping duty
unfair competition	countervailing duty	analogue market

Learning Objectives

1. Understand the definition of "dumping".
2. Be familiar with the methods to determine the normal value of the goods.
3. Understand the concept of "analogue market".
4. Understand the procedures in anti-dumping investigation and litigation.

Introduction

In international trade, the method of resorting to dumping[2] is frequently adopted by some export-oriented companies so as to expand their business volume and occupy the foreign markets. In essence, dumping is an unfair competition. It may cause injury to the relevant industries of the importing country. Hence, many countries have promulgated anti-dumping law in order to maintain foreign trade order and fair competition and to protect their domestic industries. According to the anti-dumping code in WTO, the importing country may impose anti-dumping tariff, i. e. a very high and punitive customs duty[3], upon the dumped imports, if there are sufficient evidences to prove the existence of dumping of the imports.

In economics, "dumping" can refer to any kind of predatory pricing. However, the word is now generally used only in the context of international trade law, where dumping is defined as the act of a manufacturer in one country exporting a product to another country at a price which is either below the price it charges in its home market or if it can be proven that there has been a substantial increase of a specific good; Dumping large surpluses into a market will substantially lower the market price as will introducing lower than market priced goods. The term has a negative connotation as advocates of free markets see "dumping" as a form of protectionism. Furthermore, advocates for workers and laborers believe that safeguarding businesses against predatory practices, such as dumping, help alleviate some of the harsher consequences of such practices between economies at different stages of development. The Bolkestein directive, for example, was accused in Europe of being a form of "social dumping", as it favored competition between workers, as exemplified by the Polish Plumber stereotype. While there are very few examples of a national scale dumping that succeeded in producing a national-level monopoly, there are several examples of dumping that produced a monopoly in regional markets for certain industries. Ron Chenow points to the example of regional oil monopolies in *Titan: The Life of John D. Rockefeller, Sr.* where Rockefeller receives a message from Colonel Thompson outlining an approved strategy where oil in one market, Cincinnati, would be sold at or below cost to drive competition's profits down and force them to exit the market. In another area where other independent businesses were already driven out, namely in Chicago, prices would be increased by a quarter.

A standard technical definition of dumping is the act of charging a lower price for a good in a foreign market than one charges for the same good in a domestic market. This is often referred to as selling at less than "fair value". Under the World Trade Organization (WTO) Agreement, dumping is condemned (but is not prohibited) if it causes or threatens to cause material injury to a domestic industry in the importing country.

Anti-dumping Actions

Legal Issues

If a company exports a product at a price lower than the price it normally charges in its own home market, it is said to be "dumping" the product. Opinions differ as to whether or not such practice constitutes unfair competition[4], but many governments take action against dumping to protect domestic industry. The WTO agreement does not pass judgment. Its focus is on how governments can or cannot react to dumping—it disciplines anti-dumping actions, and it is often called the "anti-dumping agreement". (This focus only on the reaction to dumping contrasts with the approach of the subsidies and countervailing measures agreement.)

The legal definitions are more precise, but broadly speaking, the WTO agreement allows governments to act against dumping where there is genuine ("material") injury to the competing domestic industry. To do so, the government has to show that dumping is taking place, calculate the extent of dumping (how much lower the export price is compared to the exporter's home market price), and show that the dumping is causing injury or threatening to cause injury.

Definitions and Extent

While permitted by the WTO, General Agreement on Tariffs and Trade (GATT) (Article Ⅵ) allows countries the option of taking action against dumping. The Anti-dumping Agreement clarifies and expands Article Ⅵ, and the two operate together. They allow countries to act in a way that would normally break the GATT principles of binding a tariff and not discriminating between trading partners—typically anti-dumping action means charging extra import duty on the particular product from the particular exporting country in order to bring its price closer to the "normal value" or to remove the injury to domestic industry in the importing country.

There are many different ways of calculating whether a particular product is being dumped heavily or only lightly. The agreement narrows down the range of possible options. It provides three methods to calculate a product's "normal value". The main one is based on the price in the exporter's domestic market. When this cannot be used, two alternatives are available—the price charged by the exporter in another country, or a calculation based on the combination of the exporter's production costs, other expenses and normal profit margins. And the agreement also specifies how a fair comparison can be made between the export price and what would be a normal price.

Calculating the extent of dumping on a product is not enough. Anti-dumping measures can only be applied if the dumping is hurting the industry in the importing country. Therefore, a detailed investigation has to be conducted according to specified rules first. The investigation must evaluate all relevant economic factors that have a bearing on the state of the industry in question. If the investigation shows dumping is taking place and domestic industry is being hurt, the exporting company can undertake to raise its price to an agreed level in order to avoid anti-dumping import duty.

Procedures in Investigation and Litigation

Detailed procedures are set out on how anti-dumping cases are to be initiated, how the investigations are to be conducted, and the conditions for ensuring that all interested parties are given an opportunity to present evidence. Anti-dumping measures must expire five years after the date of imposition, unless a review shows that ending the measure would lead to injury.

Anti-dumping investigations are to end immediately in cases where the authorities determine that the margin of dumping is, *de minimis*, or insignificantly small (defined as less than 2% of the export price of the product). Other conditions are also set. For example, the investigations also have to end if the volume of dumped imports is negligible (i. e., if the volume from one country is less than 3% of total imports of that product—although investigations can proceed if several countries, each supplying less than 3% of the imports, together account for 7% or more of total imports). The agreement says member countries must inform the Committee on Anti-dumping Practices about all preliminary and final anti-dumping actions, promptly and in detail. They must also report on all investigations twice a year. When differences arise, members are encouraged to consult each other. They can also use the WTO's dispute settlement procedure.

Actions in the United States

In the United States, domestic firms can file an antidumping petition under the regulations determined by the United States Department of Commerce, which determines "less than fair value" and the International Trade Commission, which determines "injury". These proceedings operate on a timetable governed by U. S. law. The Department of Commerce has regularly found that products have been sold at less than fair value in U. S. markets. If the domestic industry is able to establish that it is being injured by the dumping, then antidumping duties are imposed on goods imported from the dumpers' country at a percentage rate calculated to counteract the dumping margin.

Related to antidumping duties are "countervailing duties[5]". The difference is that countervailing duties seek to offset injurious subsidization while antidumping duties offset injurious dumping.

Some commentators have noted that domestic protectionism, and lack of knowledge regarding foreign cost of production, lead to the unpredictable institutional process surrounding investigation. Members of the WTO can file complaints against anti-dumping measures.

Actions in the European Union

European Union anti-dumping is under the purview of the European Council. It is governed by European Council regulation 384/96. However, implementation of anti-dumping actions (trade defense actions) is taken after voting by various committees with member state representation.

The bureaucratic entity responsible for advising member states on anti-dumping actions is the Directorate General Trade (DG Trade), based in Brussels. Community industry can apply to have an anti-dumping investigation begin. DG Trade first investigates the standing of the complainants. If they are found to represent at least 25% of community industry, the investigation will probably begin. The process is guided by quite specific guidance in the regulations. The DG Trade will make a recommendation to a committee known as the Anti-dumping Advisory Committee, on which each member state has one vote. Member states abstaining will be treated as if they voted in favor of industrial protection, a voting system which has come under considerable criticism.

As is implied by the criterion for beginning an investigation, EU anti-dumping actions are primarily considered part of a "trade defense" portfolio. Consumer interests and non-industry related interests ("community interests") are not emphasized during an investigation. An investigation typically looks for damage caused by dumping to community producers, and the level of tariff set is based on the damage done to community producers by dumping.

If consensus is not found, the decision goes to the European Council. If imposed, duties last for five years theoretically. In practice they last at least a year longer, because expiry reviews are usually initiated at the end of the five years, and during the review process the status-quo is maintained.

Analogue Market

The dumping investigation essentially compares domestic prices of the accused dumping nation with prices of the imported product on the European market. However, several rules are applied to the data before the dumping margin is calculated. Most contentious is the concept of "analogue market[6]". Some exporting nations are not granted "Market Economy Status" by the EU: China is a prime example. In such cases, the DG Trade is prevented from using domestic prices as the fair measure of the domestic price. A particular exporting industry may also lose market status if the DG Trade concludes that this industry receives government assistance. Other tests applied include the application of international accounting standards and bankruptcy laws.

The consequences of not being granted market economy status have a big impact on the investigation. For example, if China is accused of dumping widgets, the basic approach is to consider the price of widgets in China against the price of Chinese widgets in Europe. But China does not have market economy status, so Chinese domestic prices cannot be used as the reference. Instead, the DG Trade must decide upon an analogue market: a market which does have market economy status, and which is similar enough to China. Brazil and Mexico have been used, but the USA is a popular analogue market. In this case, the price of widgets in the USA is regarded as the substitute for the price of widgets in China. This process of choosing an analogue market is subject to the influence of the complainant, which has led to some criticism that it is an inherent bias in the process.

However, China is one of the countries that has the cheapest labor force. Criticisms have argued that it is quite unreasonable to compare China's goods price to the USA's as analogue. China is now developing to a more free and open market, unlike its planned-economy in the early 60s, the market in China is more willing to embrace the global competition. It is thus required to improve its market regulations and conquer the free trade barriers to improve the situation and produce a properly judged pricing level to assess the "dumping" behavior.

European Union and Common Agricultural Policy

The Common Agricultural Policy of the European Union has often been accused of dumping though significant reforms were made as part of the Agreement on Agriculture at the Uruguay round of GATT negotiations in 1992 and in subsequent incremental reforms, notably the Luxembourg Agreement in 2003. Initially the CAP sought to increase European agricultural production and provide support to European farmers through a process of market intervention whereby a special fund—the European Agricultural Guidance and Guarantee Fund (EAGGF)—would buy up surplus agricultural produce if the price fell below a certain centrally determined level (the intervention level). Through this measure European farmers were given a "guaranteed" price for their produce when sold in the European community. In addition to this internal measure a system of export reimbursements ensured that European produce sold outside of the European community would sell at or below world prices at no detriment to the European producer. This policy was heavily criticized as distorting world trade and since 1992 the policy has moved away from market intervention and towards direct payments to farmers regardless of production (a process of "decoupling"). Furthermore the payments are generally dependent on the farmer fulfilling certain environmental or animal welfare requirements so as to encourage responsible, sustainable farming in what is termed "multifunctional" agricultural subsidies—that is, the social, environmental and other benefits from subsidies that do not include a simple increase in production.

Anti-dumping Law in China

Dumping and Injury

Dumping occurs when the export price of an imported product is less than its normal value[7]. Normal value is determined according to the following methods: 1) If products identical with or similar to the imported product have comparable prices in the exporting countries' marketplace, those comparable prices shall be the normal value; 2) If products identical with or similar to the imported product do not have comparable prices in the exporting country's marketplace, the normal value shall be either (1) the comparable price of identical or similar products exported to a third country, or (2) the production cost of identical or similar products plus reasonable expenses and profit.

Export price is determined according to the following methods: 1) The price actually paid or the price that should have been paid for the imported product is the export price; 2) If no price is actually paid or should have been paid for the imported product, or its price cannot be determined, the export price shall be (1) the price for which the imported product is resold for the first time to an independent buyer, or (2) the price reconstructed according to a reasonable basis by MOC after consultation with the Customs Bureau.

The dumping margin is the amount by which the imported product's export price is less than its normal value. In determining the dumping margin, the imported product's export price and its normal value should be compared according to fair and reasonable means. Injury includes causing material injury or the threat of material injury to already established corresponding domestic industry or the creation of obstacles to the establishment of corresponding domestic industry by dumping.

In determining injuries caused by dumping to domestic industries, the following matters should be investigated: (1) The quantity of product dumped, including the total quantity of product dumped or the incremental increase in its total quantity relative to identical or similar domestic products and the possibility of large increases therein; (2) The prices of goods dumped, including reductions in the prices of goods dumped or the effect upon the prices of identical or similar domestic products; (3) The effect of the dumped product on domestic industry; (4) The dumping export company's production capacity, export capacity and inventory.

Anti-dumping Investigation

Domestic producers of products identical or similar to imported goods, or their related organizations (hereinafter referred to as "the applicant"), may submit a written application for an anti-dumping investigation to MOC in accordance with the provisions of the relevant regulations. The application should contain the following evidence: (1) The names and addresses of the applicant(s) and the producers it represents; (2) A designation and a description of the imported products, their Import Tariff Code numbers, and a designation and description of the identical or similar domestic products; (3) The imported products' quantity and prices and their effect upon domestic industry;

(4) The causal relationship between dumping and injury; (5) Other contents prescribed by MOC. The necessary evidence should be attached to the application form. After receiving an applicant's written application, MOC should examine the application and attached evidence and, after consulting with the State Economic and Trade Commission, should decide whether or not to file the case for investigation. If, under special circumstances, MOC has sufficient evidence to believe that dumping, injury and a causal relationship between the two exists, it may, after consulting with the State Economic and Trade Commission, decide on its own to file a case for investigation. The public announcement of the final ruling in an anti-dumping investigation must be made within the 12-month period beginning with the date of public announcement of the decision to file the case for investigation. Under special circumstances, that period may be extended to a total of 18 months. MOC should publicly announce its decision whether or not to file a case for investigation and notify the applicant, known exporters and importers, the exporting country's government, and other interested parties.

After the decision to file a case for investigation, MOC and the Customs Bureau shall jointly investigate the existence of dumping and determine the dumping margin, and the State Economic and Trade Commission and the relevant State Council departments shall jointly investigate the existence of injuries and determine the extent of injuries. MOC and the State Economic and Trade Commission shall separately make their initial rulings based upon the results of the investigation. MOC shall publicly announce the initial rulings. If the initial rulings establish the existence of dumping and injury, further investigations shall be made as to the dumping, dumping margin, injuries and extent of injuries in accordance with the provisions of the preceding paragraph. MOC and the State Economic and Trade Commission shall separately make their final rulings based upon the results of the subsequent investigations. MOC shall publicly announce the final rulings.

An anti-dumping investigation should be terminated and such termination publicly announced by MOC under the following circumstances: (1) The applicant withdraws the application; (2) The initial rulings do not establish the existence of dumping and injury; (3) The final rulings do not establish the existence of dumping and injury; (4) The dumping margin and the dumped product's imported quantity can be ignored.

When MOC and the Customs Bureau or the State Economic and Trade Commission and the relevant department of the State Council jointly investigate, they may distribute interrogatories to interested parties and carry out sample surveys. When requested by an interested party, an opportunity should be provided for it to express its opinion. When MOC believes it is necessary, it may dispatch personnel to the relevant countries to investigate, provided the relevant countries do not object. When MOC and the Customs Bureau or the State Economic and Trade Commission and the relevant department of the State Council jointly investigate, the interested parties shall accurately report the situation and supply the relevant materials. If they do not accurately report the situation and supply the relevant materials, or by other means hinder the investigation, MOC and the State Economic and Trade Commission may make their rulings based upon the materials available to them.

Anti-dumping Measures

If the initial ruling establishes the existence of dumping and of resultant injuries to corresponding domestic industries, the following temporary anti-dumping measures may be adopted: (1) According to prescribed procedure, a temporary anti-dumping tax may be imposed; (2) The provision of a cash deposit or other forms of guarantee may be required. The amount of temporary anti-dumping tax, cash deposit and other forms of guarantee should be consistent with the dumping margin determined by the initial ruling. MOC may propose and the State Council's Custom Tax Policy Commission shall decide upon the imposition of any temporary anti-dumping tax. MOC shall decide whether to require the provision of cash deposits and other forms of guarantee. The period for the imposition of anti-dumping taxes is the 4-month period beginning with the date of public announcement of the decision to impose the temporary measures. Under special circumstances, the period may be extended to a total of 9 months. If the exporter dumping the products or the exporting country's government promises to adopt effective measures to eliminate the injury caused to domestic industry, MOC, after consulting with the State Economic and Trade Commission, may decide to suspend the anti-dumping investigation. It should publicly announce the decision. If the exporter dumping the product or the exporting country's government fails to fulfill or withdraws the commitments, MOC, after consulting the State Economic and Trade Commission, may decide to resume the anti-dumping investigation.

If the final ruling establishes the existence of dumping and of the resultant injury to domestic industry, an anti-dumping tax may be imposed according to prescribed procedures, and MOC shall public announce the decision. MOC may propose, the State Council's Customs Tariff Policy Commission shall decide upon, and the Customs Bureau shall implement the imposition of any anti-dumping tax. The antidumping taxpayer is the importer of the dumped product. The amount of the anti-dumping tax must not exceed the dumping margin determined by the final ruling. If the amount of the anti-dumping tax determined by the final ruling is lower than the amount of the temporary anti-dumping tax, the excess tax paid shall be refunded. If the amount of the anti-dumping tax determined by the final ruling is higher than the amount of the temporary anti-dumping tax, the balance of the two taxes need not be paid. If the final ruling does not impose anti-dumping tax, the temporary anti-dumping tax collected, the cash deposit and other forms of guarantee shall be refunded.

When the following two circumstances both exist the State Council's Tariff Policy Commission, based upon MOC proposals, may decide to retroactively impose the anti-dumping tax on the dumped goods imported within the 90-day period previous to the public announcement of the decision to adopt temporary measures: (1) There a) is a history of the dumped product causing injury to domestic industry; or b) the importer of the dumped product knew or should have known that the product's exporter was dumping the product and that the dumping would cause injury to domestic industry; and, (2) A large quantity of the product dumped was imported within a short period and has already caused injury to domestic industry.

The time period for the imposition of anti-dumping taxes and price commitments prescribed pursuant to the regulations is five years. Within this time period, MOC, after consulting with the State Economic and Trade Commission, on its own or upon the requests of interested parties, may carry out a reexamination of decisions imposing anti-dumping taxes. Within a period of 12 months from the date that the reexamination begins, MOC may propose to the State Council's Customs Tariff Policy Commission that the anti-dumping tax decision be modified, revoked or maintained. The State Council's Custom Tariff Policy Commission shall make the reexamination decision, and MOC shall publicly announce the decision.

Notes

1. *Anti-dumping Law* 《反倾销法》

主要是由一国立法机关制定,由国家行政机关保证执行,为规范进口产品价格秩序,保护国内相关产业,要求进口产品相关者必须遵守的行为规则。《反倾销法》是调整进口国反倾销调查机关在对倾销进行调查、裁定和采取反倾销措施过程中所发生的各种权利与义务关系的法律规范。《反倾销法》的实施属于行政执法,也被称为准司法活动。《反倾销法》通常由国家行政机关实施,如美国的商务部和国际贸易委员会,欧盟的部长理事会和委员会,日本的大藏省和通产省,加拿大的海关和税务部,中国的商务部、海关总署等。反倾销案件直接由有关行政机关受理和裁决,适用的程序是一般行政程序。当然,《反倾销法》这种性质并不排除法院对反倾销程序进行司法审查的可能性,当事人对反倾销行政裁决不服,可以向特定法院提出司法审议的请求,但法院只是对行政机关的行政程序实施审查,而不直接受理当事人的反倾销诉讼,实际上是对行政程序进行法律监督。

本单元主要包括倾销及其界定、倾销构成要件、反倾销调查、美国和欧盟的反倾销措施和程序、中国的反倾销立法等内容,重点应把握倾销的界定、反倾销的异化趋势(西方国家所采用的替代国制度的不合理性、自由裁量权的滥用、从反不正当竞争走向贸易保护主义)以及反倾销法的重新定位。

2. dumping 倾销

依据关贸总协定第6条的规定,一国产品以低于正常价值的价格进入另一国市场,并对该国同类产业造成实质性(material)的损害或威胁,或阻碍其产业的建立,则构成倾销。倾销是一种不正当竞争(unfair competition)手段,但一些发达资本主义国家往往利用反倾销以抵制发展中国家的廉价产品进入其市场,因此,反倾销是一种贸易保护主义的手段,也是一种重要的非关税贸易壁垒(non-tariff barrier to trade)。此外,对于出口国是否为市场经济国家,一些发达国家则采取不同的方法来确定产品的正常价值。如果出口国为非市场经济国家,那么就有可能以替代国(substitute nation)的国内销售价格或其产品结构价格(structural price)来代替出口国国内的产品销售价格或其产品结构价格,因替代国往往由进口国来选定,而替代国与出口国之间存在着社会、政治、经济等方面的差异,因此,这种方法缺乏公平性,甚至带有一定的歧视性。在反倾销方面,我国出口企业也面临着同样的问题。

3. punitive customs duty 惩罚性关税

4. unfair competition 不正当竞争
   在国际贸易中,倾销(dumping)和出口补贴(export subsidy)属于不正当竞争。
5. countervailing duties 抵消性关税
   主要是指对直接或间接接受补贴的外国商品进口所征收的一种进口附加税。
6. analogue market 替代市场
   在反倾销调查中,如果认为出口国是非市场经济国家,就有可能选定一个经济发展水平与该出口国较为相似的市场经济国家作为其"替代市场"或"替代国"。
7. normal value 正常价值
   正常价值是反倾销法中一个重要的概念,正常价值通常是指在出口国的国内市场上,通过正常的销售过程,独立的消费者为该产品支付的价格。如果不存在国内销售价格或不能使用国内销售价格确定正常价值,则可用第三国出口价格或结构价格作为正常价值。第三国出口价格是指相同产品出口到一个合适的第三国,且其出口产品价格具有代表性的可比价格作为正常价值;而结构价格则是指产品在原产地的生产成本基础上加上合理的销售费、管理费和其他费用及利润所形成的价格。

Study Questions

1. What is dumping?
2. What do you think of "analogue market"?
3. Why should the importing nation take measures to stop dumping?
4. How do some western countries determine the normal price of our exports in dumping investigations?
5. What is the "structural price" of the products?

Case Study

U. S. Steel Files New Antidumping Case

Petitions for Remedies Against Surge in Chinese Tubular Goods

(Compiled by Jonathan Katz)

Jan. 7, 2010

United States Steel Corp. said Jan. 7 it has requested more duties on steel imports from China more than a week after the U. S. International Trade Commission determined that imported Chinese steel pipes adversely impacted the domestic steel industry.

This time, U. S. Steel, along with other petitioning parties, filed a "critical circumstances" complaint with the U. S. Commerce Department alleging that certain Chinese seamless steel imports spiked 290% three months after the petitioning parties initially sought antidumping and countervailing duties on seamless standard, line and pressure pipe from China.

In response, U. S. Steel is seeking retroactively imposed duties on certain imports that entered the United States after filing the petitions. In antidumping and countervailing duty investigations, remedial duties are normally effective when the Commerce Department issues a preliminary unfair trade decision. But under U. S. and international law, duties can be assessed on imports that entered the U. S. market up to 90 days prior to such a decision if evidence shows foreign producers surged into the market in an attempt to avoid tariffs.

If the petitioners are successful, remedial duties could be assessed on imports entering the market within 90 days prior to the preliminary countervailing duty decision, U. S. Steel says. The Commerce Department is scheduled to make its preliminary determination on Feb. 16, 2010.

The move comes just two days after U. S. authorities announced they had slapped tariffs on Chinese wire decking after a preliminary finding that the products were "dumped" at below market value.

About a week earlier, the Trade Commission issued a final decision saying that Chinese steel pipe imports adversely impacted the U. S. steel industry, paving the way for the Commerce Department to impose countervailing duties of up to nearly 16%.

UNIT 8 Contract Law[1]

Key Concepts

contract	damages	specific performance	consideration
offer	acceptance	misrepresentation	

Learning Objectives

1. Understand the concept of "contract".
2. Understand the offer and acceptance in conclusion of the contract.
3. Understand the concept of "consideration".
4. Be familiar with two types of misrepresentation in contract law.

A contract is a legally enforceable agreement between two or more parties with mutual obligations. The remedy at law for breach of contract is "damages" or monetary compensation. In equity, the remedy can be specific performance of the contract[2] or an injunction[3]. Both remedies award the damaged party the "benefit of the bargain" or expectation damages, which are greater than mere reliance damages, as in promissory estoppel.

Origin and Scope

Contract law is based on the principle expressed in the Latin phrase *pacta sunt servanda*, which is usually translated "agreements to be kept" but more literally means "pacts must be kept".

Contract law can be classified, as is habitual in civil law systems, as part of a general law of obligations, along with tort, unjust enrichment, and restitution.

As a means of economic ordering, contract relies on the notion of consensual exchange and has been extensively discussed in broader economic, sociological, and anthropological terms (see

"Contractual theory" below). In American English, the term extends beyond the legal meaning to encompass a broader category of agreements.

This article mainly concerns the common law. Such jurisdictions usually retain a high degree of freedom of contract, with parties largely at liberty to set their own terms. This is in contrast to the civil law, which typically applies certain overarching principles to disputes arising out of contract, as in the *French Civil Code*[4].

However, contract is a form of economic ordering common throughout the world, and different rules apply in jurisdictions applying civil law (derived from Roman law principles), Islamic law, socialist legal systems, and customary or local law.

Elements

At common law, the elements of a contract are mutual assent and consideration[5].

Mutual Assent

At common law, mutual assent is typically reached through offer and acceptance, that is, when an offer is met with an acceptance that is unqualified and that does not vary the offer's terms. The latter requirement is known as the mirror image rule[6]. If a purported acceptance does vary the terms of an offer, it is not an acceptance but a counteroffer and, therefore, simultaneously a rejection of the original offer. The *Uniform Commercial Code*[7] notably disposes of the mirror image rule in § 2-207, although the UCC only governs transactions in goods.

Offer and Acceptance[8]

The most important feature of a contract is that one party makes an offer for an arrangement that another accepts. This can be called a concurrence of wills or *consensus ad idem* (meeting of the minds) of two or more parties. The concept is somewhat contested. The obvious objection is that a court cannot read minds and the existence or otherwise of agreement is judged objectively, with only limited room for questioning subjective intention: see *Smith v. Hughes*. Richard Austen-Baker has suggested that the perpetuation of the idea of "meeting of minds" may come from a misunderstanding of the Latin term "consensus ad idem" which actually means "agreement to the [same] thing". There must be evidence that the parties had each from an objective perspective engaged in conduct manifesting their assent, and a contract will be formed when the parties have met such a requirement. An objective perspective means that it is only necessary that somebody gives the impression of offering or accepting contractual terms in the eyes of a reasonable person, not that they actually did want to form a contract.

The case of *Carlill v Carbolic Smoke Ball Company* is an example of a unilateral contract. Obligations are only imposed upon one party upon acceptance by performance of a condition. In the United States, the general rule is that in "case of doubt, an offer is interpreted as inviting the offeree to accept *either* by promising to perform what the offer requests *or* by rendering the performance, as the offeree chooses. "

Offer and acceptance does not always need to be expressed orally or in writing. An implied contract is one in which some of the terms are not expressed in words. This can take two forms. A contract which is implied in fact is one in which the circumstances imply that parties have reached an agreement even though they have not done so expressly. For example, by going to a doctor for a checkup, a patient agrees that he will pay a fair price for the service. If one refuses to pay after being examined, the patient has breached a contract implied in fact. A contract which is implied in law is also called a quasi-contract, because it is not in fact a contract; rather, it is a means for the courts to remedy situations in which one party would be unjustly enriched were he or she not required to compensate the other. For example, a plumber accidentally installs a sprinkler system in the lawn of the wrong house. The owner of the house had learned the previous day that his neighbor was getting new sprinklers. That morning, he sees the plumber installing them in his lawn. Pleased at the mistake, he says nothing, and then refuses to pay when the plumber delivers the bill. Will the man be held liable for payment? Yes, if it could be proven that the man knew that the sprinklers were being installed mistakenly, the court would make him pay because of a quasi-contract. If that knowledge could not be proven, he would not be liable. Such a claim is also referred to as "*quantum meruit*".

Consideration

Consideration is something of value given by a promissor to a promisee in exchange for something of value given by a promisee to a promissor. Typically, the thing of value is an act, such as making a payment, or a forbearance to act when one is privileged to do so, such as an adult refraining from smoking.

Consideration consists of a legal detriment and a bargain. A legal detriment is a promise to do something or refrain from doing something that you have the legal right to do, or actually doing or refraining from doing something that you don't have to do. A bargain is something the promisor (the party making promise or offer) wants, usually being one of the legal detriments. The legal detriment and bargain principles come together in consideration and create an exchange relationship, where both parties agree to exchange something that the other wishes to have.

The purpose of consideration is to ensure that there is a present bargain, that the promises of the parties are reciprocally induced. The classic theory of consideration required that a promise be of detriment to the promissor or benefit to the promisee. This is no longer the case.

Sufficiency

Consideration must be *sufficient*, but courts will not weight the *adequacy* of consideration. For instance, agreeing to sell a car for a penny may constitute a binding contract. All that must be shown is that the seller actually wanted the penny. This is known as the *peppercorn rule*. Otherwise, the penny would constitute *nominal consideration*, which is insufficient. Parties may do this for tax purposes, attempting to disguise gift transactions as contracts.

Transfer of money is typically recognized as an example of sufficient consideration, but in some cases it will not suffice, for example, when one party agrees to make partial payment of a debt in exchange for being released from the full amount.

Past consideration is not sufficient. Indeed, it is an oxymoron. For instance, in *Eastwood v. Kenyon*, the guardian of a young girl obtained a loan to educate the girl and to improve her marriage prospects. After her marriage, her husband promised to pay off the loan. It was held that the guardian could not enforce the promise because taking out the loan to raise and educate the girl was past consideration—it was completed before the husband promised to repay it.

The insufficiency of past consideration is related to the preexisting duty rule. The classic instance is *Stilk v. Myrick*, in which a captain's promise to divide the wages of two deserters among the remaining crew if they would sail home from the Baltic short-handed, was found unenforceable on the grounds that the crew were already contracted to sail the ship through all perils of the sea.

The preexisting duty rule also extends beyond an underlying contract. It would not constitute sufficient consideration for a party to promise to refrain from committing a tort or crime, for example. However, a promise from A to do something for B if B will perform a contractual obligation B owes to C, will be enforceable—B is suffering a legal detriment by making his performance of his contract with A effectively enforceable by C as well as by A.

Consideration must move from the promisee. For instance, it is good consideration for person A to pay person C in return for services rendered by person B. If there are joint promisees, then consideration need only to move from one of the promisees.

Other Jurisdictions

Some common-law and civil-law systems do not require consideration, and some commentators consider it unnecessary—the requirement of intent by both parties to create legal relations by both parties performs the same function under contract. The reason that both exist in common law jurisdictions is thought by leading scholars to be the result of the combining by 19th century judges of two distinct threads: first the consideration requirement was at the heart of the action of assumpsit, which had grown up in the Middle Ages and remained the normal action for breach of a simple contract in England & Wales until 1884, when the old forms of action were abolished; secondly, the notion of agreement between two or more parties as being the essential legal and moral foundation of contract in all legal systems, promoted by the 18th century French writer Pothier in his *Traite des Obligations*, much read (especially after translation into English in 1805) by English judges and jurists. The latter chimed well with the fashionable will theories of the time, especially John Stuart Mill's influential ideas on free will, and got grafted on to the traditional common law requirement for consideration to ground an action in assumpsit.

Civil law systems take the approach that an exchange of promises, or a concurrence of wills alone, rather than an exchange in valuable rights is the correct basis. So if you promised to give me a book, and I accepted your offer without giving anything in return, I would have a legal right to the book and you could not change your mind about giving me it as a gift. However, in common law systems the concept of *culpa in contrahendo*, a form of "estoppel", is increasingly used to create obligations during pre-contractual negotiations. Estoppel is an equitable doctrine that provides for the creation of legal obligations if a party has given an assurance and the other has relied on the assurance to his detriment. A number of commentators have suggested that consideration be abandoned, and estoppel be used to replace it as a basis for contracts. However, legislation, rather than judicial development, has been touted as the only way to remove this entrenched common law doctrine. Lord Justice Denning famously stated that "The doctrine of consideration is too firmly fixed to be overthrown by a side-wind."

Formation

In addition to the elements of a contract:

- a party must have capacity to contract;
- the purpose of the contract must be lawful;
- the form of the contract must be legal;
- the parties must intend to create a legal relationship; and
- the parties must consent.

As a result, there are a variety of affirmative defenses that a party may assert to avoid his obligation.

Affirmative Defenses

Vitiating factors constituting defences to purported contract formation include:

- mistake;
- incapacity, including mental incompetence and infancy/minority;
- duress;
- undue influence;
- unconscionability;
- misrepresentation[9]/fraud; and
- frustration of purpose.

Such defenses operate to determine whether a purported contract is either (1) void or (2) voidable. Void contracts cannot be ratified by either party. Voidable contracts *can* be ratified.

Freedom to Contract and *Hurley v. Eddingfield*

In most systems of law, parties have freedom to choose whether or not they wish to enter into a contract, absent superseding duties. In American law, one early case exemplifying this proposition is *Hurley v. Eddingfield* (1901), in which the Supreme Court of Indiana ruled in favor of a physician who voluntarily decided not to help a patient whom the physician had treated on past occasions, despite the lack of other available medical assistance and the patient's subsequent death.

In addition, for some contracts formalities must be complied with under legislation sometimes called a statute of frauds (especially transactions in real property or for relatively large cash amounts).

Invitation to Treat (also called Invitation for Offer)

Where a product in large quantities is advertised in a newspaper or on a poster, it generally is not considered an offer but instead will be regarded as an invitation to treat, since there is no guarantee that the store can provide the item for everyone who might want one. This was the basis of the decision in *Partridge v. Crittenden* a criminal case in which the defendant was charged with "offering for sale" bramble finch cocks and hens. The court held that the newspaper advertisement could only be an invitation to treat, since it could not have been intended as an offer to the world, so the defendant was not guilty of "offering" them for sale. Similarly, a display of goods in a shop window is an invitation to treat, as was held in *Fisher v. Bell* another criminal case which turned on the correct analysis of offers as against invitations to treat. In this instance the defendant was charged with "offering for sale" prohibited kinds of knife, which he had displayed in his shop window with prices attached. The court held that this was an invitation to treat, the offer would be made by a purchaser going into the shop and asking to buy a knife, with acceptance being by the shopkeeper, which he could withhold. (The law was later amended to "exposing for sale".) A display of goods on the shelves of a self-service shop is also an invitation to treat, with the offer being made by the purchaser at the checkout and being accepted by the shop assistant operating the checkout: *Pharmaceutical Society of Great Britain v. Boots Cash Chemists (Southern) Ltd*. If the person who is to buy the advertised product is of importance, for instance because of his personality, etc. , when buying land, it is regarded merely as an invitation to treat. In Carbolic Smoke Ball, the major difference was that a reward was included in the advertisement, which is a general exception to the rule and is then treated as an offer.

One of the most famous cases on invitation to treat is *Carlill v. Carbolic Smoke Ball Company*, decided in nineteenth-century England. A medical firm advertised that its new wonder drug, a smoke ball, would prevent those who used it according to the instructions from catching the flu, and if it did not, buyers would receive £100 and said that they had deposited £1,000 in the bank to show their good faith. When sued, Carbolic argued the ad was not to be taken as a serious, legally binding offer. It was merely an invitation to treat, and a gimmick (a "mere puff"). But the court of appeal held that it would appear to a reasonable man that Carbolic had made a serious offer, primarily because of the reference to the £1,000 deposited into the bank. People had given good "consideration" for it by going to the "distinct inconvenience" of using a faulty product. "Read the advertisement how you will, and twist it about as you will," said Lindley LJ, "here is a distinct promise expressed in language which is perfectly unmistakable."

Most states consider persons under the age of 18 to be minors. They have the right to cancel the contract at any time before and even after reaching the age of 18. If, however, a minor cancels the contract, the benefits that he or she received must be returned.

Contracts entered into by a minor as one party and an adult as the other party are enforceable if the adult breaches the contract. The minor can enforce the contract and collect damages by the adult's breach. However, if the minor breaches the contract, the adult does not have the legal authority to enforce the contract and cannot collect damages under the bargain principle. Promissory estoppel or unjust enrichment may be available, but generally are not.

Intention to Be Legally Bound

There is a presumption for commercial agreements that parties intend to be legally bound (unless the parties expressly state that they do not want to be bound, like in heads of agreement). On the other hand, many kinds of domestic and social agreements are unenforceable on the basis of public policy, for instance between children and parents. One early example is found in *Balfour v. Balfour*. Using contract-like terms, Mr. Balfour had agreed to give his wife £30 a month as maintenance while he was living in Ceylon (Sri Lanka). Once he left, they separated and Mr. Balfour stopped payments. Mrs. Balfour brought an action to enforce the payments. At the Court of Appeal, the Court held that there was no enforceable agreement as there was not enough evidence to suggest that they were intending to be legally bound by the promise.

The case is often cited in conjunction with *Merritt v. Merritt*. Here the court distinguished the case from *Balfour v. Balfour* because Mr. and Mrs. Merritt, although married again, were estranged at the time the agreement was made. Therefore any agreement between them was made with the intention to create legal relations.

Third Parties

The doctrine of privity of contract[10] means that only those involved in striking a bargain would have standing to enforce it. In general this is still the case, only parties to a contract may sue for the breach of a contract, although in recent years the rule of privity has eroded somewhat and third party beneficiaries have been allowed to recover damages for breaches of contracts they were not party to. In cases where facts involve third party beneficiaries or debtors to the original contracting party have been allowed to be considered parties for purposes of enforcement of the contract. A recent advance has been seen in the case law as well as statutory recognition to the dilution of the doctrine of privity of contract. The recent tests applied by courts have been the test of benefit and the duty owed test. The duty owed test looks to see if the third party was agreeing to pay a debt for the original party [needs elaboration] and whereas the benefit test looks to see if circumstances indicate that the promisee intends to give the beneficiary the benefit of the promised performance. Any defense allowed to parties of the original contract extend to third party beneficiaries. A recent example is in England, where the *Contracts (Rights of Third Parties) Act* 1999 was introduced.

Formalities and Writing

An unwritten, unspoken contract, also known as "a contract implied by the acts of the parties", which can be either implied in fact or implied in law, may also be legally binding. Contracts implied in fact are "real" contracts, that is, of no different remedy than "benefit of the bargain", as mentioned above. However, contracts implied in law are also known as quasi-contracts, and the remedy is quantum meruit, the fair market value of goods or services rendered.

Oral contracts are ordinarily valid and therefore legally binding. However, in most jurisdictions, certain types of contracts must be reduced to writing to be enforceable. This is to prevent frauds and perjuries, hence the name statute of frauds. For example, an unwritten contract would be unenforceable if for the sale of land.

Contracts that do not meet the requirements of common law or statutory Statutes of frauds are unenforceable, but are not necessarily thereby void. However, a party unjustly enriched by an unenforceable contract may be required to provide restitution for unjust enrichment. Statutes of frauds are typically codified in state statutes covering specific types of contracts, such as contracts for the sale of real estate.

In Australia and many, if not all, jurisdictions which have adopted the common law of England, for contracts subject to legislation equivalent to the Statute of frauds, there is no requirement for the entire contract to be in writing. Although for property transactions there must be a note or memorandum evidencing the contract, which may come into existence after the contract has been formed. The note or memorandum must be signed in some way, and a series of documents may be used in place of a single note or memorandum. It must contain all material terms of the contract, the subject matter and the parties to the contract. In England and Wales, the common law Statute of frauds is only now in force for guarantees, which must be evidenced in writing, although the agreement may be made orally. Certain other kinds of contract must be in writing or they are void, for instance, for sale of land under s. 52, *Law of Property Act* 1925.

If a contract is in a written form, and somebody signs it, then the signer is typically bound by its terms regardless of whether he has actually read it, provided the document is contractual in nature. However, affirmative defenses such as duress or unconscionability may enable the signer to avoid his purported obligation. Furthermore, if a party wishes to use a document as the basis of a contract, reasonable notice of its terms must be given to the other party prior to their entry into the contract. This includes such things as tickets issued at parking stations.

Bilateral and Unilateral Contracts

Contracts may be bilateral or unilateral. A bilateral contract is the kind of contract that most people think of when they think "contract" and indeed represents the vast majority of contracts. It is an agreement in which each of the parties to the contract makes a promise or set of promises to the other party or parties. For example, in a contract for the sale of a home, the buyer promises to pay the seller \$200,000 in exchange for the seller's promise to deliver title to the property.

In a unilateral contract, only one party to the contract makes a promise. A typical example is the reward contract: A promises to pay a reward to B if B finds A's dog. B is *not* under an obligation to find A's dog, but A *is* under an obligation to pay the reward to B if B does find the dog. The consideration for the contract here is B's reliance on A's promise or B giving up his legal right to do whatever he wanted at the time he was engaged in the finding of the dog.

In this example, the finding of the dog is a condition precedent to A's obligation to pay, although it is not a legal condition precedent, because technically no contract here has arisen until the dog is found (because B has not accepted A's offer until he finds the dog, and a contract requires offer, acceptance, and consideration), and the term "condition precedent" is used in contract law to designate a condition of a promise in a contract. For example, if B *promised* to find A's dog, and A promised to pay B when the dog was found, A's promise would have a condition attached to it, and offer and acceptance would already have occurred. This is a situation in which a condition precedent is attached to a bilateral contract.

Condition precedents can also be attached to unilateral contracts, however. This would require A to require a further condition to be met before he pays B for finding his dog. So, for example, A could say "If anyone finds my dog, and the sky falls down, I will give that person \$100." In this situation, even if the dog is found by B, he would not be entitled to the \$100 until the sky falls down. Therefore the sky falling down is a condition precedent to A's duty being actualized, even though they are already in a contract, since A has made an offer and B has accepted.

An offer of a unilateral contract may often be made to many people (or "to the world") by means of an advertisement. (The general rule is that advertisements are not offers.) In the situation where the unilateral offer is made to many people, acceptance will only occur on complete performance of the condition (in other words, by completing the performance that the offeror seeks, which is what the advertisement requests from the offerees—to actually find the dog). If the condition is something that only one party can perform, both the offeror and offeree are protected—the offeror is protected because he will only ever be contractually obliged to one of the many offerees, and the offeree is protected because if she does perform the condition, the offeror will be contractually obligated to pay her.

In unilateral contracts, the requirement that acceptance be communicated to the offeror is waived unless otherwise stated in the offer. The offeree accepts by performing the condition, and the offeree's performance is also treated as the price, or consideration, for the offeror's promise. The offeror is master of the offer; it is he who decides whether the contract will be unilateral or bilateral. In unilateral contracts, the offer is made to the public at large.

A bilateral contract is one in which there are duties on both sides, rights on both sides, and consideration on both sides. If an offeror makes an offer such as "If you promise to paint my house, I will give you \$ 100," this is a bilateral contract once the offeree accepts. Each side has promised to do something, and each side will get something in return for what they have done.

Uncertainty, Incompleteness and Severance

If the terms of the contract are uncertain or incomplete, the parties cannot have reached an agreement in the eyes of the law. An agreement to agree does not constitute a contract, and an inability to agree on key issues, which may include such things as price or safety, may cause the entire contract to fail. However, a court will attempt to give effect to commercial contracts where possible, by construing a reasonable construction of the contract.

Courts may also look to external standards, which are either mentioned explicitly in the contract or implied by common practice in a certain field. In addition, the court may also imply a term; if price is excluded, the court may imply a reasonable price, with the exception of land, and second-hand goods, which are unique.

If there are uncertain or incomplete clauses in the contract, and all options in resolving its true meaning have failed, it may be possible to sever and void just those affected clauses if the contract includes a severability clause. The test of whether a clause is severable is an objective test—whether a reasonable person would see the contract standing even without the clauses.

Contractual Terms

A contractual term is "any provision forming part of a contract". Each term gives rise to a contractual obligation, breach of which can give rise to litigation. Not all terms are stated expressly and some terms carry less legal weight as they are peripheral to the objectives of the contract.

Boilerplate

As discussed in Tina L. Stark's *Negotiating and Drafting Contract Boilerplate*, when lawyers refer to a "boilerplate" provision, they are referring to any standardized, "one size fits all" contract provision. But lawyers also use the term in a more narrow context to refer to certain provisions that appear at the end of the contract. Typically, these provisions tell the parties how to govern their relationship and administer the contract. Although often thought to be of secondary importance, these provisions have significant business and legal consequences. Common provisions include the governing law provision, venue, assignment and delegation provisions, waiver of jury trial provisions, notice provisions, and force majeure[11] provisions.

Classification of Term

- Condition or Warranty. Conditions are terms which go to the very root of a contract. Breach of these terms repudiates the contract, allowing the other party to discharge the contract. A warranty is not so imperative so the contract will subsist after a warranty breach. Breach of either will give rise to damages.

It is an objective matter of fact whether a term goes to the root of a contract. By way of illustration, an actress' obligation to perform the opening night of a theatrical production is a condition, whereas a singer's obligation to perform during the first three days of rehearsal is a warranty.

Statute may also declare a term or nature of term to be a condition or warranty; for example the *Sale of Goods Act* 1979 s15A provides that terms as to title, description, quality and sample (as described in the Act) are conditions save in certain defined circumstances.

- Innominate Term. Lord Diplock, in *Hong Kong Fir Shipping Co Ltd v. Kawasaki Kisen Kaisha Ltd*, created the concept of an innominate term, breach of which may or not go to the root of the contract depending upon the nature of the breach. Breach of these terms, as with all terms, will give rise to damages. Whether or not it repudiates the contract depends upon whether legal benefit of the contract has been removed from the innocent party. Megaw LJ, in 1970, preferred the legal certainty of using the classic categories of condition or warranty. This was interpreted by the House of Lords as merely restricting its application in *Reardon Smith Line Ltd. v Hansen-Tangen*.

Status as a Term

Status as a term is important as a party can only take legal action for the non fulfillment of a term as opposed to representations or mere puffery. Legally speaking, only statements that amount to a term create contractual obligations. There are various factor that a court may take into account in determining the nature of a statement. In particular, the importance apparently placed on the statement by the parties at the time the contract is made is likely to be significant. In *Bannerman v. White* it was held a term of a contract for sale and purchase of hops that they had not been treated with sulphur, since the buyer made very explicit his unwillingness to accept hops so treated, saying that he had no use for them. The relative knowledge of the parties may also be a factor, as in *Bissett v. Wilkinson* in which a statement that farmland being sold would carry 2,000 sheep if worked by one team was held merely a representation (it was also only an opinion and therefore not actionable as misrepresentation). The reason this was not a term was that the seller had no basis for making the statement, as the buyer knew, and the buyer was prepared to rely on his own and his son's knowledge of farming.

Implied Terms

A term may either be express or implied. An express term is stated by the parties during negotiation or written in a contractual document. Implied terms are not stated but nevertheless form a provision of the contract.

Terms Implied in Fact

Terms may be implied due to the facts of the proceedings by which the contract was formed. In the Australian case of *BP Refinery Westernport v. Shire of Hastings* the UK Privy Council proposed a five stage test to determine situations where the facts of a case may imply terms (this only applies to formal contracts in Australia). However, the English Court of Appeal sounded a note of caution with regard to the BP case in *Philips Electronique Grand Public SA v. British Sky Broadcasting Ltd* in which the Master of the Rolls described the test as "almost misleading" in its simplicity. The classic tests have been the "business efficacy test" and the "officious bystander test". The first of these was proposed by Lord Justice Bowen in *The Moorcock*. This test requires that a term can only be implied if it is necessary to give business efficacy to the contract to avoid such a failure of consideration that the parties cannot as reasonable businessmen have intended. But only the most limited term should then be implied—the bare minimum to achieve this goal. The officious bystander test derives its name from the judgment of Lord Justice Mackinnon in *Shirlaw v. Southern Foundries* (1926) *Ltd*, but the test actually originates in the judgment of Lord Justice Scrutton in *Reigate v. Union Manufacturing Co* (*Ramsbottom*) *Ltd*. This test is that a term can only be implied in fact if it is such a term that had an "officious bystander" listening to the contract negotiations suggested that they should include this term the parties would "dismiss him with a common 'Oh of course!'". It is at least questionable whether this is truly a separate test or just a description of how one might go about arriving at a decision on the basis of the business efficacy test.

Some jurisdictions, notably Australia, Israel and India, imply a term of *good faith* into contracts. A final way in which terms may be implied due to fact is through a previous course of dealing or common trade practice. The *Uniform Commercial Code* of the United States also imposes an implied covenant of good faith and fair dealing in performance and enforcement of contracts covered by the Code, which cannot be derogated from.

Terms Implied in Law

These are terms that have been implied into standardized relationships. Instances of this are quite numerous, especially in employment contracts and shipping contracts.

Common Law

- *Liverpool City Council v. Irwin* established a term to be implied into all contracts between tenant and landlord in multi-storey blocks that the landlord is obliged to take reasonable care to keep the common areas in a reasonable state of repair.

These terms will be implied into all contracts of the same nature as a matter of law.

Statute Law

The rules by which many contracts are governed are provided in specialized statutes that deal with particular subjects. Most countries, for example, have statutes which deal directly with sale of goods, lease transactions, and trade practices. For example, most American states have adopted Article 2 of the *Uniform Commercial Code*, which regulates contracts for the sale of goods. The most important legislation implying terms under United Kingdom law are the *Sale of Goods Act* 1979, the *Consumer Protection* (*Distance Selling*) *Regulations* 2000 and the *Supply of Goods and Services Act*

1982 which imply terms into all contracts whereby goods are sold or services provided.

Coercive vs. Voluntary Contractive Exchanges

There are a few ways of determining whether a contract has been coerced or is voluntary:

- Moral consideration: Objective consideration of right or wrong outside of the objective cause, or the perceived cause. Example: X (event) occurs everyday at 5 pm. X is wrong. Anything that avoids X is good; allowing X, even if all parties agree, is bad.
- Phenomenological consideration—what models did the participants have which influenced the perception of what was to occur or what had occurred. Example: I observe X, Y (events) every day at 5 pm. I contract against X. Today I did / did not see Y occur.
- Statistical consideration—did the participants have a statistical prediction, likelihood of an event occurring which is covered by the contract. Example: X (event) happens every day at 5 pm, I enter a contract to avoid X. X does or does not occur.

Setting Aside the Contract

There can be four different ways in which contracts can be set aside. A contract may be deemed "void", "voidable", "unenforceable" or "ineffective". Voidness implies that a contract never came into existence. Voidability implies that one or both parties may declare a contract ineffective at their wish. Unenforceability implies that neither party may have recourse to a court for a remedy. Ineffectiveness implies that the contract terminates by order of a court where a public body has failed to satisfy public procurement law. To rescind is to set aside or unmake a contract.

Misrepresentation

Misrepresentation means a false statement of fact made by one party to another party and has the effect of inducing that party into the contract. For example, under certain circumstances, false statements or promises made by a seller of goods regarding the quality or nature of the product that the seller has may constitute misrepresentation. A finding of misrepresentation allows for a remedy of rescission and sometimes damages depending on the type of misrepresentation.

There are two types of misrepresentation in contract law, fraud in the factum and fraud in inducement. Fraud in the factum focuses on whether the party in question knew they were creating a contract. If the party did not know that they were entering into a contract, there is no meeting of the minds, and the contract is void. Fraud in inducement focuses on misrepresentation attempting to get the party to enter into the contract. Misrepresentation of a material fact (if the party knew the truth, that party would not have entered into the contract) makes a contract voidable.

According to *Gordon v Selico* it is possible to make a misrepresentation either by words or by conduct, although not everything said or done is capable of constituting a misrepresentation. Generally, statements of opinion or intention are not statements of fact in the context of misrepresentation.

Both an order for specific performance and an injunction are discretionary remedies, originating for the most part in equity. Neither is available as of right and in most jurisdictions and most circumstances a court will not normally order specific performance. A contract for the sale of real property is a notable exception. In most jurisdictions, the sale of real property is enforceable by specific performance. Even in this case the defenses to an action in equity (such as laches, the *bona fide* purchaser rule, or unclean hands) may act as a bar to specific performance.

Related to orders for specific performance, an injunction may be requested when the contract prohibits a certain action. Action for injunction would prohibit the person from performing the act specified in the contract.

Procedure

In the United States, in order to obtain damages for breach of contract or to obtain specific performance or other equitable relief, the aggrieved injured party may file a civil (non-criminal) lawsuit in state court (unless there is diversity of citizenship giving rise to federal jurisdiction). If the contract contains a valid arbitration clause, the aggrieved party must submit an arbitration claim in accordance with the procedures set forth in the clause.

Many contracts provide that all disputes arising thereunder will be resolved by arbitration, rather than litigated in courts. Customer claims against securities brokers and dealers are almost always resolved by arbitration because securities dealers are required, under the terms of their membership in self-regulatory organizations such as the Financial Industry Regulatory Authority (formerly the NASD) or NYSE to arbitrate disputes with their customers. The firms then began including arbitration agreements in their customer agreements, requiring their customers to arbitrate disputes. On the other hand, certain claims have been held to be non-arbitrable if they implicate a public interest that goes beyond the narrow interests of the parties to the agreement (i. e. , claims that a party violated a contract by engaging in illegal anti-competitive conduct or civil rights violations). Arbitration judgments may generally be enforced in the same manner as ordinary court judgments. However, arbitral decisions are generally immune from appeal in the United States unless there is a showing that the arbitrator's decision was irrational or tainted by fraud. Virtually all states have adopted the *Uniform Arbitration Act* to facilitate the enforcement of arbitrated judgments. Notably, New York State, where a sizable portion of major commercial agreements are executed and performed, has not adopted the *Uniform Arbitration Act*.

In England and Wales, a contract may be enforced by use of a claim, or in urgent cases by applying for an interim injunction to prevent a breach. Likewise, in the United States, an aggrieved party may apply for injunctive relief to prevent a threatened breach of contract, where such breach would result in irreparable harm that could not be adequately remedied by money damages.

Other Contract

Online contracts, which are easily made, are usually valid on a smaller scale for a period of one to three months, while on a larger scale can last about five years. As with all things legal, especially in regards to the ever-evolving Internet, general rules like length of validity have many exceptions. All cases are evaluated on their own merits, and those merits are defined by the facts presented in each instance. It is up to the owner of the site to do what it can to guarantee enforceability of its contracts. Though 90% of people sign online contracts before reading the content, E-signature laws have made the electronic contract and signature as legally valid as a paper contract. It has been estimated that roughly one hundred and ten electronic contracts are signed every second.

Contract Theory

Contract theory is the body of legal theory that addresses normative and conceptual questions in contract law. One of the most important questions asked in contract theory is why contracts are enforced. One prominent answer to this question focuses on the economic benefits of enforcing bargains. Another approach, associated with Charles Fried, maintains that the purpose of contract law is to enforce promises. This theory is developed in Fried's book, *Contract as Promise*. Other approaches to contract theory are found in the writings of legal realists and critical legal studies theorists.

More generally, writers have propounded Marxist and feminist interpretations of contract. Attempts at overarching understandings of the purpose and nature of contract as a phenomenon have been made, notably "relational contract theory" originally developed by U. S. contracts scholars Ian Roderick Macneil and Stewart Macaulay, building at least in part on the contract theory work of U.S. scholar Lon L. Fuller, while U. S. scholars have been at the forefront of developing economic theories of contract focusing on questions of transaction cost and so-called "efficient breach" theory.

Another dimension of the theoretical debate in contract is its place within, and relationship to a wider law of obligations. Obligations have traditionally been divided into contracts, which are voluntarily undertaken and owed to a specific person or persons, and obligations in tort which are based on the wrongful infliction of harm to certain protected interests, primarily imposed by the law, and typically owed to a wider class of persons.

Recently it has been accepted that there is a third category, restitutionary obligations, based on the unjust enrichment of the defendant at the plaintiff's expense. Contractual liability, reflecting the constitutive function of contract, is generally for failing to make things better (by not rendering the expected performance), liability in tort is generally for action (as opposed to omission) making things worse, and liability in restitution is for unjustly taking or retaining the benefit of the plaintiff's money or work.

The common law describes the circumstances under which the law will recognize the existence of rights, privilege or power arising out of a promise.

Notes

1. Contract Law 合同法

本单元主要介绍合同的概念和法律性质、要约和承诺、对价、合同形式、合同种类、合同效力、虚假陈述等内容。

2. specific performance of the contract　实际履行

实际履行与禁令(injunction)是衡平法的重要违约救济制度,衡平法是为了补充和匡正当时的普通法而产生的。普通法的救济方式主要是金钱赔偿和返还财产,衡平法发展了实际履行和禁令。

3. injunction　禁令

4. *French Civil Code*　《法国民法典》

1804 年颁布的《法国民法典》又称《拿破仑法典》,是第一部资本主义国家和以资本主义经济制度为基础的近代民法典。该法典与当时的自由竞争经济条件相适应,体现了“个人最大限度的自由、法律最小限度的干预”的立法精神。其基本原则是:全体公民民事权利平等的原则、绝对所有权制度、契约自由及过失责任原则等,这些都是代表着资产阶级的自然法领域中的“天赋人权”理论在此民法典中的体现。而私权神圣的核心就是所有权绝对。由于该法典的系统性、完整性和规范性,因而对后来其他资本主义的立法产生了巨大影响,其内在的价值和思想即使在今天仍具有重要意义。

5. consideration　对价

对价又称为约因,是英美合同法中的重要概念,也是合同法上的效力原则,其本意是为换取另一个人做某事的允诺,某人付出的不一定是金钱的代价。换言之,对价是指当事人一方在获得某种利益时,必须给付对方相应的代价。对价的必要条件:对价必须合法、对价须是待履行或已履行的对价、过去的对价不能构成有效的对价、已经存在的义务和法律义务不能作为对价、对价须具有真实价值(但无须完全等价)、对价必须来自受允诺人包括其代理人、放弃有效的诉权构成对价、部分支付不能作为偿还全部债务的有效对价(但这一规则受到禁反言规则的制约)。

6. the mirror image rule　镜像规则

镜像规则是普通法上的传统制度,1887 年的 Langellier v.Shaefer 一案中曾对这一规则作出经典的归纳:“一方对另一方所发出的交易要约施加责任于前者,除非后者根据要约的条款对其予以承诺。任何对这些条款的修改和背离都将使要约无效,除非要约方同意这种修改和背离”。镜像规则要求承诺严格地与要约相符,否则将被视为反要约。《美国统一商法典》(UCC)则在相当程度上实现了对“镜像规则”的变革,集中体现在 UCC 第 2-207 条的规定上。该条第 1 款规定:明确且及时表示的承诺或者在合理时间内发出的确认书产生承诺之效力,即使它规定了与要约条款或双方约定之条款不同的附加条款,但承诺人明确表示其承诺以要约人同意该附加条款或不同条款为条件的除外。这一款的规定废弃了“镜像规则”中承诺必须与要约相一致的要求,只要是明确及时的非限定性承诺即可生效,使得格式之战下合同的成立较为轻易。UCC 考虑到,商人很少关心和阅读合同背面的一般条件,视之为陈词滥调,假如买方发出订单,卖方发回销售确认,只要双方文件中的正面条件(品种、数量、价格)相符,即使背面条款不符,合同仍可成立。UCC 的此种考虑在格式之战条件下是有其现实意义的,避免了大量正面条件已达成一致的合同因背面条款相歧而归于不成立,或将它们成立与否归因于此后捉摸不定的当事人行为,缓消了“镜像规则”所表现出来的僵硬和机械,有利于商业交易的进行。

7. *Uniform Commercial Code* 《统一商法典》

《统一商法典》是在美国统一州法全国委员会和美国法学会联合组织制定的一部示范法,1952 年正式公布。它分为 11 章(Article),以总则(General Provisions)和各分则的形式,对现实中的商事规则和商事惯例进行了归纳和制度层面的架构。基本消除了各州商法对州际交易因规定不同而造成的障碍,实现了美国商法在州际交易范围内,关于销售、票据、担保、信贷各领域规定的统一(除路易斯安那州之外的其他各州都采纳了这部法典),并为各类商事交易活动提供了优良的模式,被美国国内乃至国际商事社会广泛采用和吸收,实现了商法的国际性。

8. offer and acceptance 要约和承诺

要约是当事人一方向对方发出的希望与对方订立合同的意思表示。发出要约的一方称要约人(offeror),接收要约的一方称受要约人(offeree)。承诺是受要约人同意要约的意思表示,即受约人同意接受要约的全部条件而与要约人成立合同。承诺应当以通知的方式作出,但根据交易习惯或者要约表明可以通过行为作出承诺的除外。承诺的法律效力在于,承诺一经作出并送达要约人,合同即告成立,要约人不得加以拒绝。

9. misrepresentation 虚假陈述

虚假陈述就是主体作出的与事实不符的言词或行为。虚假陈述的情形非常复杂,它可能会诱使他人订立某项合同,也可能对他人的合法权益造成侵害,还有可能是作为违约行为的表现方式。英美法中的虚假陈述通常是指引诱他人订立合同的虚假言词或行为。

10. the doctrine of privity of contract 直接合同关系原则、合同关系不涉及第三人原则

11. force majeure 不可抗力

不可抗力条款是规定在合同订立后发生当事人在订合同时不能预见、不能避免、不可控制的意外事故,以致不能履行合同或不能如期履行合同时,遭受不可抗力的一方可以免除履行合同的责任的条款。不可抗力的法律后果是解除合同、延迟履行。不可抗力主要包括以下几种情形:自然灾害(如台风、洪水、地震等)、政府行为(如征收、征用等)、社会事件(如罢工、骚乱等)。

Study Questions

1. What is a contract?
2. How is a contract concluded?
3. How do you understand "consideration"?
4. What do you think of the remedies for breach of contract in equity?

Case Study

Gordon v Selico (1986) is an English contract law on the subject of misrepresentation by action.

Facts

Mr Gordon and Mrs Teixeira, contracted in November 1978 to purchase a 99 year lease of a flat owned by the defendant, Selico Ltd. The flat was in poor condition, as was the block that contained it, with some evidence of dry rot. Prior to the first inspection by the plaintiffs in about November 1978, the second defendants had instructed some painters to conceal patches of dry rot from view, by painting them. The plaintiffs obtained a detailed survey of the flat in February 1979, which concluded that no dry rot had been found (although only one floorboard had been lifted, and it could not be guaranteed that it did not exist elsewhere in the flat). The plaintiffs moved into their flat on January 1, 1980, and subsequently discovered extensive dry rot in the front bedroom, bathroom, and lavatory.

Judgment

Ordinarily, a misrepresentation is made by a statement of supposed fact, or otherwise a statement of intent. It was held by the Court of Appeal that the painting of dry rot to conceal it amounted to a misrepresentation. The court distinguished the set of facts from other cases, where it was held that reliance on an independent surveyor's findings defeated a claim of misrepresentation:

"Furthermore, he observed, the plaintiffs and their surveyor had ample opportunity to inspect the flat, an opportunity of which they availed themselves. In these circumstances, decisions such as *Horsfall v Thomas* and *Smith v Hughes*, precluded the plaintiffs from complaining of any misrepresentation."

Both these two cases, however, are distinguishable from the present on their facts. In the former, not only was the defect in the gun patent and discoverable on inspection, but the purchaser took no steps to inspect it, so that he did in fact not rely on any misrepresentation as to its condition which might have been made. In the latter case, the vendor did nothing to disguise the character of the oats sold. In the present case, on the learned judge's relevant findings of fact, with which we see no reason to disagree, not only was a fraudulent misrepresentation made, which was intended to mislead prospective purchasers of a lease of the property; the misrepresentation did mislead the purchasers and they acted on it to their detriment. In these circumstances, it is in our judgment no answer in law to the claim in deceit for the defendants to say that the plaintiffs or their surveyor could have discovered the dry rot on a closer inspection of Flat C or were content to purchase without any warranty as to the condition of the property; they and their surveyor were in fact misled by the cover-up operation, as they were intended to be. The general principle caveat emptor has no application where a purchaser has been induced to enter the contract of purchase by fraud. Nor can clause 4(2)(a) of the Law Society's Conditions of Sale avail a vendor in these circumstances. These subsidiary submissions made by way of defence to the claim based on deceit are not in our judgment well founded.

UNIT 9 The Law of Agency[1]

Key Concepts

agency of necessity	agency by estoppels	apparent agency
agency by ratification	breach of implied warranty of authority	

Learning Objectives

1. Understand how an agency relationship is created.
2. Be familiar with different varieties of agency.
3. Understand the duties of the agent and the principal and their liabilities to the third party.

Introduction

The agency relationship is one of the most common and important legal relationships. It is widely used in both domestic and international business environment. In international business trade, many business activities are conducted by means of agents, such as the foreign trade agent, forwarding agent, insurance agent, international settlement agent, and so on. A transaction can hardly be completed without the involvement of these agents.

Agency relationships are common in many professional areas such as:

- employment procurement
- real estate transactions (real estate brokerage, mortgage brokerage). In real estate brokerage, the buyers or sellers are the Principals themselves and the broker or his/her salesperson who represents each Principal is his/her Agent.
- financial advice (insurance agency, stock brokerage, accountancy)
- contract negotiation and promotion (business management) such as for publishing, fashion

model, music, movies, theatre, show business, and sport.

An Agent in *Commercial Law* (also referred to as a manager) is a person who is authorized to act on behalf of another (called the Principal or client) to create a legal relationship with a Third Party.

The law of agency is an area of commercial law dealing with a contractual or quasi-contractual, or non-contractual set of relationships when an agent is authorized to act on behalf of another (called the Principal) to create a legal relationship with a Third Party. Succinctly, it may be referred to as the relationship between a principal and an agent whereby the principal, expressly or impliedly, authorizes the agent to work under his control and on his behalf. The agent is, thus, required to negotiate on behalf of the principal or bring him and third parties into contractual relationship. This branch of law separates and regulates the relationships between:

- Agents and Principals;
- Agents and the Third Parties with whom they deal on their Principals' behalf; and
- Principals and the Third Parties when the Agents purport to deal on their behalf.

Authority[2]

An agent who acts within the scope of authority conferred by her principal binds the principal in the obligations she creates against third parties. There are essentially two kinds of authority recognized in the law: actual authority (whether express or implied) and apparent authority.

Actual Authority

Actual authority can be of two kinds. Either the principal may have expressly conferred authority on the agent, or authority may be implied. Authority arises by consensual agreement, and whether it exists is a question of fact. An agent, as a general rule, is only entitled to indemnity from the principal if she has acted within the scope of her actual authority, and may be in breach of contract, and liable to a third party for breach of the implied warranty of authority.

Express Actual Authority

Express actual authority means an agent has actually been expressly told she may act on behalf of a principal.

Implied Actual Authority

Implied actual authority, also called "usual authority", is authority an agent has by virtue of being reasonably necessary to carry out his express authority. As such, it can be inferred by virtue of a position held by an agent. For example, partners have authority to bind the other partners in the firm, their liability being joint and several, and in a corporation, all executives and senior employees with decision-making authority by virtue of their position have authority to bind the corporation.

Apparent Authority

Apparent authority (also called "ostensible authority") exists where the principal's words or conduct would lead a reasonable person in the third party's position to believe that the agent was authorized to act, even if the principal and the purported agent had never discussed such a relationship. For example, where one person appoints a person to a position which carries with it agency-like powers, those who know of the appointment are entitled to assume that there is apparent authority to do the things ordinarily entrusted to one occupying such a position. If a principal creates the impression that an agent is authorized but there is no actual authority, third parties are protected so long as they have acted reasonably. This is sometimes termed "agency by estoppel[3]" or the "doctrine of holding out", where the principal will be estopped from denying the grant of authority if third parties have changed their positions to their detriment in reliance on the representations made.

Rama Corporation Ltd v Proved Tin and General Investments Ltd [1952] 2 QB 147, Slade J, "Ostensible or apparent authority... is merely a form of estoppel, indeed, it has been termed agency by estoppel and you cannot call in aid an estoppel unless you have three ingredients: (i) a representation, (ii) reliance on the representation, and (iii) an alteration of your position resulting from such reliance."

In the case of *Watteau v Fenwick*, Lord Coleridge CJ on the Queen's Bench concurred with an opinion by Wills J that a third party could hold personally liable a principal who he did know about when he sold cigars to an agent that was acting outside of its authority. Wills J held that "the principal is liable for all the acts of the agent which are within the authority usually confided to an agent of that character, notwithstanding limitations, as between the principal and the agent, put upon that authority." This decision is heavily criticised and doubted, though not entirely overruled in the UK. It is sometimes referred to as "usual authority" (though not in the sense used by Lord Denning MR in *Hely-Hutchinson*, where it is synonymous with "implied actual authority"). It has been explained as a form of apparent authority, or "inherent agency power".

Authority by virtue of a position held to deter: fraud and other harms that may befall individuals dealing with agents, there is a concept of inherent agency power, which is power derived solely by virtue of the agency relation. For example, partners have apparent authority to bind the other partners in the firm, their liability being joint and several, and in a corporation, all executives and senior employees with decision-making authority by virtue of their declared position have apparent authority to bind the corporation.

Even if the agent does act without authority, the principal may ratify an unauthorized agreement entered into by an agent. It is called agency by ratification[4]. Ratification means that after the unauthorized act, the principal may agree to that act making it binding on the third party. This may be express or implied from the principal's behavior, e. g. if the agent has purported to act in a number of situations and the principal has knowingly acquiesced, the failure to notify all concerned of the agent's lack of authority is an implied ratification to those transactions and an implied grant of authority for future transactions of a similar nature.

Agency by Estoppel

It is an agency that is not created as an actual agency by a principal and an agent but that is imposed by law when a principal acts in such a way as to lead a third party to reasonably believe that another is the principal's agent and the third party is injured by relying on and acting in accordance with that belief. A principal has a duty to correct a third party's mistaken belief in an agent's authority to act on the principal's behalf. If the principal could have corrected the misunderstanding but failed to do so, he or she is estopped from denying the existence of the agency and is bound by the agent's acts in dealing with the third party.

Apparent Agency[5]

It is a legal concept in civil law system. A legal principle that an agent is deemed to have whatever power or authority a person would reasonably infer, either from the principal's representations concerning an agent's authority or from the agent's holding himself out as having proper authority. The principal may be obligated as if it had expressly granted the authority to the agent. Situation wherein the agent's conduct causes a client or prospective insured reasonably to believe that the agent has the authority to sell an insurance policy and contract on behalf of the insurance company. For example, if an agent continues to use insurance company documents, such as its application forms, rate manuals, stationery, and emblems on the door, the client has every reason to believe that the agent does in fact continue to represent the insurance company.

Agency of Necessity[6]

The origins of the doctrine of necessitous intervention by someone who is in a legal relationship with the defendant lie in the principle of agency of necessity, where an agent went beyond his or her authority by intervening on behalf of the principal in an emergency. Because of the circumstances of necessity, particularly the impracticability of the agent communicating with the principal, the courts were prepared to treat the agent as though he or she had the necessary authority to do what was reasonably necessary to save the principal's property. If an agency of necessity was established, the agent would be reimbursed for the expense incurred in rescuing the principal's property.

The doctrine of agency of necessity was initially relevant only in respect of the carriage of goods by sea, where the master took action to save the ship or cargo in an emergency. It was then extended to those cases which concerned the carriage of goods by land. This is illustrated by *The Great Northern Railway Co. v. Swaffield* where the plaintiff railway company had transported a horse to a station on behalf of the defendant. When the horse arrived there was nobody to collect it, so the plaintiff sent it to a stable. A number of months later the plaintiff paid the stabling charges and then sought to recover what it had paid from the defendant. The plaintiff's claim succeeded even though this involved the extension of the doctrine of agency of necessity to include carriers of goods by land.

There was an agency of necessity because the plaintiff was found to have had no choice but to arrange for the proper care of the horse.

Before any agency can be created by necessity, three conditions must be satisfied:

(1) It must be impossible to get the principal's instructions.

(2) There must be an actual and definite commercial necessity for the creation of the agency. Generally, there is no agency of necessity unless there is a real emergency, such as may arise out of the possession of perishable goods or of livestock requiring to be fed.

(3) The agent of necessity must act bona fide[7] in the interests of all parties concerned.

Breach of Implied Warranty of Authority[8]

A person who professes to act as agent, but has no authority from the alleged principal or has exceeded his authority, is liable in an action for breach of warranty of authority at the suit of the party with whom he professed to make the contract. The action is based, not on the original contract, but on the implied representation by the agent that he had authority to make the original contract. Points to note:

(1) The action can only be brought by the third party, not by the principal.

(2) The agent is liable whether he has acted fraudulently or innocently, and even if his authority has been terminated, without his knowledge, by death or mental disorder of the principal.

(3) The agent is not liable if his lack of authority was known to the third party, or if it was known that he did not warrant his authority or if the contract excludes his liability.

(4) If the principal gives ambiguous instructions and the agent acts on them bona fide and in a reasonable way, he will not be liable in an action for breach of warranty of authority even if he has interpreted them wrongly.

(5) The agent warrants his authority not only when he purports to contract on behalf of another but also when, purporting to act as an agent, he induces a third party to enter into any transaction with him on the faith of such agency.

(6) The measure of damages for breach of warranty of authority is the actual loss sustained.

Liabilities

Liability of Agent to Third Party

If the agent has actual or apparent authority, the agent will not be liable for acts performed within the scope of such authority, so long as the relationship of the agency and the identity of the principal have been disclosed. When the agency is undisclosed or partially disclosed, however, both the agent and the principal are liable. Where the principal is not bound because the agent has no actual or apparent authority, the purported agent is liable to the third party for breach of the implied warranty of authority.

Liability of Agent to Principal

If the agent has acted without actual authority, but the principal is nevertheless bound because the agent had apparent authority, the agent is liable to indemnify the principal for any resulting loss or damage.

Liability of Principal to Agent

If the agent has acted within the scope of the actual authority given, the principal must indemnify the agent for payments made during the course of the relationship whether the expenditure was expressly authorized or merely necessary in promoting the principal's business.

Duties

Duties of Agent to Principal

(1) Fiduciary Duty of Loyalty

The agent owes a fiduciary duty of good faith and utmost loyalty to the principal. The agent must conduct the principal's business with integrity. Therefore, the agent may not have any adverse personal financial interest in the principal's transactions during the agency. Some aspects of this duty persist even after the agency is terminated. Although the duty of loyalty may seem vague, it becomes more precise as it is applied to more specific situations. The fiduciary duty is a most basic ethical matter applicable to nearly all persons in business and government.

The ancient proviso that no person can serve two masters is at the heart of the prohibition against an agent simultaneously serving two principals in the same transaction. This would be a dual or double agency, and the agent would be unable to serve either principal fully. If the agent negotiates gains for one principal, the gains necessarily come as losses to the other. Also, dual agents are often given confidential information by either or both principals concerning key terms and the principal's willingness to sell or buy at the maximum or minimum price stated.

Conflicts of interest are not always so obvious. Sometimes a full-time agent for one party may be paid a secret bribe, gratuity, gift, or kickback by the other party. The law presumes these payments exert some influence on the agents' judgment and thereby harm the principal.

Self-dealing is another type of unethical conflict of interest in which the agent's own personal financial interests directly conflict with the principal's financial interests. Agents may not have any undisclosed, unapproved personal financial interest in a transaction in which the principal has a financial interest. The self-dealing prohibition also requires agents to refrain from competing directly with the principal while the agency is in effect. Most firms' employees are prohibited from working for competing firms or personally competing against the principal during their employment.

(2) Duty of Care

Agents must use reasonable skill and care in conducting the principals' business. They must use all the skill they possess plus any skills the agent claims and any additional skills specified in the employment contract. It is probably unethical for an agent to claim skills he or she does not really possess. Such false bravado is often the basis for liability and ethical abuse.

Professional agents such as accountants, brokers, or attorneys must exercise skill equal to other similar professionals in that region. However, the law does not imply that the agent guarantees success unless the agent specifically makes that promise. However, when an agent's negligent performance causes damage to the principal, liability questions arise. An agent may be released from liability for negligence in the employment contract.

(3) Obedience

Agents must generally obey any reasonable directions the principal provides that will impact the principal's business. Even agents given broad discretion must obey the principal's directives. Of course, an agent need not obey orders that are illegal, immoral, or unreasonable. The agent may in good faith interpret vague commands or be disobedient during an emergency if obedience would damage the principal. However, in an emergency during which the principal is unavailable for consultation, the agent could disobey the principal's directive and do as the emergency requires in good faith.

(4) Accounting

The agent's fiduciary duty requires that all property and funds belonging to the principal be accounted for adequately. This is the duty to account or provide an accounting. It requires the agent to keep accurate records and keep the agent's individual property separate from the principal's property. Upon demand, the agent must produce accurate records of receipts and disbursements to the principal. Any commingling of funds belonging to the principal and agent makes it difficult to determine the true ownership. Commingling is a fundamental ethical abuse discovered among professional agents such as accountants, real estate brokers, investment professionals, and attorneys.

(5) Communication

Agents must communicate to the principal all relevant information and notices they receive in the course of performing the principal's business. Agents are often the principal's most visible communicator because they regularly receive or provide information to third parties about the principal's business. It is probably unethical for an agent to withhold information from the principal either in sympathy for the third party or to conceal the agent's poor performance.

An agent authorized to transact the principal's business generally has authority to receive information from third parties. When third parties provide information to the agent, the law presumes the agent will comply with the duty to communicate. Knowledge or notice received by the agent is therefore imputed to the principal. After the third party gives notice to the agent, the third party is relieved from repeating the communication to the principal or to any other agent who might later replace the original agent. The principal and agent are treated as one party after information is communicated to the agent.

Duties of Principal to Agent

(1) Duty to Compensate

Normally, a duty to pay the agent is implied unless special circumstances or the relationship of the parties suggest that a gratuitous agency was intended. The agency agreement should specify the amount of compensation for the agent and when it has been earned. Many disputes arise because no clear agreement has been reached. In the absence of agreement, the agent is entitled to the customary or reasonable value of the services performed. Custom is sometimes quite clear. For example, in most communities, real estate brokers all charge the same commission rate. If there is no clear custom and the amount is in dispute, expert witnesses may testify as to what a reasonable amount would be.

(2) Duty to Reimburse and Indemnify

Sometimes agents make advances from their own funds in conducting the principal's business. If the agent is acting within the scope of her authority, the principal has a duty to reimburse the agent for expenses incurred for the principal. Also, if the agent suffers losses while acting for the principal within the scope of the agent's authority, the principal has a duty to indemnify the agent. For example, suppose David is a salesperson for a company. He is in Chicago when he is asked to go to a foreign trade show. He uses his own funds to pay workers to set up the company's booth at the show. The company has a duty to reimburse him for his expenses. However, if some fault of the agent causes a loss, the principal will not be required to indemnify the agent for the amount of the loss. And, of course, the principal is not liable for unauthorized expenses incurred by the agent.

Termination

An agent's authority can be terminated at any time. If the trust between the agent and principal has broken down, it is not reasonable to allow the principal to remain at risk in any transactions that the agent might conclude during a period of notice.

An agency may come to an end in a variety of ways:

(1) By the principal revoking the agency—However, principal cannot revoke an agency coupled with interest to the prejudice of such interest. Such agency is coupled with interest. An agency is coupled with interest when the agent himself has an interest in the subject-matter of the agency, e. g. , where the goods are consigned by an upcountry constituent to a commission agent for sale, with poor to recoup himself from the sale

proceeds, the advances made by him to the principal against the security of the goods; in such a case, the principal cannot revoke the agent's authority till the goods are actually sold, nor is the agency terminated by death or insanity.

(2) By the agent renouncing the business of agency;

(3) By the business of agency being completed;

(4) By the principal being adjudicated insolvent.

The principal also cannot revoke the agent's authority after it has been partly exercised, so as to bind the principal, though he can always do so, before such authority has been so exercised.

Further, if the agency is for a fixed period, the principal cannot terminate the agency before the time expired, except for sufficient cause. If he does, he is liable to compensate the agent for the loss caused to him thereby. The same rules apply where the agent, renounces an agency for a fixed period. Notice in this connection that want of skill, continuous disobedience of lawful orders, and rude or insulting behavior has been held to be sufficient cause for dismissal of an agent. Further, reasonable notice has to be given by one party to the other; otherwise, damage resulting from want of such notice, will have to be paid. The revocation or renunciation of an agency may be made expressly or impliedly by conduct. The termination does not take effect as regards the agent, till it becomes known to him and as regards third party, till the termination is known to them.

When an agent's authority is terminated, it operates as a termination of subagent also.

This has become a more difficult area as states are not consistent on the nature of a partnership. Some states opt for the partnership as no more than an aggregate of the natural persons who have joined the firm. Others treat the partnership as a business entity and, like a corporation, vest the partnership with a separate legal personality. Hence, for example, in English law, a partner is the agent of the other partners whereas, in Scots law where there is a separate personality, a partner is the agent of the partnership. This form of agency is inherent in the status of a partner and does not arise out of a contract of agency with a principal. In the English *Partnership Act* 1890 provides that a partner who acts within the scope of his actual authority (express or implied) will bind the partnership when he does anything in the ordinary course of carrying on partnership business. Even if that implied authority has been revoked or limited, the partner will have apparent authority unless the Third Party knows that the authority has been compromised. Hence, if the partnership wishes to limit any partner's authority, it must give express notice of the limitation to the world. However, there would be little substantive difference if English law was amended (see *Law Commission Report* 283): partners will bind the partnership rather than their fellow partners individually. For these purposes, the knowledge of the partner acting will be imputed to the other partners or the firm if a separate personality. The other partners or the firm are the principal and third parties are entitled to assume that the principal has been informed of all relevant information. This causes problems when one partner acts fraudulently or negligently and causes loss to clients of the firm. In most states, a distinction is drawn between knowledge of the firm's general business activities and the confidential affairs as they affect one client. Thus, there is no imputation if the partner is acting against the interests of the firm as a fraud. There is more likely to be liability in tort if the partnership benefited by receiving fee income for the work negligently performed, even if only as an aspect of the standard provisions of vicarious liability. Whether the injured party wishes to sue the partnership or the individual partners is usually a matter for the Plaintiff since, in most jurisdictions, their liability is joint and several[9].

Notes

1. The Law of Agency 代理法

   代理法主要介绍代理的概念、代理权产生的方式、无权代理、代理的内部关系(代理人义务、本人义务)、代理的外部关系(本人、代理人与第三人之间的关系)、代理关系终止等内容。

2. authority 授权

   为英美法中的概念,可分为明示授权(express authority)和默示授权(implied authority)。前者是指本人以明示的方式指定他人为代理人;后者是指通过对本人行为的推定而确定其存在的授权。明示授权和默示授权称为实际授权(actual authority),与实际授权相对应的则是表面授权(apparent authority),表面授权也是产生代理权的原因之一。

3. agency by estoppel 不容否认的代理

   为英美法中的概念,不容否认的代理是指本人以其言词或行为使善意第三人相信某人是其代理人,且第三人基于这种相信而改变了自己的经济地位,本人就不得否认其代理的存在,并受第三人与代理人所订合同或交易的约束。

4. agency by ratification 经追认的代理

   是指无权代理人以本人的名义实施的民商事行为,经本人追认的代理行为。经追认的代理是一种无权代理,经本人追认后该代理行为有效。

5. apparent agency 表见代理

   是指行为人虽无代理权,但善意第三人有理由相信该行为人有代理权的,该代理行为有效。表见代理实质上是无权代理,若无权代理行为均由被代理人(本人)追认决定其效力的话,会给善意第三人造成损害,因此,在表见的情形之下,规定由被代理人承担表见代理行为的法律后果,更有利于维护善意第三人的利益,保护交易安全。

6. agency of necessity 客观必需的代理

   客观必需的代理主要是在一个人受托照管另一个人的财产,为了保护这种财产而必须采取某种行动时而产生的,尽管没有得到采取这种行动的授权,但客观情况的必须视为具有此种授权。

7. bona fide 善意的、真诚的

   如:善意第三人(bona fide third party)、善意持票人(bona fide holder)、善意受让人(bona fide transferee)等。

8. breach of implied warranty of authority 违反有代理授权的默示担保

   依据英美法的解释,当代理人与第三人订立合同时,代理人对第三人有一项默示的担保,即保证他是有代理权的。值得注意的是,违反有代理授权的默示担保,该诉讼只能由第三人

提起。

9. joint and several liability　连带责任

负有连带责任的每个债务人，都负有清偿全部债务的义务，履行义务的人，有权要求其他负连带义务的人偿付他应当承担的份额。换言之，连带责任人承担了连带债务后，依法可以向其他负有连带责任的人追偿。

Study Questions

1. How can an agency relationship be created under common law system?
2. How to interpret "the agency without authority" under common law system and civil law system respectively?
3. What are the duties of the agent to the principal?
4. How to understand the legal relations between the agent, the principal and the third party?

Case Study

Facts

Mr Freeman and Mr Lockyer sued Buckhurst Park Ltd and its director, Shiv Kumar Kapoor, for unpaid fees for their architecture work on developing the Buckhurst Park Estate in Sunninghill, Berkshire. The company's articles said that all four directors of the company (another Mr Hoon, who was never there, and two nominees) were needed to constitute a quorum. Originally the company planned to simply buy and resell the land, but that fell through. Kapoor had acted alone (as if he were a managing director) in engaging the architects, without proper authority. The company argued it was not bound by the agreement.

Judge Herbert at Westminster County Court held the company was bound, and the company appealed.

Judgment

Diplock LJ held the judge was right and the company was bound to pay Freeman and Lockyer for their architecture work. He noted that if actual authority is conferred by the board without a formal resolution, this renders the board liable for a fine. If a person has no actual authority to act on a company's behalf, then a contract can still be enforced if an agent had authority to enter contracts of a different but similar kind, the person granting that authority itself had authority, the contracting party was induced by these representations to enter the agreement and the company had the capacity to act. All those conditions were fulfilled on the facts, because (1) the board knew about Kapoor's general activities and permitted him to engage in these kinds of activities; such conduct represented his authority to contract for these kinds of things; (2) the articles conferred full power to the board;

(3) Freeman and Lockyer were induced to contract by these "representations" and (4) the company had capacity.

An "actual" authority is a legal relationship between principal and agent created by a consensual agreement to which they alone are parties. Its scope is to be ascertained by applying ordinary principles of construction of contracts, including any proper implications from the express words used, the usages of the trade, or the course of business between the parties. To this agreement the contractor is a stranger; he may be totally ignorant of the existence of any authority on the part of the agent. Nevertheless, if the agent does enter into a contract pursuant to the "actual" authority, it does create contractual rights and liabilities between the principal and the contractor. It may be that this rule relating to "undisclosed principals", which is peculiar to English law, can be rationalized as avoiding circuity of action, for the principal could in equity compel the agent to lend his name in an action to enforce the contract against the contractor, and would at common law be liable to indemnify the agent in respect of the performance of the obligations assumed by the agent under the contract.

An "apparent" or "ostensible" authority, on the other hand, is a legal relationship between the principal and the contractor created by a representation, made by the principal to the contractor, intended to be and in fact acted upon by the contractor, that the agent has authority to enter on behalf of the principal into a contract of a kind within the scope of the "apparent" authority, so as to render the principal liable to perform any obligations imposed upon him by such contract. To the relationship so created the agent is a stranger. He need not be (although he generally is) aware of the existence of the representation but he must not purport to make the agreement as principal himself. The representation, when acted upon by the contractor by entering into a contract with the agent, operates as an estoppel, preventing the principal from asserting that he is not bound by the contract. It is irrelevant whether the agent had actual authority to enter into the contract.

In ordinary business dealings the contractor at the time of entering into the contract can in the nature of things hardly ever rely on the "actual" authority of the agent. His information as to the authority must be derived either from the principal or from the agent or from both, for they alone know what the agent's actual authority is. All that the contractor can know is what they tell him, which may or may not be true. In the ultimate analysis he relies either upon the representation of the principal, that is, apparent authority, or upon the representation of the agent, that is, warranty of authority.

The representation which creates "apparent" authority may take a variety of forms of which the commonest is representation by conduct, that is, by permitting the agent to act in some way in the conduct of the principal's business with other persons. By so doing the principal represents to anyone who becomes aware that the agent is so acting that the agent has authority to enter on behalf of the principal into contracts with other persons of the kind which an agent so acting in the conduct of his principal's business has usually "actual" authority to enter into.

In applying the law as I have endeavored to summarise it to the case where the principal is not a natural person, but a fictitious person, namely, a corporation, two further factors arising from the legal characteristics of a corporation have to be borne in mind. The first is that the capacity of a corporation is limited by its constitution, that is, in the case of a company incorporated under the *Companies Act*, by its memorandum and articles of association; the second is that a corporation cannot do any act, and that includes making a representation, except through its agent.

Under the doctrine of ultra vires the limitation of the capacity of a corporation by its constitution to do any acts is absolute. This affects the rules as to the "apparent" authority of an agent of a corporation in two ways. First, no representation can operate to estop the corporation from denying the authority of the agent to do on behalf of the corporation an act which the corporation is not permitted by its constitution to do itself. Secondly, since the conferring of actual authority upon an agent is itself an act of the corporation, the capacity to do which is regulated by its constitution, the corporation cannot be estopped from denying that it has conferred upon a particular agent authority to do acts which by its constitution, it is incapable of delegating to that particular agent.

To recognize that these are direct consequences of the doctrine of ultra vires is, I think, preferable to saying that a contractor who enters into a contract with a corporation has constructive notice of its constitution, for the expression "constructive notice" tends to disguise that constructive notice is not a positive, but a negative doctrine, like that of estoppel of which it forms a part. It operates to prevent the contractor from saying that he did not know that the constitution of the corporation rendered a particular act or a particular delegation of authority ultra vires the corporation. It does not entitle him to say that he relied upon some unusual provision in the constitution of the corporation if he did not in fact so rely.

The second characteristic of a corporation, namely, that unlike a natural person it can only make a representation through an agent, has the consequence that in order to create an estoppel between the corporation and the contractor, the representation as to the authority of the agent which creates his "apparent" authority must be made by some person or persons who have "actual" authority from the corporation to make the representation. Such "actual" authority may be conferred by the constitution of the corporation itself, as, for example, in the case of a company, upon the board of directors, or it may be conferred by those who under its constitution have the powers of management upon some other person to whom the constitution permits them to delegate authority to make representations of this kind. It follows that where the agent upon whose "apparent" authority the contractor relies has no "actual" authority from the corporation to enter into a particular kind of contract with the contractor on behalf of the corporation, the contractor cannot rely upon the agent's own representation as to his actual authority. He can rely only upon a representation by a person or persons who have actual authority to manage or conduct that part of the business of the corporation to which the contract relates.

The commonest form of representation by a principal creating an "apparent" authority of an agent is by conduct, namely, by permitting the agent to act in the management or conduct of the principal's business. Thus, if in the case of a company the board of directors who have "actual" authority under the memorandum and articles of association to manage the company's business permit the agent to act in the management or conduct of the company's business, they thereby represent to all persons dealing with such agent that he has authority to enter on behalf of the corporation into contracts of a kind which an agent authorized to do acts of the kind which he is in fact permitted to do usually enters into in the ordinary course of such business. The making of such a representation is itself an act of management of the company's business. Prima facie it falls within the "actual" authority of the board of directors, and unless the memorandum or articles of the company either make such a contract ultra vires the company or prohibit the delegation of such authority to the agent, the company is estopped from denying to anyone who has entered into a contract with the agent in reliance upon such "apparent" authority that the agent had authority to contract on behalf of the company.

If the foregoing analysis of the relevant law is correct, it can be summarized by stating four conditions which must be fulfilled to entitle a contractor to enforce against a company a contract entered into on behalf of the company by an agent who had no actual authority to do so. It must be shown:

(1) that a representation that the agent had authority to enter on behalf of the company into a contract of the kind sought to be enforced was made to the contractor;

(2) that such representation was made by a person or persons who had "actual" authority to manage the business of the company either generally or in respect of those matters to which the contract relates;

(3) that he (the contractor) was induced by such representation to enter into the contract, that is, that he in fact relied upon it; and

(4) that under its memorandum or articles of association the company was not deprived of the capacity either to enter into a contract of the kind sought to be enforced or to delegate authority to enter into a contract of that kind to the agent.

The confusion which, I venture to think, has sometimes crept into the cases is in my view due to a failure to distinguish between these four separate conditions, and in particular to keep steadfastly in mind (a) that the only "actual" authority which is relevant is that of the persons making the representation relied upon, and (b) that the memorandum and articles of association of the company are always relevant (whether they are in fact known to the contractor or not) to the questions (i) whether condition (2) is fulfilled, and (ii) whether condition (4) is fulfilled, and (but only if they are in fact known to the contractor) may be relevant (iii) as part of the representation on which the contractor relied...

In the present case the findings of fact by the county court judge are sufficient to satisfy the four conditions, and thus to establish that Kapoor had "apparent" authority to enter into contracts on behalf of the company for their services in connection with the sale of the company's property, including the obtaining of development permission with respect to its use. The judge found that the board knew that Kapoor had throughout been acting as managing director in employing agents and taking other steps to find a purchaser. They permitted him to do so, and by such conduct represented that he had authority to enter into contracts of a kind which a managing director or an executive director responsible for finding a purchaser would in the normal course be authorized to enter into on behalf of the company. Condition (1) was thus fulfilled. The articles of association conferred full powers of management on the board. Condition (2) was thus fulfilled. The plaintiffs, finding Kapoor acting in relation to the company's property as he was authorized by the board to act, were induced to believe that he was authorized by the company to enter into contracts on behalf of the company for their services in connection with the sale of the company's property, including the obtaining of development permission with respect to its use. Condition (3) was thus fulfilled. The articles of association, which contained powers for the board to delegate any of the functions of management to a managing director or to a single director, did not deprive the company of capacity to delegate authority to Kapoor, a director, to enter into contracts of that kind on behalf of the company. Condition (4) was thus fulfilled.

UNIT 10 Product Liability Law[1]

Key Concepts

product liability	defects	negligence	strict liability
breach of warranty	product recall		

Learning Objectives

1. Understand the rationale of strict liability.
2. Understand the essentials of the theory of negligence.
3. Be familiar with the main features of American product liability law.
4. Understand the basis of liabilities between the producer and the seller.

An Overview

Product liability law, also called "products liability", governs the liability of manufacturers, wholesalers, distributors, and vendors for damages caused by dangerous or defective products. The goal of product liability laws is to help protect consumers from dangerous products, while holding manufacturers, distributors, and retailers responsible for putting into the marketplace products that they knew or should have known were dangerous or defective. Depending upon the jurisdiction, the liability of the various parties involved as the product passes from the manufacturer to the consumer will vary.

Product liability frequently involves retail items, but can extend to pretty much anything that can be sold. It is possible, for example, for a product liability action to arise from a defect in real estate such as a leaky wall or poorly installed vapor barrier that causes mold to grow inside a wall, or from a product used in real estate, such as defective siding.

Product liability claims can be brought under a number of theories, depending upon local law.

Design Defects: Liability arises from a mistake or oversight in the design of a product, which makes it dangerous when used as intended, or when used for another reasonably foreseeable purpose.

Manufacturing Defects: Liability arises from a defect that results from the manufacturing process.

Marketing Defects: A marketing defect involves such issues as inadequate warning labels or instructions, which, for example, prevent a user from recognizing a defect in the product, or from being aware of how to safely use or apply the product. (failure to warn)

The elements of what a plaintiff must prove to prevail in a product liability action will also vary with the jurisdiction. It may be possible for a plaintiff to pursue more than one theory of liability.

Negligence[2]: In a negligence action, the plaintiff must typically demonstrate that the parties responsible for placing the product into commerce had a duty to provide the goods fit for their foreseeable uses, would have detected the defect with the exercise of reasonable care in the design, manufacture, or inspection process, failed to meet its obligations, and that the plaintiff was injured by the product as a result of the defect while engaged in a foreseeable use of the product.

Strict Liability[3]: Under a strict liability standard, once the plaintiff establishes that a product is defective, liability results from that fact alone no matter how much care was applied during design, manufacture, marketing, distribution and sale.

Breach of Warranty[4]: A warranty is essentially a contract of fitness between a manufacturer or vendor and its customer. Under a breach of express warranty theory, the plaintiff alleges the violation of the actual written warranty associated with a product. Under a breach of implied warranty theory, the plaintiff alleges that although there is no express warranty or the defect alleged is not covered by the express warranty, a defect in the goods renders them unfit for the purpose intended.

Product Liability Law in USA

After the World War Ⅱ, US economy began to develop very rapidly, many new techniques, new production procedures, product composition become more and more complex. Consequently, there occurred more and more product liability accidents. In the United States, the accidents and loss of property related to product liability began to strike the consumer considerably. For example, Consumer Product Safety Commission issued some statistics in 1986, due to safety problems of product, every year, about 36 million were injured and 30 thousand were dead. The US lawyers make their earnings in positive proportion to the compensation from the defective products. The lawyers and also the jury are inclined to show partiality to the consumer. American consumers have a strong sense of claiming damages.

Theories of Liability

In the United States, the claims most commonly associated with product liability are negligence, strict liability, breach of warranty, and various consumer protection claims. The majorities of product liability laws are determined at the state level and vary widely from state to state. Each type of product liability claim requires different elements to be proven to present a successful claim.

Types of Liability

Section 2 of the *Restatement (Third) of Torts: Products Liability* distinguishes between three major types of product liability claims:

- manufacturing defect;
- design defect;
- a failure to warn (also known as marketing defects).

However, in most states, these are not legal claims in and of themselves, but are pleaded in terms of the theories mentioned above. For example, a plaintiff might plead negligent failure to warn or strict liability for defective design. Manufacturing defects are those that occur in the manufacturing process and usually involve poor-quality materials or shoddy workmanship. Design defects occur where the product design is inherently dangerous or useless (and hence defective) no matter how carefully manufactured; this may be demonstrated either by showing that the product fails to satisfy ordinary consumer expectations as to what constitutes a safe product, or that the risks of the product outweigh its benefits. Failure-to-warn defects arise in products that carry inherent nonobvious dangers which could be mitigated through adequate warnings to the user, and these dangers are present regardless of how well the product is manufactured and designed for its intended purpose.

Breach of Warranty

Warranties are statements by a manufacturer or seller concerning a product during a commercial transaction. Warranty claims commonly require privity between the injured party and the manufacturer or seller; in plain English, this means they must be dealing with each other directly. Breach of warranty-based product liability claims usually focus on one of three types: (1) breach of an express warranty, (2) breach of an implied warranty of merchantability, and (3) breach of an implied warranty of fitness for a particular purpose. Additionally, claims involving real estate may also take the form of an implied warranty of habitability. Express warranty claims focus on express statements by the manufacturer or the seller concerning the product (e. g. , This chainsaw is useful to cut turkeys). The various implied warranties cover those expectations common to all products (e. g. , A tool is not unreasonably dangerous when used for its proper purpose), unless specifically disclaimed by the manufacturer or the seller.

Negligence

A basic negligence claim consists of proof of

(1) a duty owed;

(2) a breach of that duty;

(3) the breach was the cause in fact of the plaintiff's injury (actual cause);

(4) the breach proximately caused the plaintiff's injury;

(5) and the plaintiff suffered actual quantifiable injury (damages).

As demonstrated in cases such as *Winterbottom v. Wright*, the scope of the duty of care was limited to those with whom one was in privity. Later cases like *MacPherson v. Buick Motor Co.* broadened the duty of care to all who could be foreseeably injured by one's conduct. In common law negligence now is a tort, if the plaintiff sues the defendant in a law-court, it's not necessary to show Privity of Contract[5] between them, because this lawsuit is not made in the light of the contract. Therefore, the plaintiff may include not only the buyer, but also his relatives, friends, visitors or onlookers.

Strict Liability

Rather than focus on the behavior of the manufacturer (as in negligence), strict liability claims focus on the product itself. Under strict liability, the manufacturer is liable if the product is defective, even if the manufacturer was not negligent in making that product defective.

The difficulty with negligence is that it still requires the plaintiff to prove that the defendant's conduct fell below the relevant standard of care. However, if an entire industry tacitly settles on a somewhat careless standard of conduct, then the plaintiff may not be able to recover even though he or she is severely injured, because although the defendant's conduct caused his or her injuries, such conduct was not negligent in the legal sense. As a practical matter, with the increasing complexity of products, injuries, and medical care (which made many formerly fatal injuries survivable), it is quite a difficult and expensive task to find and retain good expert witnesses who can establish the standard of care, breach, and causation.

Therefore, in the 1940s and 1950s, many American courts departed from the *MacPherson* standard and decided that it was too harsh to require seriously injured consumer plaintiffs to prove negligence claims against manufacturers or retailers. To avoid having to deny such plaintiffs any relief, these courts began to look for facts in their cases which they could characterize as an express or implied warranty from the manufacturer to the consumer. The *res ipsa loquitur* doctrine was also stretched to reduce the plaintiff's burden of proof. Over time, the resulting legal fictions became increasingly strained.

Of the various U. S. states, California was the first to throw away the fiction of a warranty and to boldly assert the doctrine of strict liability in tort for defective products, in 1963 (under the guidance of then-Associate Justice Roger J. Traynor). See *Greenman v. Yuba Power Products*, 59 Cal. 2nd 57 (1963). The importance of *Greenman* cannot be overstated: in 1996, the Association of Trial Lawyers of America (now known as the American Association of Justice) celebrated its 50th anniversary by polling lawyers and law professors on the top ten developments in tort law during the past half-century, and *Greenman* topped the list.

In *Greenman*, Traynor cited to his own earlier concurrence in *Escola v. Coca-Cola Bottling*

Co., 24 Cal. 2nd 453,462 (1944) (Traynor, J. , concurring). In *Escola*, now widely recognized as a landmark case in American law, Justice Traynor laid the foundation for *Greenman* with these words:

Even if there is no negligence, however, public policy demands that responsibility be fixed wherever it will most effectively reduce the hazards to life and health inherent in defective products that reach the market. It is evident that the manufacturer can anticipate some hazards and guard against the recurrence of others, as the public cannot. Those who suffer injury from defective products are unprepared to meet its consequences. The cost of an injury and the loss of time or health may be an overwhelming misfortune to the person injured, and a needless one, for the risk of injury can be insured by the manufacturer and distributed among the public as a cost of doing business. It is to the public interest to discourage the marketing of products having defects that are a menace to the public. If such products nevertheless find their way into the market it is to the public interest to place the responsibility for whatever injury they may cause upon the manufacturer, who, even if he is not negligent in the manufacture of the product, is responsible for its reaching the market. However intermittently such injuries may occur and however haphazardly they may strike, the risk of their occurrence is a constant risk and a general one. Against such a risk there should be general and constant protection and the manufacturer is best situated to afford such protection.

The year after *Greenman*, the Supreme Court of California proceeded to extend strict liability to *all* parties involved in the manufacturing, distribution, and sale of defective products (including retailers) and in 1969 made it clear that such defendants were liable not only to direct customers and users, but also to any innocent bystanders randomly injured by defective products.

Since then, many jurisdictions have been swayed by Justice Traynor 's strongly persuasive arguments on behalf of the strict liability rule in *Escola*, *Greenman*, and subsequent cases—including nearly all U. S. states, the European Union, Australia, and Japan—and have adopted it either by judicial decision or by legislative act. Notably, South Africa, New Zealand, and the U. S. state of North Carolina have soundly rejected strict liability; Canada continues to officially reject it but under American influence has gradually adjusted certain aspects of negligence and warranty law to make them more favorable to consumers.

Oddly, although the *Greenman* rule was transmitted to most other states via Section 402A of the *Restatement of Torts*, *Second* (published in 1964 after *Greenman*), the Supreme Court of California refused to adopt Section 402A 's "unreasonably dangerous" limitation upon strict liability in 1972. Thus, strict liability in California is truly strict, in that the plaintiff need not show that the defect was unreasonable or dangerous. On the other hand, in California, the defendant is allowed to introduce evidence in a strict products liability action that the plaintiff contributed to his or her own injuries.

Although the Supreme Court of California has since become more conservative, it continues to endorse and expand the doctrine. In 2002 it held that strict liability for defective products even applies to makers of component products that are installed into and sold as part of real property.

Consumer Protection

In addition to the above common law claims, many states have enacted consumer protection statutes providing for specific remedies for a variety of product defects. Statutory remedies are often provided for defects which merely render the product unusable (and hence cause economic injury) but do not cause physical injury or damage to other property; the "economic loss rule" means that strict liability is generally unavailable for products that damage only themselves. The best known examples of consumer protection laws for product defects are lemon laws, which became widespread because automobiles are often an American citizen's second-largest investment after buying a home.

Defenses:

In general, the liability defenses may include:

(1) unforeseeability

(2) state of art

(3) obvious danger (also called generally known danger, the manufacturer has no duty to warn of obvious danger)

(4) inherent product danger (such as knife and medicine, elimination of such danger may change the substantial characteristics of the product)

(5) product misuse and alteration (The manufacturer has the duty to take measures to avoid the risk in reasonably foreseeable misuse and alteration)

(6) plaintiff 's fault (The plaintiff 's conduct fails to conform to generally applicable rules establishing appropriate standard of care; the recovery of damages for harm may be reduced)

Product Liability in the European Union

Moves towards a strict liability regime in Europe began with the Council of *Europe an Convention on Products Liability in Regard to Personal Injury and Death* (the Strasbourg Convention[6]) in 1977. On July 25, 1985, the European Economic Community adopted the Product Liability Directive 85/374/EEC. In language similar to Traynor's, the Directive stated that "liability without fault on the part of the producer is the sole means of adequately solving the problem, peculiar to our age of increasing technicality, of a fair apportionment of the risks inherent in modern technological production." However, the Directive also gave each member state the option of imposing a liability cap of 70 million euros per defect.

Rationale for and Debate over Strict Liability

The fundamental rationale of strict liability is to force producers to internalize the external costs they impose on society. By placing liability for all injuries caused by a product on its manufacturer, the manufacturer is forced to take into account, when deciding whether and how much to produce the product, the harm caused by it. If this internalized harm is so great that the manufacturer cannot profit from producing the product, it will discontinue the product, or sell it only at a higher price to consumers who value it especially highly (in economic terms, modify its activity level). In this way, strict liability provides a mechanism for ensuring that the societal good of products in the marketplace outweighs their societal harm.

Moreover, proponents of strict liability for defective products argue that strict liability is sensible because between two parties who are not negligent (manufacturer and consumer), one will still have to suffer the economic cost of the injury. They argue that it is preferable to place the economic costs on the manufacturer because it can better absorb them and pass them on to other consumers by the way of higher prices. As such, the manufacturer becomes the insurer of consumers that are injured by its defective products, with premiums paid by other consumers.

A related argument arises from the fact that the distribution of information about any given product is highly asymmetrical; the manufacturer of any given product is in a better position than the consumer to know of its particular dangers. Therefore, in order to fulfill the public policy of minimizing injury, it is more reasonable to impose the burden of finding and correcting such dangers upon the manufacturer as opposed to imposing the burden of finding and avoiding unsafe products upon the consumer. These arguments are often mentioned in cases of design and warning defects and less so in the case of manufacturing defects, since the latter are thought to be less preventable by the manufacturer because he is already acting with due care.

Critics charge that strict liability incentivizes product misuse (particularly in jurisdictions where this may not be a defense) and creates a moral hazard problem on the part of potential buyers. Reasoning that consumers will recover regardless of the amount of care they take in using the product, critics assert that consumers will underinvest in care even when they are the least-cost avoiders, thus leading to a lower aggregate level of care than under a negligence standard.

While proponents assert that the producer can build the cost into the price as insurance, critics argue that this assertion is ignorant of economics and only holds true in inelastic regions of the demand curve. As a result of strict liability for their products, manufacturers may not produce the socially optimal level of goods. Particularly with elastic regions of the demand curve, where consumers are very price-sensitive, the manufacturer by definition cannot pass on the economic costs to the consumers as a form of insurance without pricing many of those consumers out of the market for that good. However, because consumers are not willing to pay for this insurance, proponents of strict liability would argue that this is evidence of a product whose harm outweighs its good, in which case it should be removed from the market.

Critics also argue that applying strict liability to products results in substantially higher transaction costs. One example of these transaction costs is the creation of maintenance of legal disclaimers on products that would be unnecessary to the reasonable person—such as the improperly algorithmic "lather, rinse, repeat" instructions on shampoos and the ubiquitous "not for human consumption" labelling on an inordinate number of non-food items. This results in a waste of time and resources for the producers who have to create these warnings, decreasing the producer surplus from trade. This also lowers the consumer surplus from these transactions, as all reasonably diligent consumers will read the unnecessary instructions, whereas the consumers likely to misuse the product are unlikely to be sufficiently diligent to read the instructions.

On the other hand, strict liability likely reduces litigation costs, because a plaintiff need only prove causation, not imprudence. When it is clear that the product caused the plaintiff's harm, parties under a strict liability regime are prone to settle out of court, because only damages are in dispute.

A product recall[7] is a request to return to the maker a batch or an entire production run of a product, usually due to the discovery of safety issues. The recall is an effort to limit liability for corporate negligence (which can cause costly legal penalties) and to improve or avoid damage to publicity. Recalls are costly to a company because they often entail replacing the recalled product or paying for damage caused by use, although possibly less costly than consequential costs caused by damage to brand name and reduced trust in the manufacturer.

A country's consumer protection laws will have specific requirements in regard to product recalls. Such regulations may include how much of the cost the maker will have to bear, situations in which a recall is compulsory (usually because the risk is big enough), or penalties for failure to recall. The firm may also initiate a recall voluntarily, perhaps subject to the same regulations as if the recall were compulsory. In the case of a compulsory recall, consumers who fail to dispose of it or return it to the manufacturer for replacement or refund could be fined for as much as $5 000.

Product Liability Law in Japan

Introduction of the Product Liability System

Through the rapid development of science and technology and aggressive innovation in economic activities, Japan has attained a society of mass production and mass consumption. On the other hand, because consumers use and consume high-tech and complicated products daily, their safety primarily depends on product manufacturers.

Therefore, in order to change the principle of liability for damages in product-related accidents from "negligence" to "defect", and relieve the injured persons in a swift and appropriate manner, the *Product Liability Law* shall come into force from July 1, 1995. With the introduction of the Product Liability system, it is expected that the way of thinking and the approach concerning product safety of both the industry business segment and the consumer segment will change and improve.

Definition of Product Liability

Product Liability shall be defined as liability for damages in such case as follows: In the case where due to a defect in the delivered product, a life, a body or property of another person (including a third party not using or consuming the product directly, and a legal person as well as a natural person) is injured, the person who manufactured, processed, imported or put his name, etc. on the product as business is liable for damages of the injured person.

Significance of Introduction of the Product Liability Law

Previously in Japan, claims for damages have usually been made based on the *Civil Code Article No. 709* in case the injury is caused by a defect in the product. The *Civil Code Article No. 709* employs the "fault-based liability (negligence) principle", and requires the "intention or fault" of the manufacturer, etc. as a condition for liability.

The *Product Liability Law* takes the "defect in the product" as a condition for liability instead of the "intention or fault" of the manufacturer, etc. Therefore, after introduction of the *Product Liability Law*, the injured has only to verify the "defect in the product" for claiming damages.

Civil Code Article No. 709	**Product Liability Law**
· The damage · The intention or fault of the accused · The causal relationship between the damage and the intention or fault	· The damage · The defect in the product (at the time distribution commences) · The causal relationship between the damage and the defect

The *Product Liability Law* can be said to employ the "liability without fault principle[8]", that is, the manufacturer, etc. is liable for damages if the injury is caused by a defect in the product regardless of whether it was his intention or fault. However, the manufacturer, etc. is not liable when there is no defect in the product. As the *Product Liability Law* is a means for claiming damages, the plaintiff side bears the burden of proof[9] for the above-mentioned 1) —3). The enactment of the *Product Liability Law* means a change in the liability rule from fault-based liability principle to defect-based liability principle.

Points of the Product Liability Law

Scope of the Product

By definition, "product" means movable property manufactured or processed. Therefore, incorporeal property such as services, information, software, electricity, etc. , and immovables are not the object of the Law. Moreover, agricultural, forestal, marine and mineral products which are not processed artificially are not the object of the Law.

Parties Subject to Liability

Parties subject to liability are as follows: Any person who puts his name, etc. on the product with such titles as "manufacturer" or "importer", or any person who puts his name, etc. on the product in a manner mistakable for its manufacturer or importer. (For instance, any person selling OEM[10] products using his company brand name.) Any person who, by putting his name, etc. on the product, may be recognized as its manufacturer-in-fact, in the light of a manner concerning manufacturing, processing, importation or sales, and other circumstances. (For instance, any person, even though he puts his name, etc. on the product with such titles as "seller" or "sales agency", who is socially recognized as its manufacturer-in-fact or is a sole distributor of the product.)

Concept of the Term "Defect"

A "defect" does not mean mere lack of quality of the product, but means lack of safety in the product which may cause the injury to life, body, or property. In the law, the term "defect" is defined as "lack of safety that the product ordinarily should provide", taking into account "the nature of the product", "the ordinarily foreseeable manner of use of the product", "the time when the manufacturer, etc. delivered the product", and other circumstances concerning the product. These three above-mentioned circumstances include such respective factors, as are presented below. In the actual trial, while the weight of each factor is different depending on individual cases, these factors are comprehensively taken into account in judging whether the product is defective or not. "The nature of the product" means the circumstances of the product itself, including factors such as the following: representation of the product (instructions, warnings, etc. to prevent accidents) effectiveness and usefulness of the product (compared to its danger), cost vs. effect (the safety standard of products in the same price range), probability of occurrence of accident and its extent ordinary use period and durable period of the product "The ordinarily foreseeable manner of use of the product" means the circumstances concerning use of the product, including factors such as the following reasonably foreseeable use of the product possibility of preventing damage from occurring by the product user. "The time when the manufacturer, etc. delivered the product" means the circumstances when the manufacturer, etc. delivered the product, including factors such as the following: situation at the time the product was delivered (the safety level required in society at the time the product was delivered), technological capabilities (the prior state of safety regulations and possibility of alternative design).

Exemptions(Development Risk Defense)

The *Product Liability Law* admits "Development Risk Defense" as an exemption. This means the manufacturer, etc. shall not be liable for damages, if the manufacturer, etc. proves that the state of "scientific or technical knowledge" at the time when the manufacturer, etc. delivered the product was not such as to enable the existence of the defect in the product to be discovered. "Scientific or technical knowledge" means all the established knowledge that could influence the decision on the existence of the defect, and not the knowledge held by a peculiar person but the total knowledge that objectively exists in society. Component or Raw Material Manufacturer 's Defense Insofar as components or raw materials are "products" movable property manufactured or processed, their manufacturers are also subject to liability in the Law. However, if the manufacturer, etc. of a component or raw material proves that the defect is substantially attributable to compliance with the instructions concerning the specifications given by the assembling manufacturer who incorporates the component or raw material into another product, and that the manufacturer, etc. is not negligent on occurrence of the defect, the manufacturer of the component or raw material shall not be liable for damages.

Time Limitations

The right for damages provided in the Law shall be extinguished by prescription if the injured person or his legal representative does not exercise their rights within the following period: A period of three years from the time when the injured person or his legal representative becomes aware of the damage and the liable party for the damage (short-term negative prescription); A period of ten years from the time when the manufacturer, etc. delivered the product (long-term liable period).

Concerning introduction of the *Product Liability Law*, the cooperation of all divisions of a company is indispensable. Namely, not only development, design, manufacturing and quality control divisions, but also general affairs, law and consumer divisions, etc. are recommended to cooperate with each other on product safety measures.

In case injury to life, body, or property is caused by a defect in the product, all product-related manufacturers as well as the assembling manufacturer of the finished product shall be liable jointly and severally for the damages described in the Law.

Comparison of Japan's Product liability Law with Product Liability System of EU and USA

	Japan	**European Union**	**USA**
	The P L Law	EC Product Liability Directive (Council Directive of 25 July, 1985)	Judicial Precedents
Principle Liability for Damages	Liability without fault principle (Defect-based liability principle)		
Burden of Proof (Adoption of Presumption Rule)	The plaintiff side bears the burden of proof of damage, defect and causal relationship between defect and damage.		
	No	No	No
	(flexible application of empirical rules and inference)		Preponderance of the evidence discovery
Adoption of Development Risk Defense	Yes	Yes	Yes
		(option: adopted by 12 of 14 countries)	(state of the art defense)

(continued)

Liable Period	10 years from the delivery of the product (10 years from the time the damage arises in case such damage as caused by accumulation of substances or others)	10 years from the delivery of the product	10 years from the delivery of the product (in many states)

Product Liability Law in China

Brief Introduction

In 1986, the *General Principles of the Civil Law* was passed by the NPC (National People's Congress), in which there is one Article (Article 122) governing the product liability, which is taken as a formal beginning of the legislation on product liability of China, saying that "if a substandard product causes property damage or physical injury to others, the manufacturer or seller shall bear civil liability according to law".

In 1993, the *Product Quality Law* of PRC (amended in 2000), the amendment strengthens the product quality supervision system and enlarges the categories of the damages for personal injury.

Liability Basis

The producer shall undertake the strict liability for the damages or injuries caused by the defective products, whereas the seller undertakes fault-based liability. The producer and the seller shall undertake joint and several liability. If the liability falls on the producer, but the seller has made compensation, the seller shall have the right to recover the loss from the producer, and vice versa.

Defenses

The producer may exempt himself from the liability if he can prove the existence of any of the following circumstances:

(1) The product has not been put in circulation;

(2) The defect causing the damage did not exist at the time when the product was put in circulation;

(3) The science and technology at the time the product was put into circulation was at a level incapable of detecting the defect.

Limitation Period

The limitation period to bring an action of product liability is 2 years from the date when the plaintiff knew or should have known the infringement of his rights and interests; 10 years from the date when the product was delivered to the first user or consumer.

Notes

1. Product Liability Law　产品责任法
   产品责任是指产品生产者、销售者因生产、销售有缺陷产品致使他人遭受人身伤害、财产损失所应承担的赔偿责任。产品责任法是确定生产者、销售者承担此种民事责任的法律规范的总称,旨在保护广大用户、消费者的合法权益。产品责任法主要包括产品责任含义、产品缺陷(瑕疵)、责任主体、归责原则、举证责任、赔偿范围、诉讼时效、抗辩事由等内容。
2. negligence　疏忽
   疏忽是指产品的生产者或销售者未尽到相应的注意义务(duty of care),致使产品有缺陷,由于这种缺陷使消费者的人身或财产遭到损害,对此,产品生产者或销售者应承担责任。这是建立在过失责任理论之上的,这种疏忽在英美法上是一种侵权行为。
3. strict liability　严格责任
   严格责任是一种不以过错为要件的责任形态,只要某种行为客观上造成危害后果,不论行为人主观上有无过错,就应承担责任。在《产品责任法》中,只要产品存在缺陷,对使用者或消费者具有不合理的危险并因此造成人身或财产伤害,该产品的生产者或销售者就应承担赔偿责任。严格责任为英美法系中的一个概念,大陆法系通常采用无过错责任(liability without fault)。
4. warranty　担保
   担保分为明示担保(express warranty)与默示担保(implied warranty),前者是指产品的生产者对其产品所做的明示说明,包括对其性能、质量、用途等的介绍。产品制造者应保证其产品质量达到其所明示说明的质量标准,如果达不到这一标准而给他人造成损害,则认为是违反明示担保,应当承担相应的法律责任。默示担保具有两层含义:对产品商销性(merchantability)的默示担保与产品适合特定用途(fitness of particular purpose)的默示担保。产品制造者虽然没有作出明示的说明,也应担保其产品一般的效用,具有平均的品质且不含有隐蔽缺陷;还应担保其产品适合某一特定用途。否则,因产品缺陷造成买受人损害,则认为产品制造人违反默示担保,应当承担赔偿责任。担保理论的局限性主要是,受害人应与产品的生产、销售者之间存在合同关系,否则难以援引该理论提供法律救济。
5. Privity of Contract　直接合同关系原则、合同关系不涉及第三人原则
   是指消费者只有同生产者、销售者之间存在直接合同关系(主要指买卖合同关系),才能依合同就缺陷产品对自己造成的人身、财产损害要求生产者、销售者承担民事责任,即“无合同则无责任”规则。
6. *The Strasbourg Convention*　《斯特拉斯堡公约》
   其全称为《关于人身伤亡产品责任欧洲公约》(*European Convention on Products Liability in*

Regard to Personal Injury and Death),欧洲理事会于 1977 年 1 月 27 日在法国斯特拉斯堡通过该公约。

7. product recall　产品召回

产品召回是指生产商将已经送到批发商、零售商或最终用户手上的产品收回。产品召回的典型原因是所售出的产品被发现存在缺陷。产品召回制度则是针对厂家原因造成的批量性问题而采取的处理办法。

8. liability without fault principle　无过错责任原则

是指没有过错造成他人损害的,依法律规定应由与造成损害原因有关的人承担民事责任的原则。英美法称之为"严格责任"。我国民法通则规定的典型的适用无过错责任的案件有:产品缺陷致人损害、高度危险作业致人损害、环境污染致人损害、地面施工致人损害、饲养的动物致人损害等损害赔偿案件。

9. burden of proof　举证责任

其一般原则是指"谁主张,谁举证",而"举证责任倒置"是这一原则的例外。

10. OEM　原始设备制造商、原厂委托制造

其全称为 Original Equipment Manufacturer,按原单位(品牌单位)委托合同进行产品开发和制造,用原单位商标,由原单位销售或经营的合作经营生产方式,又称为"代工生产"或"贴牌生产"。相关用语如 ODM (Original Design Manufacturer)原始设计制造商、原厂委托设计,以及 OBM(Original Brand Manufacturer),原始品牌制造商,即生产商自行创立产品品牌。

Study Questions

1. What are the main theories involved in the product liability law?
2. Briefly describe the differences of the product liability law of Japan, USA and EU.
3. Try to define such terms as strict liability, absolute liability, liability without fault, fault-based liability and joint and several liability.
4. Discuss the liability defenses involved in the product liability law.

UNIT 11 World Trade Organization[1]

Key Concepts

"Green Room" negotiation	MFN	GATT
the Bretton Woods System	de facto	National Treatment

Learning Objectives

1. Understand the fundamental principles of WTO.
2. Understand the differences between WTO and GATT.
3. An understanding of how WTO functions.

An Overview

The WTO is an international organization designed to supervise and liberalize international trade. The WTO came into being on January 1, 1995, and is the successor to the General Agreement on Tariffs and Trade (GATT), which was created in 1947, and operated for almost five decades as a *de facto*[2] international organization.

To ensure that the world economy did not fall back into 1920s-30s isolationism, the General Agreement on Tariffs and Trade (GATT) was initiated over 1947-1948 under the United Nations umbrella. From that time until 1994, (when it was replaced by the WTO), GATT oversaw seven rounds of multilateral trade agreements that boosted world trade from $ 2 trillion to $ 4 trillion between 1980-1994.

GATT's main objective was tariff reduction, and in this it was highly successful, reducing tariffs on manufactured goods from a 1945 average of 40% down to the year 2000 level of about 4%. In the 1990s, as tariff concerns diminished, the emphasis switched to non-tariff barriers to international trade. GATT member realized the need for a new organization—created in 1995, the WTO focused on trade in services.

The World Trade Organization deals with the rules of trade between nations at a near-global level; it is responsible for negotiating and implementing new trade agreements, and is in charge of policing member countries' adherence to all the WTO agreements, signed by the bulk of the world's trading nations and ratified in their parliaments.

The WTO is governed by a Ministerial Conference[3], which meets every two years; a General Council, which implements the conference's policy decisions and is responsible for day-to-day administration; and a director-general[4], who is appointed by the Ministerial Conference. The WTO's headquarters are in Geneva, Switzerland.

The WTO's stated goal is to improve the welfare of the peoples of its member countries, specifically by lowering trade barriers and providing a platform for negotiation of trade. Its main mission is "to ensure that trade flows as smoothly, predictably and freely as possible". This main mission is further specified in certain core functions serving and safeguarding five fundamental principles, which are the foundation of the multilateral trading system.

History of WTO

The WTO's predecessor, the General Agreement on Tariffs and Trade (GATT), was established after World War Ⅱ in the wake of other new multilateral institutions dedicated to international economic cooperation—notably the Bretton Woods institutions known as the World Bank and the International Monetary Fund. A comparable international institution for trade, named the International Trade Organization was successfully negotiated. The ITO was to be a United Nations specialized agency and would address not only trade barriers but other issues indirectly related to trade, including employment, investment, restrictive business practices, and commodity agreements. But the ITO treaty was not approved by the U. S. and a few other signatories and never went into effect.

From Geneva to Tokyo Rounds of Negotiations

Seven rounds of negotiations occurred under GATT. The first real GATT trade rounds concentrated on further reducing tariffs. Then, the Kennedy Round in the mid-1960s brought about a GATT anti-dumping Agreement and a section on development. The Tokyo Round during the 1970s was the first major attempt to tackle trade barriers that do not take the form of tariffs, and to improve the system, adopting a series of agreements on non-tariff barriers, which in some cases interpreted existing GATT rules, and in others broke entirely new ground. Because these plurilateral agreements were not accepted by the full GATT membership, they were often informally called "codes". Several of these codes were amended in the Uruguay Round, and turned into multilateral commitments accepted by all WTO members. Only four remained plurilateral (those on government procurement, bovine meat, civil aircraft and dairy products), but in 1997 WTO members agreed to terminate the bovine meat and dairy agreements, leaving only two.

Uruguay Round

Well before GATT 's 40th anniversary, its members concluded that the GATT system was straining to adapt to a new globalizing world economy. In response to the problems identified in the 1982 Ministerial Declaration (structural deficiencies, spill-over impacts of certain countries' policies on world trade GATT could not manage etc.), the eighth GATT round—known as the Uruguay Round—was launched in September 1986, in Punta del Este, Uruguay.

It was the biggest negotiating mandate on trade ever agreed: the talks were going to extend the trading system into several new areas, notably trade in services and intellectual property, and to reform trade in the sensitive sectors of agriculture and textiles; all the original GATT articles were up for review. The Final Act concluding the Uruguay Round and officially establishing the WTO regime was signed April 15, 1994, during the ministerial meeting at Marrakesh, Morocco, and hence is known as the *Marrakesh Agreement.*

The GATT still exists as the WTO 's umbrella treaty for trade in goods, updated as a result of the Uruguay Round negotiations (a distinction is made between *GATT* 1994, the updated parts of GATT, and *GATT* 1947, the original agreement which is still the heart of GATT 1994). GATT 1994 is not however the only legally binding agreement included via the Final Act at Marrakesh; a long list of about 60 agreements, annexes, decisions and understandings was adopted. The agreements fall into a structure with six main parts:

- The Agreement Establishing the WTO;
- Goods and investment—the Multilateral Agreements on Trade in Goods including the GATT 1994 and the Trade Related Investment Measures;
- Services—the General Agreement on Trade in Services;
- Intellectual Property—the Agreement on Trade-Related Aspects of Intellectual Property Rights (TRIPS);
- Dispute Settlement (DSU);
- Reviews of Governments' trade Policies (TPRM).

Doha Round

The Doha Development Round started in 2001 and continues today. The WTO launched the current round of negotiations, the Doha Development Agenda (DDA) or Doha Round, at the fourth ministerial conference in Doha, Qatar in November 2001. The Doha round was to be an ambitious effort to make globalization more inclusive and help the world's poor, particularly by slashing barriers and subsidies in farming. The initial agenda comprised both further trade liberalization and new rule-making, underpinned by commitments to strengthen substantial assistance to developing countries.

The negotiations have been highly contentious and agreement has not been reached, despite the intense negotiations at several ministerial conferences and at other sessions. Disagreements still continue over several key areas including agriculture subsidies.

Ministerial Conferences

The topmost decision-making body of the WTO is the Ministerial Conference, which usually meets every two years. It brings together all members of the WTO, all of which are countries or customs unions. The Ministerial Conference can take decisions on all matters under any of the multilateral trade agreements. The inaugural ministerial conference was held in Singapore in 1996. Disagreements between largely developed and developing economies emerged during this conference over four issues initiated by this conference, which led to them being collectively referred to as the "Singapore issues". The second ministerial conference was held in Geneva in Switzerland. The third conference in Seattle, Washington ended in failure, with massive demonstrations and police and National Guard crowd control efforts drawing worldwide attention. The fourth ministerial conference was held in Doha in the Persian Gulf nation of Qatar. The Doha Development Round was launched at the conference. The conference also approved the joining of China, which became the 143rd member to join. The fifth ministerial conference was held in Cancún, Mexico, aiming at forging agreement on the Doha round. An alliance of 22 southern states, the G20 developing nations (led by India, China, Brazil, ASEAN led by the Philippines), resisted demands from the North for agreements on the so-called "Singapore issues" and called for an end to agricultural subsidies within the EU and the US. The talks broke down without progress.

The sixth WTO ministerial conference was held in Hong Kong from 13-18 December, 2005. It was considered vital if the four-year-old Doha Development Agenda negotiations were to move forward sufficiently to conclude the round in 2006. In this meeting, countries agreed to phase out all their agricultural export subsidies by the end of 2013, and terminate any cotton export subsidies by the end of 2006. Further concessions to developing countries included an agreement to introduce duty free, tariff free access for goods from the Least Developed Countries, following the Everything but Arms initiative of the European Union—but with up to 3% of tariff lines exempted. Other major issues were left for further negotiation to be completed by the end of 2010. The WTO General Council, on 26 May, 2009, agreed to hold a seventh WTO ministerial conference session in Geneva from 30 November-3 December 2009. A statement by chairman Amb. Mario Matus acknowledged that the prime purpose was to remedy a breach of protocol requiring two-yearly "regular" meetings, which had lapsed with the Doha Round failure in 2005, and that the "scaled-down" meeting would not be a negotiating session, but "emphasis will be on transparency and open discussion rather than on small group processes and informal negotiating structures". The general theme for discussion was "The WTO, the Multilateral Trading System and the Current Global Economic Environment".

Functions of WTO

Among the various functions of the WTO, these are regarded by analysts as the most important:

- It oversees the implementation, administration and operation of the covered agreements.
- It provides a forum for negotiations and for settling disputes.

- Additionally, it is the WTO's duty to review the national trade policies, and to ensure the coherence and transparency of trade policies through surveillance in global economic policy-making.
- Another priority of the WTO is the assistance of developing, least-developed and low-income countries in transition to adjust to WTO rules and disciplines through technical cooperation and training.
- The WTO is also a center of economic research and analysis: regular assessments of the global trade picture in its annual publications and research reports on specific topics are produced by the organization.
- Finally, the WTO cooperates closely with the two other components of the Bretton Woods system[5], the IMF[6] and the World Bank[7].

Principles of the Trading System

The WTO establishes a framework for trade policies; it does not define or specify outcomes. That is, it is concerned with setting the rules of the trade policy games. Five principles are of particular importance in understanding both the pre-1994 GATT and the WTO:

1. Non-discrimination

It has two major components: the most favored nation[8] (MFN) rule, and the national treatment[9] policy. Both are embedded in the main WTO rules on goods, services, and intellectual property, but their precise scope and nature differ across these areas. The MFN rule requires that a product made in one member country be treated no less favorably that a very similar good that originated in any other country. "Grant someone a special favor and you have to do the same for all other WTO members." According to national treatment, imported and locally-produced goods should be treated equally (at least after the foreign goods have entered the market). National treatment ensures that liberalization commitments are not offset through the imposition of domestic taxes and similar measures.

2. Reciprocity

It reflects both a desire to limit the scope of free-riding that may arise because of the MFN rule, and a desire to obtain better access to foreign markets. A related point is that for a nation to negotiate, it is necessary that the gain from doing so be greater than the gain available from unilateral liberalization; reciprocal concessions intend to ensure that such gains will materialize.

3. Binding and Enforceable Commitments

The tariff commitments made by WTO members in a multilateral trade negotiation and on accession are enumerated in schedules (lists) of concessions. These schedules establish "ceiling bindings"[10]: a country can change its bindings, but only after negotiating with its trading partners, which could mean compensating them for loss of trade. If satisfaction is not obtained, the complaining country may invoke the WTO dispute settlement procedures.

4. Transparency

The WTO members are required to publish their trade regulations, to maintain institutions allowing for the review of administrative decisions affecting trade, to respond to requests for information by other members, and to notify changes in trade policies to the WTO. These internal transparency requirements are supplemented and facilitated by periodic country-specific reports (trade policy reviews) through the Trade Policy Review Mechanism (TPRM)[11]. The WTO system tries also to improve predictability and stability, discouraging the use of quotas and other measures used to set limits on quantities of imports.

5. Safety Valves

In specific circumstances, governments are able to restrict trade. There are three types of provisions in this direction: articles allowing for the use of trade measures to attain non-economical objectives; articles aimed at ensuring "fair competition"; and provisions permitting intervention in trade for economic reasons.

Formal Structure

According to WTO rules, all WTO members may participate in all councils, committees, etc. , except Appellate Body[12], Dispute Settlement Panels[13], and plural-lateral committees.

Highest Level: Ministerial Conference

The topmost decision-making body of the WTO is the Ministerial Conference, which has to meet at least every two years. It brings together all members of the WTO, all of which are countries or separate customs territories. The Ministerial Conference can make decisions on all matters under any of the multilateral trade agreements.

Second Level: General Council

The daily work of the ministerial conference is handled by three groups: the General Council, the Dispute Settlement Body, and the Trade Policy Review Body. All three consist of the same membership—representatives of all WTO members—but each meets under different rules.

(1) The General Council—is the WTO 's highest-level decision-making body in Geneva, meeting regularly to carry out the functions of the WTO. It has representatives (usually ambassadors or equivalent) from all member governments and has the authority to act on behalf of the ministerial conference which only meets about every two years. The council acts on behalf on the Ministerial Council on all WTO affairs.

(2) The Dispute Settlement Body—Made up of all member governments, usually represented by ambassadors or equivalent.

(3) The Trade Policy Review Body (TPRB)—the WTO General Council meets as the Trade Policy Review Body to undertake trade policy reviews of Members under the TRPM. The TPRB is thus open to all WTO Members.

Third Level: Councils for Trade

The Councils for Trade work under the General Council. There are three councils—Council for Trade in Goods[14], Council for Trade—Related Aspects of Intellectual Property Rights[15], and Council for Trade in Services[16]—each council works in different fields. Apart from these three councils, six other bodies report to the General Council reporting on issues such as trade and development, the environment, regional trading arrangements and administrative issues.

(1) Council for Trade in Goods—The workings of the General Agreement on Tariffs and Trade (GATT) which covers international trade in goods, are the responsibility of the Council for Trade in Goods. It is made up of representatives from all WTO member countries.

(2) Council for Trade-Related Aspects of Intellectual Property Rights—Information on intellectual property in the WTO, news and official records of the activities of the TRIPS Council, and details of the WTO's work with other international organizations in the field.

(3) Council for Trade in Services—The Council for Trade in Services operates under the guidance of the General Council and is responsible for overseeing the functioning of the General Agreement on Trade in Services (GATS). It's open to all WTO members, and can create subsidiary bodies as required.

Fourth Level: Subsidiary Bodies

There are subsidiary bodies under each of the three councils:

(1) The Goods Council—subsidiary under the Council for Trade in Goods. It has 11 committees consisting of all member countries, dealing with specific subjects such as agriculture, market access, subsidies, and anti-dumping measures and so on. Committees include the following: Information Technology Agreement (ITA), Committee State Trading Enterprises.

(2) Textiles Monitoring Body—Consists of a chairman and 10 members acting under it. The next two groups dealing with notifications—process by which governments inform the WTO about new policies and measures in their countries.

(3) The Services Council—subsidiary under the Council for Trade in Services which deals with financial services, domestic regulations and other specific commitments.

(4) Dispute Settlement Panels and Appellate Body—subsidiary under the Dispute Settlement Body to resolve disputes and the Appellate Body to deal with appeals.

Other Committees

Committees on:

Trade and Environment

Trade and Development (Subcommittee on Least-Developed Countries)

Regional Trade Agreements

Balance of Payments Restrictions

Budget, Finance and Administration

Working Parties on Accession

Working Groups on Trade, Debt and Finance

Trade and Technology Transfer

The WTO operates on a one country, one vote system, but actual votes have never been taken. Decision-making is generally by consensus, and relative market size is the primary source of bargaining power. The advantage of consensus decision-making is that it encourages efforts to find the most widely acceptable decision. Main disadvantages include large time requirements and many rounds of negotiation to develop a consensus decision, and the tendency for final agreements to use ambiguous language on contentious points that makes future interpretation of treaties difficult.

Because WTO negotiations proceed not by consensus of all members, but by a process of informal negotiations between small groups of countries, such negotiations are often called "Green Room" negotiations[17] (after the color of the WTO Director-General's Office in Geneva), or "Mini-Ministerial"[18], when they occur in other countries. These processes have been regularly criticized by many of the WTO's developing country members which are often totally excluded from the negotiations.

The Free Trade-Protectionism Debate

Free trade has very much become associated with world development. As one has increased, so generally has the other. Yet, in particular countries and for specific industries, arguments for protectionism have been pitted against those of free trade.

Pro-free-trade[19] arguments include:

(1) Free trade promotes global competition, which benefits consumers through increased varieties of products and lower prices. Countries specialize and export those goods in which they have comparative advantages and import products that they produce less effectively than other nations. One ongoing debate has been whether the price advantages resulting from developing-nation cost structures are passed on to customers in developed nations in the form of lower prices, or whether developing-nation cost benefits simply result in increased margins for importing retailers or other channel intermediaries in advanced markets.

(2) The economic interdependencies of trade and global commerce make countries less likely to go to war. One reason why the European Economic Community[20] was formed so soon after World War Ⅱ was that countries with commercial interdependencies and regular dialogs were less likely to enter into political-military conflicts. One problem has been that commercial disputes have taken the place of military rivalries as forums for country-based competition.

(3) The uneven distribution of global resources, particularly in commodities, makes trade inevitable. Concentrations of resources, such as oil in the Middle East, timber in South America and Asia, or gold and diamonds in South Africa, make trade inevitable as nations share resources distributed through world trade. However, commodity prices on world markets have rarely kept pace with global inflation, resulting in diminished purchasing power for developing country providers.

Efforts to increase commodity prices such as oil have generally been resisted in the developed nations as inflationary, and continued low commodity prices limit developing-country industrialization efforts.

(4) Trade helps emerging economies develop through technology transfers. The rise in world-development standards eases suffering in poor nations by contributing to their economic growth. South Korea's export-based growth strategy contributed to the raising of its GDP per capita from $87 in 1962 to over $10,000 in 1995. As technology transfers have become more frequent, so more countries acquire the skills to compete worldwide. Over the long-term, these nations can become major global competitors to developed-country firms.

(5) World trade encourages efficient use of global resources. Competition forces countries to focus on industries in which they are competitive. For example, developing nations can use their surplus workers to compete in labor-intensive industries, such as textiles. Developed countries can use their educated and skilled workforces to be manufacturing centers for technically advanced (capital intensive) goods and services such as high-tech or financial services.

(6) Global competition forces companies to become more efficient and innovative. Many of the management philosophies and techniques of the 1990s (total quality management, reengineering, etc.) have been transferred internationally by corporations in their quests to attain competitive advantages at national-market and global levels.

(7) Trade as a source of global education has made countries and peoples increasingly aware of world events and problems. Global media give instantaneous news coverage worldwide, educating national publics and broadening their appreciation of foreign markets. Similarly, increased product varieties educate consumers about labor-saving devices and alternative-consumption styles. A downside to this argument is that, while such products and promotions stimulate consumers toward higher standards of consumption, they also create frustrations for consumers too poor to participate fully in consumption-based societies (e.g., developing countries).

(8) Exporting creates jobs. Estimates during the 1970s put job creation at 20,000 jobs per $1 billion in export trade. Estimates for the 1990s place this figure at about 7,000 jobs per $1 billion in exports. For countries like Japan, a $100 billion trade surplus means about 700,000 additional jobs.

Protectionist/anti free-trade arguments tend to be country or industry-focused and include the following:

(1) Job loss: Global competition through imports causes unemployment in national economies. If exporting creates 7,000 jobs per $1 billion in exports, then it can be argued that imports replace jobs at a similar rate. Thus, a U.S. trade deficit of $400 billion would be worth 2.8 million jobs if it were erased overnight.

(2) Low developing country wage rates represent unfair competition: Industrialized countries argue that emergent-nation wage rates are too low. For example, they may not include payroll taxes (e.g., social security, unemployment benefits). Another complaint is that many countries do not adhere to established labor practices (e.g., 40 or 48-hour work weeks, five-day schedules, etc.). Developing countries have actively lobbied against low-wage arguments at the WTO, claiming that

their cheap labor is a legitimate competitive advantage. They further argue that worker productivity in many industries is determined not by labor costs, but by the amount of capital backing up labor. In this case, it would be the developed nations that have "unfair" advantages. The WTO does condemn some labor practices, such as the use of child and prison labor in international trade. However, even the child-labor argument has its adherents, as in some cases, children become major financial contributors for families in dire economic circumstances. Problems occur, however, in some cases when children must work in dangerous conditions (e.g., brick-making) and endure long work hours and harsh discipline. While sweat-shop conditions are common in developing countries, they also occur in North America and Western Europe, particularly with immigrant labor.

(3) Infant industry[21] argument: Start-up industries, especially in emergent nations, often need time to build up experience and scale economies before being exposed to international competition. The automobile industries in South Korea and Brazil matured under this regimen. Problems occur as industries in this situation often lack incentives to attain inter-national competitiveness, and protection becomes difficult to remove.

(4) Strategic industry arguments: There are some industries that governments label "strategic" and which are sheltered from international competition. In the post-1945 period, these included infrastructure industries such as mail services, airlines, telecommunications, and energy (e.g., utilities). Governments argued that such sectors should remain in the public domain for national security reasons. However, with the de-escalation of East-West tensions, national security issues have become less pronounced, and many infrastructure industries have been privatized and opened up to international competition.

However, there remain a number of sectors that national governments deem "strategic" and where some protectionism is practiced. One of these is agriculture. The EU maintains a protectionist stance on agriculture through its common agricultural policy (CAP). Under CAP, European prices are set according to the least effective producer to ensure continuous agricultural supplies. Other countries (notably the U.S.) argue that non-protected markets for agricultural produce would benefit world consumers through lower prices. While this is a valid argument, there are fears that dependencies on foreign food supplies could be disastrous in the event of crop failures, and that nations should have the right to ensure their own food supplies, even at higher prices.

Many countries, for similar reasons, prefer to maintain their own military and defense industries to prevent excessive dependence on foreign contractors. While this may result in high-priced defense systems and less-than-globally-optimal weapons, this type of protection insulates governments from political pressures that could accrue from such dependencies. Similarly, there are restrictions on trade in nuclear technologies to ensure that they do not fall into hostile hands.

(5) "Uneven playing fields": Some countries are alleged to practice "managed trade policies", whereby governments effectively shield domestic producers from the full forces of global competition through (often) subtle non-tariff barriers. Japan has for many years maintained a significant balance of trade surplus with the outside world and managed import-price competition

through tight control of domestic distribution channels. Foreign companies and products have little choice but to distribute products through inefficient multi-layered channels that stifle price competition at the retail level. This has limited competitive options for foreign companies in the Japanese market and opened Japan up to charges of protectionism. Both the EU and the U. S. have been active in pressuring Japan to secure the same access to the Japanese market as Japanese companies enjoy in North America and Western Europe.

(6) Managed trade accounts: Countries often restrict trade to a level where export earnings in convertible currencies cover import bills. This prevents major trade-balance deficits and accumulations of hard-currency debts with the rest of the world. While this limits trade and national economic development in the short term, there are fewer pressures on national exchange-rate values, and adequate foreign-currency reserves can be maintained.

(7) Free trade and economic restructuring: Free trade has significant repercussions as resources are moved out of uncompetitive sectors into industries with secure long-term prospects. In industrialized economies, politicians recognize that unskilled labor suffers disproportionately when jobs are transferred to developing countries. While conventional economic wisdom suggests that advanced countries should export high-tech and knowledge-intensive products, retraining poorly educated and unskilled workers is a difficult task. Trends away from manufacturing employment are complemented by increases in service industries. But the hollowing out of national manufacturing sectors remains a governmental concern in maturing economics.

(8) Cultural protectionism: Some countries restrict foreign influences (often including imports and foreign direct investments) to preserve their national cultures. Not all nations want unrestricted access to Western products. Canada maintains curbs on U.S. "cultural imperialism" by limiting sales of U.S. textbooks, curtailing the amount of foreign content in domestic radio stations, and taxing Canadian ads in Canadian editions of U. S. magazines. Similarly countries with strong national cultures (e.g., France) or profoundly religious convictions (e.g., Middle East) are skeptical of Western materialism and hype.

National Infrastructure Development: World Bank Group

UN and World Bank concerns with national infrastructure development stem from their recognition of "persistent global problems", including poverty and inadequacies in food supplies, sanitation, water, education, and physical infrastructures.

The World Bank Group is made up of five organizations that use global financial markets to provide capital for national infrastructure developments. The first loans were originally made to finance the reconstruction of Western Europe and Japan after World War Ⅱ. Today the group provides loans and assistance to promote economic growth in the developing world. Note though that capital is raised on international money markets and that, while poorer countries (< $925 per capita) pay little by way of interest charges and have long payback periods, most World Bank activities have market-related interest rates and short grace periods before repayment begins.

Private Sector Infrastructure Developments

Trade liberalization and increasing investments by international corporations has led to major improvements in the coordination of corporate activities. Linkages among company subsidiaries, suppliers, production facilities, distributors, and customers have all been enhanced through improvements in transportation and communications infrastructures.

Private sector contributions to world infrastructure development include the following:

(1) Internationalization of channels: as retailers, such as Laura Ashley, Carrefour, Benetton, Wal-Mart, and Home Depot, have capitalized on global demand homogenization to go abroad in significant numbers.

(2) Electronic commerce: using the Internet, international credit cards, and electronic transfers of funds have facilitated online sales, promotions to customers, and enhanced communications within international corporations.

Internally, companies have been quick to embrace the new technology in building global communications networks. A *Computer World* survey of forty-seven global companies found that thirty-five had global communications networks, with a further nine aiming to have their own networks by the year 2000. Firms have been able to integrate supply chains from demand monitoring at retail through to purchasing, production, and distribution functions. The full effects of IT technologies on supply-chain strategies are assessed later.

Externally, Internet effects on global commerce have been notable, as E-commerce has come online. While North America accounted for two-thirds of Internet users in 1998, the non-U. S. share of E-commerce revenues was expected to increase from 11% in 1998 to 23% World wide-web sites are expected to be major facilitators of global trade as:

- Sales orders and inquiries can be received 24 hours a day.
- Current product lines and brochures can be promoted.
- Some frustrations of international communications can he avoided. For example, miscommunications through verbal exchanges are avoided through written messages; missed telephone connections are avoided; and time can be taken to compile and compose detailed written responses.
- Communications are less affected by time differences.
- Internet remains an inexpensive means of communication.

(3) Shipping developments: Improvements in shipping have made trans-Atlantic crossing in 100 hours (as opposed to a week or more) likely in the foreseeable future. Mergers have affected the shipping industry as national and regional carriers have combined to provide seamless shipping services on a global basis land inter-modal alliances among airlines, shipping, and trucking firms are providing complete services across water and land.

(4) Growth in international air express services has doubled from 480,000 packages in 1992 to over 1 million deliveries per day for a growth rate of over 20% per year (versus rates of 7% for the

world air-cargo industry generally). Competition among express carriers (DHL Worldwide, FedEx, UPS, and TNT/GD) has put pressures on traditional air carriers to make the industry more attractive to prospective users. So efficient have these companies become that firms like FedEx have become the logistics arms of major international corporations in 2003.

(5) Satellite technology has made global communications a reality. Recent advances have greatly expanded the variety, availability, and potential uses for satellite technology, whose costs have decreased with mass-market usage, especially in mobile communications. Lockheed Martin, Loral Space and Communications, Boeing, and TRW are current leaders in the field, though they face increasing competition from Russian and Asian companies.

(6) Global media developments proliferated over the 1990s and into the new millennium. From a broadcast perspective, global television has become a reality. CNN International carries news and current events into most countries; the Discovery channel is broadcast in twenty languages into 143 countries; ESPN International takes sports into 157 million households globally and in twenty languages. Broadcast media are also regional. MBC is an Arabic news and entertainment channel; AXN is an eleven country Asian entertainment network; Sony operates a Hindi-language network across India and for Indians in Western Europe; Latin America has Discovery TV networks (four channels), Fox Kids, and sports networks. Print media have also expanded globally. Britain 's Financial Times is distributed in 140 countries, Newsweek in 190 nations, and Fortune has Asian, North American, Latin American, European, and Chinese editions.

Notes

1. World Trade Organization　世界贸易组织

世界贸易组织(World Trade Organization,简称 WTO),成立于 1995 年 1 月 1 日,总部设在日内瓦。WTO 的前身为 1947 年创立的关税及贸易总协定(General Agreement on Tariffs and Trade,简称 GATT)。世贸组织是一个独立于联合国的永久性国际组织。该组织的基本原则和宗旨是通过实施市场开放、非歧视和公平贸易等原则,来达到推动实现世界贸易自由化的目标。与关贸总协定相比,世贸组织管辖的范围除传统的和乌拉圭回合新确定的货物贸易外,还包括长期游离于关贸总协定外的知识产权、投资措施和非货物贸易(服务贸易)等领域,而 GATT 只适用于商品货物贸易。世贸组织具有法人地位,它在调解成员争端方面具有更高的权威性和有效性。世贸组织的最高决策权力机构是部长会议(Ministerial Conference),至少每两年召开一次会议。下设总理事会(General Council)和秘书处,负责世贸组织日常会议和工作。总理事会设有货物贸易、非货物贸易(服务贸易)、知识产权三个理事会(Council for Trade in Goods, Council for Trade in Services, Council for Trade-Related Aspects of Intellectual Property Rights)和贸易与发展、预算二个委员会。总理事会还下设贸易政策核查机构,它监督着各个委员会并负责起草国家政策评估报告。对美国、欧盟、日本、加拿大每两年起草一份政策评估报告,对最发达的 16 个国家每 4 年一次,对发展中国家每 6 年一次。上诉法庭负责对成员间发生的分歧进行仲裁。世贸组织成员资格分为两种,即创始成员和新加入成员。创始成员必须是关贸总协定的缔约方(contracting parties),世贸组织在接纳新成员时,须在部长级大会上由三分之二多数成员投票表决通过。

2. de facto 事实上(的)

3. Ministerial Conference 部长会议

世贸组织的最高决策权力机构是部长会议(Ministerial Conference),至少每两年召开一次会议。

4. director-general 总干事

5. Bretton Woods System 布雷顿森林体系

1944 年,来自 44 个国家的顶级经济学家在新罕布什尔州的布雷顿森林庄园济济一堂,共商世界经济的未来大计。他们的协定将大大影响世界经济格局。由美国主导确立的一种金融制度与三个新机构闪亮登场(固定汇率制、国际货币基金组织、国际复兴与开发银行、关税及贸易总协定)。

6. IMF 国际货币基金组织

为了监督货币兑换,布雷顿森林会议的代表们建立了一个被称为国际货币基金组织的国际性机构。该基金的成员将达成汇率管理协定以促进货币价值的稳定。为了帮助贸易及其他商业活动进行必要的货币兑换,国际货币基金组织建立了全球范围的多边付款制度来提供资金互助安排,成员国可以用本国货币购买外币。如果可能,成员国可以用外汇买回本国货币。为了帮助各国避免资金流动不畅问题,基金组织将提供货币储备或银行贷款帮助成员国克服国际收支的短期失衡。

7. the World Bank 世界银行

布雷顿森林会议建立的第二个机构为国际复兴与开发银行,更通俗的名称为世界银行。建立该机构有两个主要目标:第一,提供长期低息贷款以重建遭受战争创伤的欧洲和亚洲;第二,重建任务完成后,目标将转为开发贷款,同样以长期、低息方式提供。人们原本希望世界银行创造出一个国际贸易与合作得以蓬勃开展的稳定与富裕的世界。而世界银行采取自愿认缴股本的方式并实行权数投票表决制,这意味着世界银行将成为财大气粗的经济大国的工具。

8. the most favored nation 最惠国

最惠国待遇(Most Favored-Nation Treatment)是指缔约国一方现在或将来给予任何第三国的一切减让、特权或优惠,必须同等地给予缔约国的另一方。签订这种条款的目的旨在消除双方之间在通商、航海、关税、移民、投资等方面的歧视,以促进彼此的贸易往来和经济发展。

9. the national treatment 国民待遇

国民待遇原则是国际贸易领域和投资领域中的核心原则之一,其基本内涵是指一国以对待本国国民之同样方式对待外国国民。即外国人与本国人享有同等的待遇。传统的国民待遇仅局限于民事领域,随着国际经济交往的日益频繁,其内容逐渐延伸到国际投资领域,并成为该领域普遍遵循的基本法则。“次国民待遇”,即外国人在东道国所享受的待遇可以低于东道国的本国国民。“超国民待遇”的基本含义就是东道国给予外国公民或法人,在货物贸易、服务贸易、投资、知识产权等方面的待遇,高于其给本国公民或法人的待遇。

10. ceiling bindings 上限约束

即确定对进口农产品新的最高关税,通常高于乌拉圭回合前的实际税率。

11. Trade Policy Review Mechanism　贸易政策审议机制
    贸易政策审议机制(Trade Policy Review Mechanism, TPRM)是指世界贸易组织对各成员(国家/地区)的贸易政策、做法及其对多边贸易体制的影响定期进行全面评价和评估的制度。它与争端解决机制和贸易谈判机制一起构成世界贸易组织的三大机制。
12. Appellate Body　上诉机构
    例如:standing Appellate Body:常设上诉机构。WTO 争端解决机制规定了专家组报告的准自动通过规则,而不需要以前 GATT 体制的多数同意原则。通过由七名独立专家组成的常设上诉机构对专家组报告进行审查的上诉机制,为可能错误的专家组报告提供了额外的保障。
13. Dispute Settlement Panels　争端解决小组
14. Council for Trade in Goods　货物贸易理事会
    负责《1994 年关贸总协定》及其他货物贸易协议的有关事宜。
15. Council for Trade-Related Aspects of Intellectual Property Rights　与贸易有关的知识产权理事会
    监督执行与贸易有关的知识产权协定。
16. Council for Trade in Services　服务贸易理事会
    监督执行服务贸易总协定及分部门协议的有关事宜。
17. "Green Room" negotiations　绿屋会谈、密室谈判
    "绿屋会议"(the Green Room Meeting)的说法始于乌拉圭回合,因为当时的 GATT 总理事的办公室是绿色的,而在那里举行的会议多是排外的、不公开的,所以人们就把这种排外的、不透明、不民主的决策方式称作"绿屋会议"或"密室谈判"。
18. Mini-Ministerial　微型(小型)部长级会议
19. pro-free-trade　赞成自由贸易
    pro-:支持;anti-:反对;the pros and cons 赞成和反对的论据(意见)。
20. the European Economic Community　欧洲经济共同体
21. infant industry　幼稚产业
    是指某一产业处于发展初期,基础和竞争力薄弱但经过适度保护能够发展成为具有潜在比较优势的新兴产业。

Study Questions

1. What is the WTO's primary purpose?
2. What are the differences between WTO and GATT?
3. What are the fundamental principles of WTO?
4. What are the main functions of WTO?
5. What do you think of "Green Room" negotiations?
6. How do you understand Bretton Woods System?

UNIT 12 International Monetary Fund and the World Bank

Key Concepts

IMF	international balance of payments	SDR	IBRD	IDA
IFC	MIGA	ICSID		

Learning Objectives

1. Understand the concept of SDR.
2. Be familiar with the role of IMF.
3. Understand the role of the World Bank.
4. Be familiar with the main services to be provided by the World Bank.

International Monetary Fund[1]

The International Monetary Fund is a specialized agency of the United Nations system set up by treaty in 1945 to help promote the health of the world economy. Headquartered in Washington, D. C., it is governed by its almost global membership of 184 countries.

1. The IMF 's Purposes

The purposes of the International Monetary Fund are: (1) To promote international monetary cooperation through a permanent institution which provides the machinery for consultation and collaboration[2] on international monetary problems. (2) To facilitate the expansion and balanced growth of international trade, and to contribute thereby to the promotion and maintenance of high levels of employment and real income and to the development of the productive resources of all members as primary objectives of economic policy. (3) To promote exchange stability, to maintain orderly exchange arrangements among members, and to avoid competitive exchange depreciation[3].

(4) To assist in the establishment of a multilateral system of payments in respect of current transactions between members and in the elimination of foreign exchange restrictions which hamper the growth of world trade. (5) To give confidence to members by making the general resources of the Fund temporarily available to them under adequate safeguards, thus providing them with opportunity to correct maladjustments in their balance of payments without resorting to measures destructive of national or international prosperity. (6) In accordance with the above, to shorten the duration and lessen the degree of disequilibrium in the international balances of payments[4] of members.

To serve these purposes, the IMF: (1) monitors economic and financial developments and policies, in member countries and at the global level, and gives policy advice to its members based on its more than fifty years of experience; (2) lends to member countries with balance of payments problems, not just to provide temporary financing but to support adjustment and reform policies aimed at correcting the underlying problems; (3) provides the governments and central banks of its member countries with technical assistance and training in its areas of expertise. For example:

As the only international agency whose mandated activities involve active dialogue with virtually every country on economic policies, the IMF is the principal forum for discussing not only national economic policies in a global context, but also issues important to the stability of the international monetary and financial system. These include countries' choice of exchange rate arrangements, the avoidance of destabilizing international capital flows, and the design of internationally recognized standards and codes for policies and institutions.

By working to strengthen the international financial system and to accelerate progress toward reducing poverty, as well as promoting sound economic policies among all its member countries, the IMF is helping to make globalization work for the benefit of all.

2. The Origins of IMF

The IMF was conceived in July 1944 at a United Nations conference held at Bretton Woods, New Hampshire[5], U. S. A. when representatives of 45 governments agreed on a framework for economic cooperation designed to avoid a repetition of the disastrous economic policies that had contributed to the Great Depression of the 1930s[6].

During that decade, as economic activity in the major industrial countries weakened, countries attempted to defend their economies by increasing restrictions on imports; but this just worsened the downward spiral in world trade, output, and employment. To conserve dwindling reserves of gold and foreign exchange, some countries curtailed their citizens' freedom to buy abroad, some devalued their currencies, and some introduced complicated restrictions on their citizens' freedom to hold foreign exchange. These fixes, however, also proved self-defeating, and no country was able to maintain its competitive edge for long. Such "beggar-thy-neighbor" policies[7] devastated the international economy; world trade declined sharply, as did employment and living standards in many countries.

As World War Ⅱ came to a close, the leading allied countries considered various plans to restore order to international monetary relations, and at the Bretton Woods conference the IMF emerged. The country representatives drew up the charter of an international institution to oversee the international monetary system and to promote both the elimination of exchange restrictions relating to trade in goods and services, and the stability of exchange rates.

The IMF came into existence in December 1945, when the first 29 countries signed its Articles of Agreement. The statutory purposes of the IMF today are the same as when they were formulated in 1944. Since then, the world has experienced unprecedented growth in real incomes. And although the benefits of growth have not flowed equally to all—either within or among nations—most countries have seen increases in prosperity that contrast starkly with the interwar period, in particular. Part of the explanation lies in improvements in the conduct of economic policy, including policies that have encouraged the growth of international trade and helped smooth the economic cycle of boom and bust. The IMF is proud to have contributed to these developments.

In the decades since World War II, apart from rising prosperity, the world economy and monetary system have undergone other major changes—changes that have increased the importance and relevance of the purposes served by the IMF, but that have also required the IMF to adapt and reform. Rapid advances in technology and communications have contributed to the increasing international integration of markets and to closer linkages among national economies. As a result financial crises, when they erupt, now tend to spread more rapidly among countries.

In such an increasingly integrated and interdependent world, any country's prosperity depends more than ever both on the economic performance of other countries and on the existence of an open and stable global economic environment. Equally, economic and financial policies that individual countries follow affect how well or how poorly the world trade and payments system operate. Globalization thus calls for greater international cooperation, which in turn has increased the responsibilities of international institutions that organize such cooperation—including the IMF.

The IMF's purposes have also become more important simply because of the expansion of its membership. The number of IMF member countries has more than quadrupled from the 45 states involved in its establishment, reflecting in particular the attainment of political independence by many developing countries and more recently the collapse of the Soviet bloc.

The expansion of the IMF's membership, together with the changes in the world economy, have required the IMF to adapt in a variety of ways to continue serving its purposes effectively.

3. SDR[8]

The SDR, or special drawing right, is an international reserve asset introduced by the IMF in 1969 (under the First Amendment to its Articles of Agreement) out of concern among IMF members that the current stock, and prospective growth, of international reserves might not be sufficient to support the expansion of world trade. The main reserve assets were gold and U. S. dollars, and members did not want global reserves to depend on gold production, with its inherent uncertainties, and continuing U. S. balance of payments deficits, which would be needed to provide continuing growth in U. S. dollar reserves. The SDR was introduced as a supplementary reserve asset, which the IMF could "allocate" periodically to members when the need arose, and cancel, as necessary.

SDRs—sometimes known as "paper gold"[9] although they have no physical form—have been allocated to member countries (as book-keeping entries[10]) as a percentage of their quotas. So far, the IMF has allocated SDR 21.4 billion (about $ 29 billion) to member countries. The last allocation took place in 1981, when SDR 4.1 billion was allocated to the 141 countries that were then members of the IMF. Since 1981, the membership has not seen a need for another general allocation of SDRs, partly because of the growth of international capital markets. In September 1997, however, in light of the IMF's expanded membership—which included countries that had not received an allocation—the Board of Governors proposed a Fourth Amendment to the Articles of Agreement. When approved by the required majority of member governments, this will authorize a special one-time "equity" allocation of SDR 21.4 billion, to be distributed so as to raise all members' ratios of cumulative SDR allocations to quotas to a common benchmark.

IMF member countries may use SDRs in transactions among themselves, with 16 "institutional" holders of SDRs, and with the IMF. The SDR is also the IMF's unit of account. A number of other international and regional organizations and international conventions use it as a unit of account, or as a basis for a unit of account.

The SDR's value is set daily using a basket of four major currencies: the euro, Japanese yen, pound sterling, and U. S. dollar. On August 1, 2001, SDR 1 = US $ 1. 26. The composition of the basket is reviewed every five years to ensure that it is representative of the currencies used in international transactions, and that the weights assigned to the currencies reflect their relative importance in the world's trading and financial systems.

4. Adapting to Meet New Challenge

As the development of the world economy since 1945 has brought new challenges, the work of the IMF has evolved and the institution has adapted so as to be able to continue serving its purposes effectively. Especially since the early 1990s, enormous economic challenges have been associated with globalization—the increasing international integration of markets and economies. These have included the need to deal with turbulence in emerging financial markets, notably in Asia and Latin America; to help a number of countries make the transition from central planning to market-oriented systems and enter the global market economy; and to promote economic growth and poverty reduction in the poorest countries at risk of being left behind by globalization.

The IMF has responded partly by introducing reforms aimed at strengthening the architecture—or framework of rules and institutions—of the international monetary and financial system and by enhancing its own contribution to the prevention and resolution of financial crises. It has also given new emphasis to the goals of enhancing economic growth and reducing poverty in the world's poorest countries. And reform is continuing.

The World Bank[11]

The World Bank was established on July 1, 1944 by a conference of 44 governments in Bretton Woods, New Hampshire, USA. The "World Bank" is the name that has come to be used for the

International Bank for Reconstruction and Development (IBRD)[12] and the International Development Association (IDA)[13], a trust fund managed by the IBRD to provide grants and interest-free credits[14] to the world's poorest countries. Together these organizations provide low-interest loans, interest-free credit, and grants to developing countries.

In addition to IBRD and IDA, three other organizations make up the World Bank Group. The International Finance Corporation (IFC)[15] promotes private sector investment by supporting high-risk sectors and countries. The Multilateral Investment Guarantee Agency (MIGA)[16] provides political risk insurance (guarantees) to investors in and lenders to developing countries. And the International Center for Settlement of Investment Disputes (ICSID)[17] settles investment disputes between foreign investors and their host countries.

The World Bank Group consists of five closely associated institutions, all owned by member countries that carry ultimate decision-making power. As explained below, each institution plays a distinct role in the mission to fight poverty and improve living standards for people in the developing world. The term "World Bank Group" encompasses all five institutions. The term "World Bank" refers specifically to two of the five, IBRD and IDA.

1.The International Bank for Reconstruction and Development (IBRD)

IBRD was established in 1945 with 184 members. It aims to reduce poverty in middle-income and creditworthy poorer countries by promoting sustainable development, through loans, guarantees, and non-lending—including analytical and advisory—services. IBRD does not maximize profit but has earned a net income each year since 1948. Its profits fund several developmental activities and ensure financial strength, which enables low-cost borrowings in capital markets, and good terms for borrowing clients. Owned by member countries, IBRD links voting power to members' capital subscriptions—in turn based on a country's relative economic strength.

2. The International Development Association (IDA)

IDA was established in 1960 with 162 members. Contributions to IDA enable the World Bank to provide $6—7 billion per year in interest-free credits to the world's 78 poorest countries, home to 2.4 billion people. This support is vital because these countries have little or no capacity to borrow on market terms. In most of these countries incomes average under just $500 a year per person, and many people survive on much less. IDA helps provide access to better basic services (such as education, health care, and clean water and sanitation) and supports reforms and investments aimed at productivity growth and employment creation.

3. The International Finance Corporation (IFC)

IFC was established in 1956 with 175 members. IFC's mandate is to further economic development through the private sector. Working with business partners, it invests in sustainable private enterprises in developing countries and provides long-term loans, guarantees, and risk management and advisory services to its clients. IFC invests in projects in regions and sectors underserved by private investment and finds new ways to develop promising opportunities in markets deemed too risky by commercial investors in the absence of IFC participation.

4. The Multilateral Investment Guarantee Agency

MIGA was established in 1988 with 157 members. It helps encourage foreign investment in developing countries by providing guarantees to foreign investors against losses caused by noncommercial risks, such as expropriation, currency inconvertibility and transfer restrictions, and war and civil disturbances. Furthermore, MIGA provides technical assistance to help countries disseminate information on investment opportunities. The agency also offers investment dispute mediation on request.

5. The International Center for Settlement of Investment Disputes (ICSID)

ICSID was established in 1966 with 134 members. It helps to encourage foreign investment by providing international facilities for conciliation and arbitration of investment disputes, in this way helping to foster an atmosphere of mutual confidence between states and foreign investors. Many international agreements concerning investment refer to ICSID's arbitration facilities. ICSID also has research and publishing activities in the areas of arbitration law and foreign investment law.

Notes

1. International Monetary Fund　国际货币基金组织

   成立于1946年,其基本职能是向会员国提供短期信贷,缓解成员国的国际收支困难;建立和维持规范性的国际货币体系,维持汇率稳定;与成员国及有关国际组织协商解决国际金融货币问题。其宗旨是:促进国际货币合作;便利国际贸易的扩大和平衡发展;稳定国际汇兑;避免竞争性外汇贬值;协助建立货币交易的多边支付制度并消除妨碍世界贸易的外汇管制。IMF的资金来源于会员国认缴的份额(份额目前以该组织创立的记账单位SDR来表示,它相当于股东加入股份公司的股金)、借款(向会员介入资金)、信托基金(Trust fund)(所持有的黄金出售后所得之利润作为信托基金)等。IMF的贷款对象仅限于会员国政府。值得注意的是,IMF的贷款方式为,会员国向IMF借款和还款分别采用所谓“购买”(purchase)和“购回”(re-purchase)的方式。所谓“购买”或称“提款”(drawing),即指借款国用相当于借款额的本国货币来购买弥补国际收支逆差的外汇。(这在技术上虽不同于一般的国际借贷,但效果却是一样的,从IMF角度看,会员国借款则改变了IMF持有的货币构成。)所谓“购回”,是指借款国还款时,要用自己原来所借外汇购回本国货币。
2. the machinery for consultation and collaboration　协商与合作机制
3. to avoid competitive exchange depreciation　避免竞争性货币贬值
4. the international balances of payments　国际收支平衡
5. Bretton Woods, New Hampshire　美国新罕布什尔州布雷顿森林(小镇)

   第二次世界大战结束前,美国与英国等44国同盟国代表于1944年7月在此地举行国际货币金融会议,并决定创建IMF。
6. the Great Depression of the 1930s　20世纪30年代的(经济)大萧条

7. “beggar-thy-neighbor” policies　损人利己的政策
8. SDR　为 special drawing right 的缩写形式,特别提款权。
就 SDR 应注意几点:(1)SDR 是 IMF 于 1969 年 9 月创设的一种储备资产和记账单位,作为成员国在普通提款权以外的一种特别使用资金的权利,按成员国在 IMF 中的认缴份额比例分配。(2)成员国分配到的 SDR,可通过基金组织换取外汇,可同黄金、外汇一起作为成员国的国际储备,故又称“纸黄金”。(创设时 SDR 是一种有黄金保值的记账单位,每单位含金量为 0.888 671 克纯金,与当时的美元等值。)(3)成员国使用 SDR 无须偿还,所持 SDR 超过其累计分配额时,可获得利息,不足部分则须支付利息。(4)SDR 是成员国在 IMF“特别提款权账户”中的一种账面资产,只能用于成员国政府间结算,或向其他成员国换取外汇弥补国际收支逆差,或偿还 IMF 的贷款,但它不能兑换成黄金,不能直接作为支付手段。
9. “paper gold”　纸黄金
10. as book-keeping entries　作为记账单位
11. The World Bank　世界银行
成立于 1944 年,世界银行集团由国际复兴开发银行、国际金融公司、国际开发协会组成,广义上还包括解决投资争端国际中心和多边投资担保机构。其宗旨是:通过提供资金、经济和技术咨询、鼓励国际投资等方式,帮助成员国,特别是发展中国家提高生产能力,促进经济和社会进步,改善和提高人民生活水平。其主要职能是:对成员国政府、政府机构或政府所担保的私人企业发放用于市场目的的长期贷款,开始主要为重建西欧经济提供资金,后来转向发展中国家提供资金以支持其经济发展。
12. the International Bank for Reconstruction and Development (IBRD)　国际复兴开发银行
13. the International Development Association(IDA)　国际开发协会
14. interest-free credits　无息贷款。low-interest loans 为低息贷款
15. The International Finance Corporation (IFC)　国际金融公司
16. The Multilateral Investment Guarantee Agency (MIGA)　多边投资担保机构
17. the International Center for Settlement of Investment Disputes (ICSID)　解决投资争端国际中心

Study Questions

1. What is the purpose of the establishment of IMF?
2. Briefly describe the role of IMF.
3. Why is SDR also called “paper gold”?
4. Briefly describe the role of the World Bank.
5. Briefly describe the roles of the members of the World Bank Group.

UNIT 13 TRIMs Agreement[1]

Key Concepts

TRIMs	national treatment	general elimination of quantitative restrictions
transparency	requirements of local contents	requirements of balance of trade

Learning Objectives

1. Be familiar with main contents of TRIMs.
2. Understand TRIMs elimination and transitional period.
3. Understand WTO members' commitment to their obligations.
4. Understand the principle of transparency.

An Overview

In the late 1980s, there was a significant increase in foreign direct investment throughout the world. However, some of the countries receiving foreign investment imposed numerous restrictions on that investment designed to protect and foster domestic industries, and to prevent the outflow of foreign exchange reserves. Examples of these restrictions include local content requirements (which require that locally-produced goods be purchased or used), manufacturing requirements (which require the domestic manufacturing of certain components), trade balancing requirements, domestic sales requirements, technology transfer requirements, export performance requirements (which require the export of a specified percentage of production volume), local equity restrictions, foreign exchange restrictions, remittance restrictions, licensing requirements, and employment restrictions. These measures can also be used in connection with fiscal incentives as opposed to requirement. Some of these investment measures distort trade in violation of GATT Article Ⅲ and Ⅺ, and are therefore prohibited. Until the completion of the Uruguay Round negotiations, which produced a well-rounded Agreement on Trade-Related Investment Measures (hereinafter the "*TRIMs Agreement*"), the few international agreements providing disciplines for measures restricting foreign investment provided only limited guidance in terms of content and country coverage. The *OECD Code* on Liberalization of Capital Movements, for example, requires members to liberalize restrictions on direct investment in a broad range of areas. The *OECD Code*'s efficacy, however, is limited by the numerous reservations made by each of the members. In addition, there are other international treaties, bilateral and multilateral, under which signatories extend most-favoured-nation treatment to direct investment. Only a few such treaties, however, provide national treatment for direct investment. Moreover, although the *APEC Investment Principles* adopted in November 1994 provide rules for investment as a whole, including non-discrimination and national treatment, they have no binding force.

GATT 1947 prohibited investment measures that violated the principles of national treatment[2] and the general elimination of quantitative restrictions[3], but the extent of the prohibitions was never clear. The *TRIMs Agreement*, however, contains statements prohibiting any TRIMs that are inconsistent with the provisions of Articles Ⅲ or XI of GATT 1994. In addition, it provides an illustrative list that explicitly prohibits local content requirements, trade balancing requirements, foreign exchange restrictions and export restrictions (domestic sales requirements) that would violate Article Ⅲ: 4 or Ⅺ: 1 of GATT 1994. TRIMs prohibited by the Agreement include those that are mandatory or enforceable under domestic law or administrative rulings, or those with which compliance is necessary to obtain an advantage (such as subsidies or tax breaks). Indeed, the *TRIMs Agreement* is not intended to impose new obligations, but to clarify the pre-existing GATT 1947 obligations. Under the WTO *TRIMs Agreement*, countries are required to rectify any measures inconsistent with the Agreement, within a set period of time, with a few exceptions.

What Is a TRIM?

The Agreement did not define TRIMs, but provided an illustrative list as follows:

TRIMs that are inconsistent with the obligation of national treatment provided for in paragraph 4 of Article Ⅲ of GATT 1994 include those which are mandatory or enforceable under domestic law or under administrative rulings, or compliance with which is necessary to obtain an advantage[4], and which require: a) the purchase or use by an enterprise of products of domestic origin or from any domestic source, whether specified in terms of particular products, in terms of volume or value of products, or in terms of a proportion of volume or value of its local production[5]; or b) that an enterprise's purchases or use of imported products be limited to an amount related to the volume or value of local products that it exports[6].

TRIMS that are inconsistent with the obligation of general elimination of quantitative restrictions provided for in paragraph 1 of Article XI of GATT 1994 include those which are mandatory or enforceable under domestic law or under administrative rulings, or compliance with which is necessary to obtain an advantage, and which restrict: a) the importation by an enterprise of products used in or related to its local production, generally or to an amount related to the volume or value of local production that it exports[7]; b) the importation by an enterprise of products used in or related to its local production by restricting its access to foreign exchange to an amount related to the foreign exchange inflows attributable to the enterprise[8]; or c) the exportation or sale for export by an enterprise of products, whether specified in terms of particular products, in terms of volume or value of products, or in terms of a proportion of volume or value of its local production[9]. The lack of a precise definition means that the issue is not always clear-cut and there has been considerable disagreement as to whether or not certain measures are covered by the Agreement.

Examples of TRIMs Explicitly Prohibited by the *TRIMs Agreement*

Local Content Requirement

Measures requiring the purchase or use by an enterprise of domestic products, whether specified in terms of particular products, in terms of volume or value of products, or in terms of a proportion of volume or value of its local production. (Violation of GATT Article Ⅲ: 4)

Trade Balancing Requirements

Measures requiring that an enterprise's purchases or use of imported products be limited to an amount related to the volume or value of local products that it exports. (Violation of GATT Article Ⅲ: 4)

Measures restricting the importation by an enterprise of products used in or related to its local production, generally or to an amount related to the volume or value of local production that it exports. (Violation of GATT Article XI:1)

Foreign Exchange Restrictions

Measures restricting the importation by an enterprise of products (parts and other goods) used in or related to its local production by restricting its access to foreign exchange to an amount related to the foreign exchange inflows attributable to the enterprise. (Violation of GATT Article XI:1)

Export Restrictions (Domestic Sales Requirements)

Measures restricting the exportation or sale for export by an enterprise of products, whether specified in terms of particular products, in terms of volume or value of products, or in terms of a proportion of volume or value of its local production. (Violation of GATT Article Ⅺ: 1)

TRIMs Elimination and Transition Periods[10]

Under the Agreement member states were given 90 days to notify the WTO of any existing TRIMs. There were 43 notifications by 24 developing countries (19 related to the auto industry and 10 to the agri-food industry). Member states were then given a "transition period" during which their notified TRIMs were to be eliminated. The length of time was based on a state's level of development, i. e. developed countries were given 2 years; developing countries were given 5 years;

and least-developed countries were given 7 years. Therefore all developing countries should have implemented the TRIMs agreement and eliminated their regulations by 1 January, 2000.

However, Article 5. 3 of the Agreement permits developing and least-developed countries to apply for an extension of the transition period. 10 WTO members have so far submitted transitional period extension requests (Annex 2). It is likely that a number of other countries will seek extended transitional periods, but are waiting to see what happens with the "first batch". The requests range from Chile 1 year to Pakistan 7 years.

Since 1995 the TRIMs obligations that new members face on accession to the WTO depend on the terms of their accession. So far all acceding countries have agreed to implement the TRIMs agreement upon accession regardless of whether they are developing countries or not.

Exceptions for Developing Countries

Developing countries are permitted to retain TRIMs that constitute a violation of GATT Article Ⅲ or XI, provided the measures meet the conditions of GATT Article XVⅢ which allows specified derogation from the GATT provisions, by virtue of the economic development needs of developing countries.

Transparency[11]

Members reaffirm, with respect to TRIMs, their commitment to obligations on transparency and notification in Article X of GATT 1994, in the undertaking on "Notification" contained in the *Understanding Regarding Notification, Consultation, Dispute Settlement and Surveillance* adopted on 28 November, 1979 and in the *Ministerial Decision on Notification Procedures* adopted on 15 April, 1994.

Each Member shall notify the Secretariat of the publications in which TRIMs may be found, including those applied by regional and local governments and authorities within their territories. Each Member shall accord sympathetic consideration to requests for information, and afford adequate opportunity for consultation, on any matter arising from this Agreement raised by another Member. In conformity with Article X of GATT 1994 no Member is required to disclose information the disclosure of which would impede law enforcement or otherwise be contrary to the public interest or would prejudice the legitimate commercial interests of particular enterprises, public or private.

Extension Request Negotiations

Discussions about extension requests take place within the WTO Council for Trade in Goods (CTG). The countries submit an extension request to the CTG and then have to justify the request in the face of detailed questioning from other members—the US, EC and Japan have usually been the most active.

The first round of extension requests have now been largely settled. Argentina, Colombia, Malaysia, Mexico, Pakistan, the Philippines, Romania and Thailand have accepted the Chair of the CTG's "two by two" proposal in November 2000. This involves automatic 2 year extensions until the end of 2001 with requests for additional extensions for a maximum period of two years to be submitted by 31 August, 2001 (though requests arriving after this date will be considered). These further extensions would need to be accompanied by a reasonable phase out plan for the remaining TRIMs. The extensions are not guaranteed and will be dealt with on a case by case basis. Chile's request for an extension until 31 December, 2001 had already been agreed.

The only country yet to come to an agreement is Egypt, whose application for an extension was made after 31 December, 1999. If this is not accepted by the CTG the request would have to be treated as a waiver under GATT Article IX (Annex 3).

TRIMs Review

There will be a joint WTO/UNCTAD study on TRIMs. This will be an examination of how governments have used TRIMs as policy tools for industrial development and their effect on international trade, investment flows, economic growth, etc.

Notes

1. TRIMs Agreement: *Trade Related Investment Measures Agreement* 《与贸易有关的投资措施协议》简称 TRIMs 协议。一般来说,投资与贸易是相互促进的,但有时东道国的一些投资措施会对货物贸易产生限制、扭曲作用,从而对国际贸易的自由发展带来负面影响。因此,为了禁止那些限制、扭曲贸易的投资措施,自 1986 年开始的乌拉圭回合谈判,投资措施被列入多边贸易谈判的议题,TRIMs 协议是其所取得的成果之一,并成为 WTO 法律体制的有机组成部分。
2. national treatment 国民待遇
   即外国投资者应享有与东道国国民同等的待遇。
3. general elimination of quantitative restrictions 普遍取消数量限制
4. those which are mandatory or enforceable under domestic law or under administrative rulings, or compliance with which is necessary to obtain an advantage.
   依照国内法律或行政法规规定的那些强制性或可予强制执行的措施,或者为了取得一项利益而需遵循的那些措施。
5. the purchase or use by an enterprise of products of domestic origin or from any domestic source, whether specified in terms of particular products, in terms of volume or value of products, or in terms of a proportion of volume or value of its local production.
   (要求)企业购买或使用国内产的或源于国内渠道的产品,而不论按其具体产品、具体产品的数量或价值进行规定,还是按当地产品的数量或价值的比例进行规定。此条规定的是当地成分要求。
6. that an enterprise's purchases or use of imported products be limited to an amount related to the volume or value of local products that it exports.
   (要求)企业购买或使用的进口产品限定在其当地产品出口数量或价值的一定范围内。此条规定的是贸易平衡要求。

7. restrict the importation by an enterprise of products used in or related to its local production, generally or to an amount related to the volume or value of local production that it exports.
一般性地限制企业进口用于当地生产或与其有关的产品,或按企业出口产品的数量或价值对其进口产品进行限制。
8. restrict the importation by an enterprise of products used in or related to its local production by restricting its access to foreign exchange to an amount related to the foreign exchange inflows attributable to the enterprise.
通过将企业用汇限制在其创汇的一定额度内以限制其进口用于当地生产或与此有关的产品。即进口用汇限制。
9. restrict the exportation or sale for export by an enterprise of products, whether specified in terms of particular products, in terms of volume or value of products, or in terms of a proportion of volume or value of its local production.
限制企业出口或销售其出口的产品,而不论按其具体产品、具体产品的数量或价值进行限制,还是按当地产品的数量或价值的比例进行限制。此条实际上规定的是国内销售要求。
10. transition periods　过渡期
11. transparency　透明度
即信息公开和披露要求,每一成员方应遵守其在透明度和通知方面所承诺的义务。

Study Questions

1. What is the quantitative restriction?
2. What is the national treatment?
3. With respect to investment issues, what are the main differences between TRIMs Agreement and GATS?
4. What are the main exceptional provisions in TRIMs Agreement?
5. Briefly explain the principle of transparency.

UNIT 14 Introduction to Intellectual Property[1]

Key Concepts

intellectual property	intangible assets	patent	trademark
copyright	trade secret		

Learning Objectives

1. Understand the concept and features of intellectual property.
2. Understand the history of intellectual property .
3. Be familiar with the definitions of patent, trademark, trade secret and copyright.
4. Be familiar with the international conventions for the protection of intellectual property.

An Overview

Intellectual property (IP) is a term referring to a number of distinct types of creations of the mind for which a set of exclusive rights are recognized—and the corresponding fields of law. Under intellectual property law, owners are granted certain exclusive rights to a variety of intangible assets[2], such as musical, literary, and artistic works; discoveries and inventions; and words, phrases, symbols, and designs. Common types of intellectual property include copyrights[3], trademarks[4], patents[5], industrial design rights and trade secrets[6] in some jurisdictions.

Although many of the legal principles governing intellectual property have evolved over centuries, it was not until the 19th century that the term intellectual property began to be used, and not until the late 20th century that it became commonplace in the United States. The *British Statute of Anne* 1710 and the *Statute of Monopolies* 1623 are now seen as the origins of copyright and patent law respectively.

Modern usage of the term intellectual property goes back at least as far as 1867 with the founding of the North German Confederation whose constitution granted legislative power over the protection of intellectual property (*Schutz des geistigen Eigentums*) to the confederation. When the administrative secretariats established by the *Paris Convention*[7] (1883) and the *Berne Convention*[8] (1886) merged in 1893, they located in Berne, and also adopted the term intellectual property in their new combined title, the United International Bureaux for the Protection of Intellectual Property. The organization subsequently relocated to Geneva in 1960, and was succeeded in 1967 with the establishment of the World Intellectual Property Organization[9] (WIPO) by treaty as an agency of the United Nations. According to Lemley, it was only at this point that the term really began to be used in the United States (which had not been a party to the *Berne Convention*), and it did not enter popular usage until passage of the *Bayh-Dole Act* in 1980.

> "The history of patents does not begin with inventions, but rather with royal grants by Queen Elizabeth I (1558-1603) for monopoly privileges... Approximately 200 years after the end of Elizabeth's reign, however, a patent represents a legal [right] obtained by an inventor providing for exclusive control over the production and sale of his mechanical or scientific invention... [demonstrating] the evolution of patents from royal prerogative to common-law doctrine."

In an 1818 collection of his writings, the French liberal theorist, Benjamin Constant, argued against the recently introduced idea of "property which has been called intellectual". The term intellectual property can be found used in an October 1845 Massachusetts Circuit Court ruling in the patent case *Davoll et al. v. Brown*, in which Justice Charles L. Woodbury wrote that "only in this way can we protect intellectual property, the labors of the mind, productions and interests are as much a man's own... as the wheat he cultivates, or the flocks he rears". The statement that "discoveries are... property" goes back earlier. Section 1 of the *French Law* of 1791 stated, "All new discoveries are the property of the author; to assure the inventor the property and temporary enjoyment of his discovery, there shall be delivered to him a patent for five, ten or fifteen years." In Europe, French author A. Nion mentioned *propriété intellectuelle* in his *Droits Civils des Auteurs, Artistes et Inventeurs*, published in 1846.

The concept's origins can potentially be traced back further. Jewish law includes several considerations whose effects are similar to those of modern intellectual property laws, though the notion of intellectual creations as property does not seem to exist—notably the principle of Hasagat Ge'vul (unfair encroachment) was used to justify limited-term publisher (but not author) copyright in the 16th century. The Talmud contains the prohibitions against certain mental crimes (further elaborated in the Shulchan Aruch), notably Geneivat da'at (literally "mind theft"), which some have interpreted as prohibiting theft of ideas, though the doctrine is principally concerned with fraud and deception, not property.

Patent

A patent is a set of exclusive rights granted by a state (national government) to an inventor or their assignee for a limited period of time in exchange for a public disclosure of an invention.

The procedure for granting patents, the requirements placed on the patentee, and the extent of the exclusive rights vary widely between countries according to national laws and international agreements. Typically, however, a patent application must include one or more claims defining the invention which must be new, non-obvious, and useful or industrially applicable. In many countries, certain subject areas are excluded from patents, such as business methods, treatment of the human body, and mental acts. The exclusive right granted to a patentee in most countries is the right to prevent others from making, using, selling, or distributing the patented invention without permission. It is just a right to prevent others' use. A patent does not give the proprietor of the patent the right to use the patented invention, should it fall within the scope of an earlier patent.

Under the *World Trade Organization's (WTO) Agreement on Trade-Related Aspects of Intellectual Property Rights*, patents should be available in WTO member states for any inventions, in all fields of technology, and the term of protection available should be the minimum twenty years. Different types of patents may have varying patent terms (i. e. , durations).

The term patent usually refers to an exclusive right granted to anyone who invents any new, useful, and non-obvious process, machine, article of manufacture, or composition of matter, or any new and useful improvement thereof, and claims that right in a formal patent application. The additional qualification utility patent is used in the United States to distinguish it from other types of patents (e. g. design patents) but should not be confused with utility models granted by other countries. Examples of particular species of patents for inventions include biological patents, business method patents, chemical patents and software patents.

Some other types of intellectual property rights are referred to as patents in some jurisdictions: industrial design rights are called design patents in some jurisdictions (they protect the visual design of objects that are not purely utilitarian), plant breeders' rights are sometimes called plant patents, and utility models or Gebrauchsmuster are sometimes called petty patents or innovation patents. This article relates primarily to the patent for an invention, although so-called petty patents and utility models may also be granted for inventions.

Certain grants made by the monarch in pursuance of the royal prerogative were sometimes called letters patent, which was a government notice to the public of a grant of an exclusive right to ownership and possession. These were often grants of a patent-like monopoly and predate the modern origins of the patent system. For other uses of the term patent, see notably land patents, which were land grants by early state governments in the USA, and printing patent, a precursor of modern copyright. These meanings reflect the original meaning of letters patent that had a broader scope than current usage.

Trademark

A trademark, trade mark, or trade-mark is a distinctive sign or indicator used by an individual, business organization, or other legal entity to identify that the products or services to consumers with which the trademark appears originate from a unique source, and to distinguish its products or services from those of other entities.

A trademark may be designated by the following symbols:

- ™(for an unregistered trade mark, that is, a mark used to promote or brand goods)
- ℠(for an unregistered service mark, that is, a mark used to promote or brand services)
- ®(for a registered trademark)

A trademark is typically a name, word, phrase, logo, symbol, design, image, or a combination of these elements. There is also a range of non-conventional trademarks comprising marks which do not fall into these standard categories, such as those based on color, smell, or sound.

The owner of a registered trademark may commence legal proceedings for trademark infringement to prevent unauthorized use of that trademark. However, registration is not required. The owner of a common law trademark may also file suit, but an unregistered mark may be protectable only within the geographical area within which it has been used or in geographical areas into which it may be reasonably expected to expand.

The term trademark is also used informally to refer to any distinguishing attribute by which an individual is readily identified, such as the well-known characteristics of celebrities. When a trademark is used in relation to services rather than products, it may sometimes be called a service mark, particularly in the United States.

The essential function of a trademark is to exclusively identify the commercial source or origin of products or services, such that a trademark, properly called, indicates source or serves as a badge of origin. In other words, trademarks serve to identify a particular business as the source of goods or services. The use of a trademark in this way is known as trademark use. Certain exclusive rights attach to a registered mark, which can be enforced by way of an action for trademark infringement, while unregistered trademark rights may be enforced pursuant to the common law tort of passing off.

It should be noted that trademark rights generally arise out of the use or to maintain exclusive rights over that sign in relation to certain products or services, assuming there are no other trademark objections.

Different goods and services have been classified by the International (Nice) Classification of Goods and Services into 45 Trademark Classes (1 to 34 cover goods, and 35 to 45 services). The idea of this system is to specify and limit the extension of the intellectual property right by determining which goods or services are covered by the mark, and to unify classification systems around the world.

Trade Secret

A trade secret is a formula, practice, process, design, instrument, pattern, or compilation of information which is not generally known or reasonably ascertainable, by which a business can obtain an economic advantage over competitors or customers. In some jurisdictions, such secrets are referred to as "confidential information" or "classified information".

The precise language by which a trade secret is defined varies by jurisdiction (as do the particular types of information that are subject to trade secret protection). However, there are three factors that, although subject to differing interpretations, are common to all such definitions. A trade secret is information that:

- is not generally known to the public;
- confers some sort of economic benefit on its holder (where this benefit must derive specifically from its not being generally known, not just from the value of the information itself);
- is the subject of reasonable efforts to maintain its secrecy.

By comparison, under US law, "A trade secret, as defined under 18 U. S. C. § 1839 (3) (A), (B) (1996), has three parts: (1) information; (2) reasonable measures taken to protect the information; and (3) which derives independent economic value from not being publicly known."

A company can protect its confidential information through non-compete and non-disclosure contracts[10] with its employees (within the constraints of employment law, including only restraint that is reasonable in geographic and time scope). The law of protection of confidential information effectively allows a perpetual monopoly in secret information—it does not expire as would a patent. The lack of formal protection, however, means that a third party is not prevented from independently duplicating and using the secret information once it is discovered.

The sanctioned protection of such type of information from public disclosure is viewed as an important legal aspect by which a society protects its overall economic vitality. A company typically invests money, time and energy (work) into generating information regarding refinements of processes and operations. If competitors had access to the same knowledge, the first company's ability to survive or maintain its market dominance or market position and market share would be impaired. Where trade secrets are recognized, the creator of knowledge regarded as a "trade secret" is entitled to regard such "special knowledge" as intellectual property.

In the United States, trade secrets are not protected by law in the same manner as trademarks or patents. Specifically, both trademarks and patents are protected under federal statutes, the *Lanham Act* and *Patent Act*, respectively. Instead, trade secrets are protected under state laws, and most states have ratified the *Uniform Trade Secrets Act* (UTSA), except for Massachusetts, New York, New Jersey, North Carolina, and Texas. One of the differences between patents and trademarks, on the one hand, and trade secrets, on the other, is that trade secret is protected only when the secret is not disclosed.

Copyright

Copyright is a set of exclusive rights granted to the author or creator of an original work, including the right to copy, distribute and adapt the work. In most jurisdictions copyright arises upon fixation and does not need to be registered. Copyright owners have the exclusive statutory right to exercise control over copying and other exploitation of the works for a specific period of time, after which the work is said to enter the public domain. Uses covered under limitations and exceptions to copyright, such as fair use, do not require permission from the copyright owner. All other uses require permission. Copyright owners can license or permanently transfer or assign their exclusive rights to others.

Initially copyright law applied to only the copying of books. Over time other uses such as translations and derivative works were made subject to copyright. Copyright now covers a wide range of works, including maps, sheet music, dramatic works, paintings, photographs, architectural drawings, sound recordings, motion pictures and computer programs. The *British Statute of Anne* 1709, full title *An Act for the Encouragement of Learning, by vesting the Copies of Printed Books in the Authors or Purchasers of such Copies, during the Times therein Mentioned*, was the first copyright statute. Today copyright laws are partially standardized through international and regional agreements such as the *Berne Convention* and the *WIPO Copyright Treaty*. Although there are consistencies among nations' copyright laws, each jurisdiction has separate and distinct laws and regulations covering copyright. National copyright laws on licensing, transfer and assignment of copyright still vary greatly between countries and copyrighted works are licensed on a territorial basis. Some jurisdictions also recognize moral rights of creators, such as the right to be credited for the work.

Notes

1. intellectual property　知识产权

   是指"权利人对其所创作的智力劳动成果所享有的专有权利",一般只在有限时间期内有效。各种智力创造比如发明、文学和艺术作品,以及在商业中使用的标志、名称、图像以及外观设计,都可被认为是某一个人或组织所拥有的知识产权。知识产权是指对智力劳动成果依法所享有的占有、使用、处分和收益的权利。知识产权是一种无形财产,它与房屋、汽车等有形财产一样,都受到国家法律的保护,都具有价值和使用价值。它有两类:一类是版权,另一类是工业产权。版权是指著作权人对其文学作品享有的署名、发表、使用以及许可他人使用和获得报酬等的权利;工业产权则是包括发明专利、实用新型专利、外观设计专利、商标、服务标记、厂商名称、货源名称或原产地名称等的独占权利。

2. intangible assets　无形资产

   专利权、商标权等称为无形资产。

3. copyrights　著作权、版权

   是指文学、艺术和自然科学、社会科学作品的作者及其相关主体依法对作品所享有的人身

权利和财产权利。

4. trademarks 商标

商标是用以区别商品和服务不同来源的商业性标志,由文字、图形、字母、数字、三维标志、颜色组合或者上述要素的组合构成。商标权是商标注册人依法支配其注册商标并禁止他人侵害的权利,包括商标注册人对其注册商标的排他使用权、收益权、处分权、续展权和禁止他人侵害的权利。

5. patents 专利

是指发明创造人或其权利受让人对特定的发明创造在一定期限内依法享有的独占实施权,是知识产权的一种。

6. trade secrets 商业秘密

是指不为公众所知悉、能为权利人带来经济利益、具有实用性并经权利人采取保密措施的技术信息和经营信息。

7. the *Paris Convention* 《巴黎公约》

全称为《保护工业产权巴黎公约》(*Paris Convention on the Protection of Industrial Property*),于1883年3月20日在巴黎签订,1884年7月7日生效。《巴黎公约》的调整对象即保护范围是工业产权,包括发明专利权、实用新型、工业品外观设计、商标权、服务标记、厂商名称、产地标记或原产地名称以及制止不正当竞争等。

8. the *Berne Convention*(1886) 《伯尔尼公约》

全称为《保护文学和艺术作品伯尔尼公约》(*Berne Convention for the Protection of Literary and Artistic Works*),是关于著作权保护的国际条约,于1886年在瑞士伯尔尼签订。截至2004年12月31日,缔约方总数为157个国家,1992年10月15日中国成为该公约成员国。

9. the World Intellectual Property Organization 世界知识产权组织

简称WIPO。总部设在瑞士日内瓦的世界知识产权组织,是联合国组织系统中的16个专门机构之一,是一个致力于促进使用和保护人类智力作品的国际组织。它管理着涉及知识产权保护各个方面的24项(16部关于工业产权,7部关于版权,加上建立世界知识产权组织公约)国际条约。

10. non-disclosure contracts 保密合同、保密协议

Study Questions

1. What are the legal features of intellectual property?
2. Try to define patent, trademark, trade secret and copyright.
3. Try to list important international conventions for the protection of intellectual property.
4. What is WIPO?

UNIT 15 Introduction to Paris Convention for the Protection of Industrial Property[1]

Key Concepts

industrial property	national treatment	right of priority	compulsory license
well-known marks	independence of patent	unfair competition	

Learning Objectives

1. Understand the scope of industrial property.
2. Understand the implications of national treatment.
3. Understand the independence of patent.
4. Be familiar with well-known marks and their protection.

This convention was first passed on March 20, 1883, in Paris. It was revised at Brussels, Belgium, on December 14, 1900, at Washington, United States, on June 2, 1911, at Hague, Netherlands, on November 6, 1925, at London, United Kingdom, on June 2, 1934, at Lisbon, Portugal, on October 31, 1958, and at Stockholm, Sweden, on July 14, 1967, and was amended on September 28, 1979.

The Convention now has 173 contracting member countries, which makes it one of the most widely adopted treaties worldwide. China has acceded to this convention in 1985. The *Paris Convention* is administered by the World Intellectual Property Organization (WIPO), based in Geneva, Switzerland.

Scope of Industrial Property[2]

The protection of industrial property has as its object patents, utility models, industrial designs, trademarks, service marks, trade names, indications of source or appellations of origin, and the repression of unfair competition[3]. Industrial property shall be understood in the broadest sense and shall apply not only to industry and commerce proper, but likewise to agricultural and extractive industries and to all manufactured or natural products, for example, wines, grain, tobacco leaf, fruit, cattle, minerals, mineral waters, beer, flowers, and flour. Patents shall include the various kinds of industrial patents recognized by the laws of the countries of the Union, such as patents of importation, patents of improvement, patents and certificates of addition, etc.

National Treatment[4]

Nationals of any country of the Union shall, as regards the protection of industrial property, enjoy in all the other countries of the Union the advantages that their respective laws now grant, or may hereafter grant, to nationals; all without prejudice to the rights specially provided for by this Convention. Consequently, they shall have the same protection as the latter, and the same legal remedy against any infringement of their rights, provided that the conditions and formalities imposed upon nationals are complied with.

Nationals of countries outside the Union who are domiciled or who have real and effective industrial or commercial establishments in the territory of one of the countries of the Union shall be treated in the same manner as nationals of the countries of the Union.

Right of Priority[5]

Any person who has duly filed an application for a patent, or for the registration of a utility model, or of an industrial design, or of a trademark, in one of the countries of the Union, or his successor in title, shall enjoy, for the purpose of filing in the other countries, a right of priority. Any filing that is equivalent to a regular national filing under the domestic legislation of any country of the Union or under bilateral or multilateral treaties concluded between countries of the Union shall be recognized as giving rise to the right of priority. The periods of priority referred to above shall be twelve months for patents and utility models, and six months for industrial designs and trademarks.

If the last day of the period is an official holiday, or a day when the Office is not open for the filing of applications in the country where protection is claimed, the period shall be extended until the first following working day.

Any person desiring to take advantage of the priority of a previous filing shall be required to make a declaration indicating the date of such filing and the country in which it was made. Each country shall determine the latest date on which such declaration must be made.

The countries of the Union may require any person making a declaration of priority to produce a copy of the application (description, drawings, etc.) previously filed. The copy, certified as correct by the authority which received such application, shall not require any authentication, and may in any case be filed, without fee, at any time within three months of the filing of the subsequent application. They may require it to be accompanied by a certificate from the same authority showing the date of filing, and by a translation.

Independence of Patents

Patents applied for in the various countries of the Union by nationals of countries of the Union shall be independent of patents obtained for the same invention in other countries, whether members of the Union or not.

The foregoing provision is to be understood in an unrestricted sense, in particular, in the sense that patents applied for during the period of priority are independent, both as regards the grounds for nullity and forfeiture, and as regards their normal duration.

Patents obtained with the benefit of priority shall, in the various countries of the Union, have a duration equal to that which they would have, had they been applied for or granted without the benefit of priority.

Compulsory Licenses[6]

Each country of the Union shall have the right to take legislative measures providing for the grant of compulsory licenses to prevent the abuses which might result from the exercise of the exclusive rights conferred by the patent, for example, failure to work.

Forfeiture of the patent[7] shall not be provided for except in cases where the grant of compulsory licenses would not have been sufficient to prevent the said abuses. No proceedings for the forfeiture or revocation of a patent may be instituted before the expiration of two years from the grant of the first compulsory license.

A compulsory license may not be applied for on the ground of failure to work or insufficient working before the expiration of a period of four years from the date of filing of the patent application or three years from the date of the grant of the patent, whichever period expires last; it shall be refused if the patentee justifies his inaction by legitimate reasons. Such a compulsory license shall be non-exclusive and shall not be transferable, even in the form of the grant of a sub-license, except with that part of the enterprise or goodwill which exploits such license.

The protection of industrial designs shall not, under any circumstance, be subject to any forfeiture, either by reason of failure to work or by reason of the importation of articles corresponding to those which are protected.

If, in any country, use of the registered mark is compulsory, the registration may be cancelled only after a reasonable period, and then only if the person concerned does not justify his inaction.

Concurrent use of the same mark on identical or similar goods by industrial or commercial establishments considered as co-proprietors of the mark according to the provisions of the domestic law of the country where protection is claimed shall not prevent registration or diminish in any way the protection granted to the said mark in any country of the Union, provided that such use does not result in misleading the public and is not contrary to the public interest.

Period of Grace for the Payment of Fees for the Maintenance of Rights[8]

A period of grace of not less than six months shall be allowed for the payment of the fees prescribed for the maintenance of industrial property rights, subject, if the domestic legislation so provides, to the payment of a surcharge.

The countries of the Union shall have the right to provide for the restoration of patents which have lapsed by reason of non-payment of fees.

Conditions of Registration; Independence of Protection of Same Mark in Different Countries

The conditions for the filing and registration of trademarks shall be determined in each country of the Union by its domestic legislation. However, an application for the registration of a mark filed by a national of a country of the Union in any country of the Union may not be refused, nor may a registration be invalidated, on the ground that filing, registration, or renewal, has not been effected in the country of origin. A mark duly registered in a country of the Union shall be regarded as independent of marks registered in the other countries of the Union, including the country of origin.

Well-Known Marks

The countries of the Union undertake, ex officio[9] if their legislation so permits, or at the request of an interested party, to refuse or to cancel the registration, and to prohibit the use, of a trademark which constitutes a reproduction, an imitation, or a translation, liable to create confusion, of a mark considered by the competent authority of the country of registration or use to be well known in that country as being already the mark of a person entitled to the benefits of this Convention and used for identical or similar goods. These provisions shall also apply when the essential part of the mark constitutes a reproduction of any such well-known mark or an imitation liable to create confusion therewith.

Assignment of Marks

When, in accordance with the law of a country of the Union, the assignment of a mark is valid only if it takes place at the same time as the transfer of the business or goodwill to which the mark belongs, it shall suffice for the recognition of such validity that the portion of the business or goodwill located in that country be transferred to the assignee, together with the exclusive right to manufacture in the said country, or to sell therein, the goods bearing the mark assigned.

The foregoing provision does not impose upon the countries of the Union any obligation to regard as valid the assignment of any mark the use of which by the assignee would, in fact, be of such a nature as to mislead the public, particularly as regards the origin, nature, or essential qualities, of the goods to which the mark is applied.

Protection of Marks

Every trademark duly registered in the country of origin shall be accepted for filing and protected as is in the other countries of the Union, subject to the reservations indicated in this Article. Such countries may, before proceeding to final registration, require the production of a certificate of registration in the country of origin, issued by the competent authority. No authentication shall be required for this certificate.

Shall be considered the country of origin the country of the Union where the applicant has a real and effective industrial or commercial establishment, or, if he has no such establishment within the Union, the country of the Union where he has his domicile, or, if he has no domicile within the Union but is a national of a country of the Union, the country of which he is a national.

In determining whether a mark is eligible for protection, all the factual circumstances must be taken into consideration, particularly the length of time the mark has been in use.

No trademark shall be refused in the other countries of the Union for the sole reason that it differs from the mark protected in the country of origin only in respect of elements that do not alter its distinctive character and do not affect its identity in the form in which it has been registered in the said country of origin.

Unfair Competition[10]

The countries of the Union are bound to assure to nationals of such countries effective protection against unfair competition. Any act of competition contrary to honest practices in industrial or commercial matters constitutes an act of unfair competition. The following in particular shall be prohibited: 1) all acts of such a nature as to create confusion by any means whatever with the establishment, the goods, or the industrial or commercial activities, of a competitor; 2) false allegations in the course of trade of such a nature as to discredit the establishment, the goods, or the industrial or commercial activities, of a competitor; 3) indications or allegations the use of which in the course of trade is liable to mislead the public as to the nature, the manufacturing process, the characteristics, the suitability for their purpose, or the quantity, of the goods.

Notes

1. *Paris Convention for the Protection of Industrial Property* 《保护工业产权巴黎公约》
简称《巴黎公约》,该公约于 1883 年在巴黎通过,目前,多数成员国采用 1967 年斯德哥尔摩修订的版本。我国于 1985 年成为该公约的成员国。巴黎公约旨在保护工业产权,包括专利、实用新型、外观设计、商标、服务标记、厂商名称、货源标记(indications of source)和原产地标记(appellation of origin)、制止不正当竞争(repression of unfair competition),而国民待遇原则、优先权原则和专利独立性原则为巴黎公约的三个基本原则。该公约历经一百多年，至今仍发挥着重要作用。

2. scope of industrial property　工业产权范围

   巴黎公约对工业产权作了广义的解释。

3. The protection of industrial property has as its object patents, utility models, industrial designs, trademarks, service marks, trade names, indications of source or appellations of origin, and the repression of unfair competition. 工业产权保护的对象包括专利、实用新型、外观设计、商标、服务标记、商号（厂商名称）、货源标记或原产地名称以及制止不正当竞争。

4. national treatment　国民待遇

   即在保护工业产权方面，成员国的国民在联盟其他国家内享有该国现在授予或将来可能授予该国国民保护的权利。简而言之，在工业产权保护方面，外国人应享有本国人同等的待遇。

5. right of priority　优先权

   即指特定的申请人在某一成员国提出工业产权申请的基础上，如在一定期限内就同一申请也在其他成员国提出时，那么，第一次的申请日则被视为其后的申请日。换言之，在申请时间方面，后面的申请享有等同于第一次申请日的优先地位。

6. compulsory licenses　强制许可

   旨在防止专利权人在行使专利权时有可能产生的滥用独占权（abuses of exclusive right）现象，例如，不实施专利（failure to work）。

7. forfeiture of the patent　丧失专利权

8. period of grace for the payment of fees for the maintenance of rights　交纳专利维持费的宽限期

9. ex officio　[拉]依职权

10. unfair competition　不正当竞争

    《巴黎公约》对不正当竞争作了原则性的规定，即在商业活动中的一切违背诚信的行为均属不正当竞争行为。例如，在商业活动制造混淆、诋毁商誉及误导公众的行为为不正当竞争。

Study Questions

1. What is the industrial property?
2. Briefly describe the principles of *Paris Convention*.
3. What is the role of *Paris Convention*?
4. What do you think of the principle of the national treatment which the developing countries shall follow?
5. What are the other international treaties on intellectual property?

UNIT 16 Disputes Settlement in International Trade[1]

Key Concepts

conciliation	mediation	arbitration	alternative dispute resolution
arbitral awards	arbitration agreement	DSU	DSB
appellate review	Appellate Body		

Learning Objectives

1. Understand the features and advantages of arbitration.
2. Be familiar with arbitration agreement (clauses).
3. Understand international commercial arbitration.
4. Understand its vital role of the dispute settlement system in WTO.
5. Understand the main contents of DSU and the functions of DSB.
6. Be familiar with the procedures for the settlement of disputes in WTO.

Arbitration

Arbitration, a form of alternative dispute resolution[2] (ADR), is a legal technique for the resolution of disputes outside the courts, where the parties to a dispute refer it to one or more persons (the "arbitrators", "arbiters" or "arbitral tribunal[3]"), by whose decision (the "award") they agree to be bound. It is a settlement technique in which a third party reviews the case and imposes a decision that is legally binding for both sides. Other forms of ADR include mediation[4] (a form of settlement negotiation facilitated by a neutral third party) and non-binding resolution by experts. Arbitration is often used for the resolution of commercial disputes, particularly in the context of international commercial transactions.

Arbitration is a proceeding in which a dispute is resolved by an impartial adjudicator whose decision the parties to the dispute have agreed, or legislation has decreed, will be final and binding. Arbitration is not the same as:

· judicial proceedings, although in some jurisdictions, court proceedings are sometimes referred as arbitrations

· alternative dispute resolution (or ADR)

· expert determination

· mediation

Advantages of Arbitration

Parties often seek to resolve their disputes through arbitration because of a number of perceived potential advantages over judicial proceedings:

· when the subject matter of the dispute is highly technical, arbitrators with an appropriate degree of expertise can be appointed (as one cannot "choose the judge" in litigation)

· arbitration is often faster than litigation in court

· arbitration can be cheaper and more flexible for businesses

· arbitral proceedings and an arbitral award are generally non-public, and can be made confidential

· in arbitral proceedings the language of arbitration may be chosen, whereas in judicial proceedings the official language of the country of the competent court will be automatically applied

· because of the provisions of the *New York Convention* 1958[5], arbitration awards are generally easier to enforce in other nations than court judgments

· in most legal systems there are very limited avenues for appeal of an arbitral award, which is sometimes an advantage because it limits the duration of the dispute and any associated liability

Arbitration Agreement[6]

In theory, arbitration is a consensual process; a party cannot be forced to arbitrate a dispute unless he agrees to do so. In practice, however, many fine-print arbitration agreements are inserted in situations in which consumers and employees have no bargaining power. Moreover, arbitration clauses are frequently placed within sealed users' manuals within products, within lengthy click-through agreements on websites, and in other contexts in which meaningful consent is not realistic. Such agreements are generally divided into two types:

· agreements which provide that, if a dispute should arise, it will be resolved by arbitration. These will generally be normal contracts, but they contain an arbitration clause

· agreements which are signed after a dispute has arisen, agreeing that the dispute should be resolved by arbitration (sometimes called a "submission agreement")

Agreements to refer disputes to arbitration generally have a special status in the eyes of the law. For example, in disputes on a contract, a common defence is to plead the contract is void and thus any claim based upon it fails. It follows that if a party successfully claims that a contract is void, then each clause contained within the contract, including the arbitration clause, would be void. However, in most countries, the courts have accepted that:

1. a contract can only be declared void by a court or other tribunal; and

2. if the contract (valid or otherwise) contains an arbitration clause, then the proper forum to determine whether the contract is void or not, is the arbitration tribunal.

Arguably, either position is potentially unfair; if a person is made to sign a contract under duress, and the contract contains an arbitration clause highly favourable to the other party, the dispute may still referred to that arbitration tribunal. Conversely a court may be persuaded that the arbitration agreement itself is void having been signed under duress. However, most courts will be reluctant to interfere with the general rule which does allow for commercial expediency; any other solution (where one first had to go to court to decide whether one had to go to arbitration) would be self defeating.

Sources of Law

States regulate arbitration through a variety of laws. The main body of law applicable to arbitration is normally contained either in the national *Private International Law Act* (as is the case in Switzerland) or in a separate law on arbitration (as is the case in England). In addition to this, a number of national procedural laws may also contain provisions relating to arbitration.

By far the most important international instrument on arbitration law is the 1958 *New York Convention* on Recognition and Enforcement of Foreign Arbitral Awards. Some other relevant international instruments are:

- *The Geneva Protocol* of 1923
- *The Geneva Convention* of 1927
- *The European Convention* of 1961
- *The Washington Convention* of 1965 (governing settlement of international investment disputes)
- *The UNCITRAL Model Law* (providing a model for a national law of arbitration)
- *The UNCITRAL Arbitration Rules*[7] (providing a set of rules for an ad hoc arbitration)

Arbitral Tribunal

The term arbitral tribunal is used to denote the arbitrator or arbitrators sitting to determine the dispute. The composition of the arbitral tribunal can vary enormously, with either a sole arbitrator sitting, two or more arbitrators, with or without a chairman or umpire, and various other combinations.

In most jurisdictions, an arbitrator enjoys immunity from liability for anything done or omitted whilst acting as arbitrator unless the arbitrator acts in bad faith.

Arbitrations are usually divided into two types:

- *ad hoc* arbitrations and administered arbitrations.

In *ad hoc* arbitrations, the arbitral tribunals are appointed by the parties or by an appointing authority chosen by the parties. After the tribunal has been formed, the appointing authority will normally have no other role and the arbitration will be managed by the tribunal.

In administered arbitration, the arbitration will be administered by a professional arbitration institution providing arbitration services, such as the LCIA in London, or the ICC in Paris, or the American Arbitration Association in the United States. Normally the arbitration institution also will be the appointing authority.

Arbitration institutions tend to have their own rules and procedures, and may be more formal. They also tend to be more expensive, and, for procedural reasons, slower.

Duties of the Tribunal

The duties of a tribunal will be determined by a combination of the provisions of the arbitration agreement and by the procedural laws which apply in the seat of the arbitration. The extent to which the laws of the seat of the arbitration permit "party autonomy" (the ability of the parties to set out their own procedures and regulations) determines the interplay between the two.

However, in almost all countries the tribunal owes several non-derogable duties. These will normally be:

· to act fairly and impartially between the parties, and to allow each party a reasonable opportunity to put their case and to deal with the case of their opponent (sometimes shortened to: complying with the rules of "natural justice"); and

· to adopt procedures suitable to the circumstances of the particular case, so as to provide a fair means for resolution of the dispute.

Arbitral Awards[8]

Although arbitration awards are characteristically an award of damages against a party, in many jurisdictions tribunals have a range of remedies that can form a part of the award. These may include:

1. payment of a sum of money (conventional damages)
2. the making of a "declaration" as to any matter to be determined in the proceedings
3. in some jurisdictions, the tribunal may have the same power as a court to:
   1) order a party to do or refrain from doing something ("injunctive relief")
   2) to order specific performance of a contract
   3) to order the rectification, setting aside or cancellation of a deed or other document
4. In other jurisdictions, however, unless the parties have expressly granted the arbitrators the right to decide such matters, the tribunal's powers may be limited to deciding whether a party is entitled to damages. It may not have the legal authority to order injunctive relief, issue a declaration, or rectify a contract, such powers being reserved to the exclusive jurisdiction of the courts.

Enforcement of Arbitration Awards

One of the reasons that arbitration is so popular in international trade as a means of dispute resolution, is that it is often easier to enforce an arbitration award in a foreign country than it is to enforce a judgment of the court.

Under the *New York Convention* 1958, an award issued a contracting state can generally be freely enforced in any other contracting state, only subject to certain, limited defenses.

Only foreign arbitration awards can be subject to recognition and enforcement pursuant to the *New York Convention*. An arbitral decision is foreign where the award was made in a state other than the state of recognition or where foreign procedural law was used.

Virtually every significant commercial country in the world is a party to the Convention, but relatively few countries have a comprehensive network for cross-border enforcement of judgments of the court.

The other characteristic of cross-border enforcement of arbitration awards that makes them appealing to commercial parties is that they are not limited to awards of damages. Whereas in most countries only monetary judgments are enforceable in the cross-border context, no such restrictions are imposed on arbitration awards and so it is theoretically possible (although unusual in practice) to obtain an injunction or an order for specific performance in an arbitration proceeding which could then be enforced in another *New York Convention* contracting state.

The *New York Convention* is not actually the only treaty dealing with cross-border enforcement of arbitration awards. The earlier *Geneva Convention on the Execution of Foreign Arbitral Awards* 1927 remains in force, but the success of the *New York Convention* means that the *Geneva Convention* is rarely utilized in practice.

Article V of the *New York Convention* provides an exhaustive list of grounds on which enforcement can be challenged. These are generally narrowly construed by the courts in arbitration centres to uphold the pro-enforcement bias of the Convention.

Costs

In many legal systems—both common law and civil law—it is normal practice for the courts to award legal costs against a losing party, with the winner becoming entitled to recover an approximation of what it spent in pursuing its claim (or in defense of a claim). The United States is a notable exception to this rule, as except for certain extreme cases, a prevailing party in a US legal proceeding does not become entitled to recoup its legal fees from the losing party.

Like the courts, arbitral tribunals generally have the same power to award costs in relation to the determination of the dispute. In international arbitration as well as domestic arbitrations governed by the laws of countries in which courts may award costs against a losing party, the arbitral tribunal will also determine the portion of the arbitrators' fees that the losing party is required to bear.

International Commercial Arbitration[9]

The resolution of disputes under international commercial contracts is widely conducted under the auspices of several major international institutions and rule making bodies. The most significant are the International Chamber of Commerce (ICC), the International Centre for Dispute Resolution (ICDR), the international branch of the American Arbitration Association, the London Court of International Arbitration (LCIA), the Hong Kong International Arbitration Centre, and the Singapore International Arbitration Centre (SIAC). Specialist ADR bodies also exist, such as the World Intellectual Property Organisation (WIPO), which has an arbitration and mediation center and a panel of international neutrals specialising in intellectual property and technology related disputes. A number of arbitral institutions have adopted the *UNCITRAL Rules* for use in international cases.

The most salient feature of the rules of the ICC is its use of the "terms of reference". The "terms of reference" is a summary of the claims and issues in dispute and the particulars of the procedure, and it is prepared by the tribunal and signed by the parties near the beginning of the proceedings.

In a more recent development, the Swiss Chambers of Commerce of Industry of Basel, Berne, Geneva, Lausanne, Lugano, Neuchâtel and Zurich have adopted a new set of *Swiss Rules of Commercial Mediation* that are designed to integrate fully with the *Swiss Rules of International Arbitration* that were previously adopted by these chambers to harmonize international arbitration and mediation proceedings across Switzerland. For a recent paper on these two sets of ADR rules and how they may be combined.

The Dispute Settlement System of WTO[10]

Dispute settlement is regarded by the World Trade Organization (WTO) as the central pillar of the multilateral trading system, and as the organization's unique contribution to the stability of the global economy. A dispute arises when one member country adopts a trade policy measure or takes some action that one or more fellow members considers to a breach of WTO agreements or to be a failure to live up to obligations. By joining the WTO, member countries have agreed that if they believe fellow members are in violation of trade rules, they will use the multilateral system of settling disputes instead of taking action unilaterally—this entails abiding by agreed procedures (Dispute Settlement Understanding) and respecting judgments, primarily of the Dispute Settlement Body[11] (DSB), the WTO organ responsible for adjudication of disputes. A former WTO Director-General characterized the WTO dispute settlement system as "the most active international adjudicative mechanism in the world today".

Dispute Settlement Understanding

In 1994, the WTO members agreed on the Understanding on Rules and Procedures Governing the Settlement of Disputes or Dispute Settlement Understanding[12] (DSU) (annexed to the Final Act signed in Marrakesh in 1994). Pursuant to the rules detailed in the DSU, member states can engage in consultations to resolve trade disputes pertaining to a "covered agreement" or, if unsuccessful, have a WTO panel hear the case. The priority, however, is to settle disputes, through consultations if possible. By January 2008, only about 136 of the nearly 369 cases had reached the full panel process. The operation of the WTO dispute settlement process involves the parties and third parties to a case and may also involve the DSB panels, the Appellate Body, the WTO Secretariat, arbitrators, independent experts, and several specialized institutions. The General Council discharges its responsibilities under the DSU through the Dispute Settlement Body (DSB). Like the General Council, the DSB is composed of representatives of all WTO Members. The DSB is responsible for administering the DSU, i. e. for overseeing the entire dispute settlement process. It also has the authority to establish panels, adopt panel and Appellate Body reports, maintain surveillance of implementation of rulings and recommendations, and authorize the suspension of obligations under the covered agreements. The DSB meets as often as necessary to adhere to the timeframes provided for in the DSU.

From Complaint to Final Report

If a member state considers that a measure adopted by another member state has deprived it of a benefit accruing to it under one of the covered agreements, it may call for consultations with the other member state. If consultations fail to resolve the dispute within 60 days after receipt of the request for consultations, the complainant state may request the establishment of a Panel. It is not possible for the respondent state to prevent or delay the establishment of a Panel, unless the DSB by consensus decides otherwise. The panel, normally consisting of three members appointed *ad hoc* by the Secretariat, sits to receive written and oral submissions of the parties, on the basis of which it is expected to make findings and conclusions for presentation to the DSB. The proceedings are confidential, and even when private parties are directly concerned, they are not permitted to attend or make submissions separate from those of the state in question. Disputes can also arise under non-violation nullification of benefits claims. The final version of the panel's report is distributed first to the parties; two weeks later it is circulated to all the members of the WTO. In sharp contrast with other systems, the report is required to be adopted at a meeting of the DSB within 60 days of its circulation, unless the DSB by consensus decides not to adopt the report or a party to the dispute gives notice of its intention to appeal. A party may appeal a panel report to the standing Appellate Body, but only on issues of law and legal interpretations developed by the panel. Each appeal is heard by three members of the permanent seven-member Appellate Body set up by the Dispute Settlement Body and broadly representing the range of WTO membership. Members of the Appellate Body have four-year terms. They must be individuals with recognized standing in the field of law and international trade, not affiliated with any government. The Appellate Body may uphold, modify or reverse the panel's legal findings and conclusions. Normally appeals should not last more than 60 days, with an absolute maximum of 90 days. The possibility for appeal makes the WTO dispute resolution system unique among the judicial processes of dispute settlement in general public international law.

Members may express their views on the report of the Appellate Body, but they cannot derail it. The DSU states unequivocally that an Appellate Body report shall be adopted by the DSB and unconditionally accepted by the parties, unless the DSB decides by consensus within thirty days of its circulation not to adopt the report. Unless otherwise agreed by the parties to the dispute, the period from establishment of the panel to consideration of the report by the DSB shall as a general rule not exceed nine months if there is no appeal, and twelve months if there is an appeal.

Compliance

The DSU addresses the question of compliance and retaliation. Within thirty days of the adoption of the report, the member concerned is to inform the DSB of its intentions in respect of implementation of the recommendations and rulings. If the member explains that it is impracticable to comply immediately with the recommendations and rulings, it is to have a "reasonable period of time" in which to comply. If no agreement is reached about the reasonable period for compliance, that issue is to be the subject of binding arbitration; the arbitrator is to be appointed by agreement of the parties. If there is a disagreement as to the satisfactory nature of the measures adopted by the respondent state to comply with the report, that disagreement is to be decided by a panel, if possible the same panel that heard the original dispute, but apparently without the possibility of appeal from its decision. The DSU provides that even if the respondent asserts that it has complied with the recommendation in a report, and even if the complainant party or the panel accepts that assertion, the DSB is supposed to keep the implementation of the recommendations under surveillance.

Compensation and Retaliation

If all else fails, two more possibilities are set out in the DSU:

- If a member fails within the "reasonable period" to carry out the recommendations and rulings, it may negotiate with the complaining state for a mutually acceptable compensation. Compensation is not defined, but may be expected to consist of the grant of a concession by the respondent state on a product or service of interest to the complainant state.
- If no agreement on compensation is reached within twenty days of the expiry of the "reasonable period", the prevailing state may request authorization from the DSB to suspend application to the member concerned of concessions or other obligations under the covered agreements. The DSU makes clear that retaliation is not favored, and sets the criteria for retaliation. In contrast to prior GATT practice, authorization to suspend concessions in this context is semi-automatic, in that the DSB "shall grant the authorization [...] within thirty days of the expiry of the reasonable period", unless it decides by consensus to reject the request. Any suspension or concession or other obligation is to be temporary. If the respondent state objects to the level of suspension proposed or to the consistency of the proposed suspension with the DSU principles, still another arbitration is provided for, if possible by the original panel members or by an arbitrator or arbitrators appointed by the Director-General, to be completed within sixty days from expiration of the reasonable period.

While such "retaliatory measures" are a strong mechanism when applied by economically powerful countries like the United States or the European Union, when applied by economically weak countries against stronger ones, they can often be ignored. This has been the case, for example, with the March 2005 Appellate Body ruling in case DS 267, which declared US cotton subsidies illegal. Whether or not the complainant has taken a measure of retaliation, surveillance by the DSB is to continue, to see whether the recommendations of the panel or the Appellate Body have been implemented.

Developing Countries

Like most of the agreements adopted in the Uruguay Round, the DSU contains several provisions directed to developing countries. The Understanding states that members should give "special attention" to the problems and interests of developing country members. Further, if one party to a dispute is a developing country, that party is entitled to have at least one panelist who comes from a developing country. If a complaint is brought against a developing country, the time for consultations (before a panel is convened) may be extended, and if the dispute goes to a panel, the deadlines for the developing country to make its submissions may be relaxed. Also, the Secretariat is authorized to make a qualified legal expert available to any developing country on request. Formal complaints against least developed countries are discouraged, and if consultations fail, the Director-General and the Chairman of the DSB stand ready to offer their good offices before a formal request for a panel is made. As to substance, the DSU provides that the report of panels shall "explicitly indicate" how account has been taken of the "differential and more favorable treatment" provisions of the agreement under which the complaint is brought. Whether or not a developing country is a party to a particular proceeding, "particular attention" is to be paid to the interests of the developing countries in the course of implementing recommendations and rulings of panels. In order to assist developing countries in overcoming their limited expertise in WTO law and assist them in managing complex trade disputes, an Advisory Centre on WTO Law was established in 2001. The aim is to level the playing field for these countries and customs territories in the WTO system by enabling them to have a full understanding of their rights and obligations under the *WTO Agreement*.

Notes

1. disputes settlement in international trade 国际贸易争端解决
2. alternative dispute resolution (ADR) 选择性争端解决方式(或诉讼外争端解决方式)
   ADR 机制是一种独立或相对独立于法院诉讼的非诉讼纠纷解决方式。这一概念源于美国,原指 21 世纪逐步发展起来的各种诉讼外争端解决方式,现已发展为世界各国普遍存在着的民事诉讼制度以外的非诉讼争端或纠纷解决程序或机制的总称。

3. arbitral tribunal 仲裁庭

是指负责审理和裁决提交仲裁争议案件的临时组织。一般由首席仲裁员(或仲裁长)一人和仲裁员两人组成,如果双方当事人共同选定独任仲裁员一人,则由独任仲裁员单独成立仲裁庭。通常在争议案件审理终结并作出裁决后,仲裁庭即告解散。

4. mediation 调解

5. the *New York Convention* 1958 1958 年《纽约公约》

其全称为 1958 年《联合国承认和执行外国仲裁裁决的公约》(*Convention on the Recognition and Enforcement of Foreign Arbitral Awards*)

6. arbitration agreement 仲裁协议

是指双方当事人在自愿、协商、平等、互利的基础之上将他们之间已经发生或者可能发生的争议提交仲裁解决的书面文件,是申请仲裁的必备材料。

7. *The UNCITRAL Arbitration Rules* 《联合国国际贸易法委员会仲裁规则》

其英文全称为 *United Nations Commission on International Trade Law Arbitration Rules*

8. arbitral awards 仲裁裁决

仲裁裁决是指仲裁庭对当事人之间所争议的事项作出的裁决。仲裁实行一裁终局制度,裁决自作出之日起发生法律效力。任何一方当事人不履行仲裁裁决的,另一方当事人可以向人民法院申请强制执行,受申请的人民法院应当执行。根据我国参加的《纽约公约》的规定,我国仲裁机构作出的仲裁裁决,也可以在其他缔约国得到承认和执行,如果被执行人或者其财产不在中国境内的,当事人可以直接向有管辖权的外国法院申请承认和执行。

9. international commercial arbitration 国际商事仲裁

10. The Dispute Settlement System of WTO 世界贸易组织争议解决机制

该机制适用世贸组织成员之间因执行 WTO 协议而产生的争议。因此,争议的主体为该组织的成员,而各缔约方所属的自然人、法人,则不能成为该争议解决机制的主体。该机制的主要目标是确保 WTO 各项协议的实施,废除各国与 WTO 协议不一致的有关规定。

11. Dispute Settlement Body (DSB) 争议解决机构

这是 WTO 争议解决机制设立的专门的争议解决机构,DBS 解决的争议不仅包括传统的货物贸易争议(如有关反倾销、补贴与反补贴等方面的争议),而且还包括知识产权保护和服务贸易而引起的争议。

12. Dispute Settlement Understanding (DSU) 关于争议解决规则与程序的谅解书

DSU 应为 Dispute Settlement Understanding 的缩略形式。根据这一谅解书规定,在 WTO 框架下解决争议,主要经历协商(即争议各方必须先自行协商解决)、专家小组设立及对争议事项审查、上诉评审程序、执行程序(如果一方不执行,那么 DSB 授权申诉方中止给对方的减让或对其所承担的其他义务,即所谓的"交叉报复")等四个阶段。

Study Questions

1. What are the main features and advantages of arbitration?
2. Try to know other forms of alternative dispute resolution and their differences.
3. What are the main contents of arbitration agreement?
4. Under what circumstances may a dispute be submitted to DSB for settlement?
5. Briefly describe the procedures for the settlement of disputes in WTO.

References

[1] Chen Jianping. *Legal English in International Business*. Hangzhou: Zhejiang University Press, 2004.

[2] Ewan McKendrick. *Contract Law—Text, Cases and Materials*. Oxford University Press, 2005.

[3] Jia Hao. *Comparing UCP* 500 *and UCP* 600*—an Efficient Way to Learn UCP* 600, LC VIEWS Newsletter NO. 90, January 2007.

[4] John Mo. *International Commercial Law* 4th ed. Butterworths: LexisNexis, 2009.

[5] John Shijian Mo. *International Commercial Law* 1st ed. Beijing: Chinese Legal Press, 2004.

[6] P. S. Atiyah. *The Rise and Fall of Freedom of Contract*. New York:Clarendon Press, 1979.

[7] Randy E. Barnett. *Contracts*. Aspen Publishers, 2003.

[8] R August. *International Business Law: Text, Cases, and Readings*. New Jersey: Pearson/Prentice Hall, 2009.

[9] Schmitthoff. *The Law and Practice of International Trade* 11*th ed*. Thomson Sweet & Maxwell, 2007.

[10] B Mercurio et al. *International Business Law*.Oxford: Oxford University Press, 2010.

[11] S Lester et al. *World Trade Law Text, Materials and Commentary*. Oxford: Hart Publishing, 2008.

[12] Yu Jinsong & Wu Zhipan. *International Economic Law* 1*st ed*. Beijing: Peking University Press, 2000.